STEP THREE - DEVELOPING GIFTS AND SKILLS

TEACHER MANUAL

DR. HENDRIK VORSTER

STEP THREE - DEVELOPING GIFTS AND SKILLS

-- Teacher Manual --

Discipleship Foundations Step 3 – Gifts and Skills Development (Teacher Manual)
By Dr. Hendrik J. Vorster

A practical guide to learn the Values and Spiritual Disciplines of the Kingdom of God, as taught by Lord Jesus Christ.

Apart from this Handbook, you will also need the following items to complete your study:

A New International Version of the Bible
A pen or pencil to write the answers.
Coloured pencils (red, blue, green and yellow).

For more copies and information please visit and write to us at: www.churchplantinginstitute.com
resources@churchplantinginstitute.com

Copyright © churchplantingdoctor.com All rights reserved.

No part of this publication may be reproduced, stored in a retrieval system, or transmitted in any form or by any means, electronic, mechanical, photocopying, recording or otherwise, without written permission from churchplantingdoctor.com

Scripture taken from the HOLY BIBLE,
New International Version
Copyright 1973, 1978, 1984, 2011 Biblica.
Used by permission of Zondervan.

Church Planting Doctor is a Registered Ministry of Cornerstone Ministries International.

ISBN 13-978-1-7338266-8-6

INDEX

Gift discovery weekend encounter
- Session 1 – Introduction to Spiritual Gifts
- Session 2 - The Ministerial Office Gifts
- Session 3 – The Service Gifts
- Session 4 – The Supernatural Gifts
- Session 5 – Discovering your Spiritual Gifts

Survey of the Bible weekend encounter
- Session 1 – Survey of the Bible
- Session 2 – Making most of my time in the Word

Faith sharing weekend encounter
- Session 1 – Introduction in sharing our faith
- Session 2 – Sharing our faith in a practical way
- Session 3 – The practical gospel message

Overcoming weekend encounter
- Session 1 – Introduction
- Session 2 – Cares of the world
- Session 3 – Fear and Unbelief
- Session 4 – Unforgiveness
- Session 5 – Lust of the flesh
- Session 6 – Faith and Obedience

Shepherd Leader weekend encounter
- Introduction
- Session 1 – The Biblical Shepherd
- Session 2 – The heart of a Shepherd
- Session 3 – The purpose of a Shepherd
- Session 4 – Developing deep and meaningful relationships

Session 5 – Practical keys
Session 6 – Practical application
Session 7 - Consecration

Other Books by Dr Hendrik J. Vorster

Endnotes

PART I
GIFTS DISCOVERY WEEKEND ENCOUNTER

WEEKEND ONE

ENCOUNTER SCHEDULE

- Session 1 – Introduction to Spiritual Gifts
- Session 2 - The Ministerial Office Gifts
- Session 3 – The Service Gifts
- Session 4 – The Supernatural Gifts
- Session 5 – Discovering your Spiritual Gifts
- Session 6 - Vorster Spiritual Gifts Questionnaire
- Session 7 - Vorster Gifts Score Sheet

1

INTRODUCTION
SESSION ONE

God saved us to _serve_!
God saved us to serve. To serve the purpose of God well, we need to be appropriately equipped.

God equips us with Spiritual *Gifts* to serve!

The way God equips His people is by giving them Gifts and Abilities, and we call these Spiritual Gifts. Knowing and Understanding Spiritual Gifts and how God uses these in and through our lives, empowers us to minister more effectively to the Building up of the Body of Christ.

What Is a Spiritual Gift?

> *"A Spiritual Gift is a distinguishing _ability_ given to us, by the Holy Spirit, specifically to build the Body of Christ up for their _edification_."*

Spiritual Gifts

The Bible teaches that every believer is, and should function as, a vital part of the body of Christ. God has bestowed many gifts upon His church. He has endowed the members with special abilities and ministries for the benefit of the body as a whole, both locally and worldwide.

Natural **abilities are not Spiritual Giftedness**

Let's first discuss talents, or natural abilities. A natural ability may be something you're born with, like physical co-ordination. Or it may be a talent you've developed through the years, such as playing a musical instrument.

These natural abilities or talents may be useful or entertaining, but they deal primarily with the surfaces of life. The root concern of one's relationship with God is left untouched. Abilities and talents affect people on a temporary basis, not an eternal basis, and spiritual growth isn't necessary for their development.

Spiritual Gifts are therefore abilities graciously given to us by the Holy Spirit. The purpose for the activation of these Gifts in our lives are for the building up and edification of the Body of Christ.

The Nature of Spiritual Gifts

1. Spiritual Gifts are "Supernatural" abilities, powers and operations.

Spiritual Gifts are bestowed, by the Holy Spirit, for the use of Believers only.

> *1 Corinthians 12:7 (NIV)*
> *"Now to each one the manifestation of the Spirit is given for the common good."*

Spiritual gifts are not just human talents, they are Divinely Inspired abilities, powers and operations. The Bible does not isolate a particular set of gifts as being more supernatural than others.

> *1 Corinthians 12:28 (NIV)*
> *"And **God has placed in the church** first of all apostles, second prophets, third teachers, then miracles, then gifts of healing, of helping, of guidance, and of different kinds of tongues."*

The gifts of healings and tongues are right in the midst of the gifts of helps and administration. Even though some Gifts seem to be more explicitly prominent and visible than others, they operate by the same Holy Spirit, for the same purpose.

2. Spiritual Gifts are "Gracious Gifts" for Believers.

Spiritual gifts are gifts given graciously to His people. The word for gifts is "charismata" which literally means "graciously given." This means that it is graciously given for our use. It is given for a purpose.

> *1 Peter 4:10 (NIV)*
> *Each of you should use whatever gift you have received to serve others, **as faithful stewards of God's grace** in its various forms.*

3. Spiritual gifts are to be "used", and not treated or treasured just like ordinary trophies.

We are all encouraged to serve and use our Gifts in the measure of faith we received. We should be humbled by the fact that we have been blessed to possess Spiritual Gifts.

> *1 Peter 4:10 (NIV)*
> ***Each of you should use whatever gift you have received to serve others**, as faithful stewards of God's grace in its various forms.*

4. Spiritual gifts operate by "faith" and must be "developed" and nurtured.

Spiritual Gifts are received by impartation, through the laying on of hands.

> *1 Timothy 4:14 (NIV)*
> *Do not neglect your gift, **which was given you through prophecy when the body of elders laid their hands on you.***

> *2 Timothy 1:6 (NIV)*
> *"For this reason I remind you to fan into flame the gift of God, which is in you through the laying on of my hands."*

Spiritual Gifts are exercised according to one's faith.

> *Romans 12:6 (NIV)*
> *"We have different gifts, according to the grace given to each of us. If your gift is prophesying, then **prophesy in accordance with your faith**; if it is serving, then serve; if it is teaching, then teach; if it is to encourage, then give encouragement; if it is giving, then give generously; if it is to lead, do it diligently; if it is to show mercy, do it cheerfully."*

Spiritual Gifts are subject to the will of the user.

> *1 Corinthians 14:32 (NIV)*
> *"The spirits of prophets are subject to the control of prophets."*

The Bible teaches that Spiritual Gifts should be encouraged and nurtured.

> *1 Corinthians 14:1 (NIV)*
> *Follow the way of love **and eagerly desire gifts of the Spirit,** especially prophecy.*

1 Corinthians 14:12 (NIV)
"So it is with you. **Since you are eager for gifts of the Spirit, try to excel** in those that build up the church."

1 Corinthians 14:39 (NIV)
Therefore, my brothers and sisters, **be eager to prophesy,** and do not forbid speaking in tongues.

2 Timothy 1:6 (NIV)
"For this reason I remind you to **fan into flame the gift of God,** which is in you through the laying on of my hands."

We should be eager for Spiritual Gifts.

1 Corinthians 12:31 (NIV)
"31 Now **eagerly desire the greater gifts.** Love Is Indispensable, And yet I will show you the most excellent way."

1 Corinthians 14:1 (NIV)
"1 Follow the way of love and eagerly desire gifts of the Spirit, especially prophecy."

1 Corinthians 14:12 (NIV)
12 So it is with you. **Since you are eager for gifts of the Spirit, try to excel** in those that build up the church.

5. Spiritual Gifts are given for the "upbuilding" of the Body of Christ.

The true purpose of Spiritual Gifts is for edification.

1 Corinthians 12:7 (NIV)
"Now to each one the manifestation of **the Spirit is given for the common good.**"

1 Corinthians 14:4 (NIV)
Anyone who speaks in a tongue edifies themselves, **but the one who prophesies edifies the church.**

1 Corinthians 14:26 (NIV)
What then shall we say, brothers and sisters? When you come together, each of you has a hymn, or a word of instruction, a revelation, a tongue or an interpretation. **Everything must be done so that the church may be built up.**

Spiritual Gifts are to bring glory to the Lord Jesus.

1 Peter 4:10,11 (NIV)
"Each of you should use whatever gift you have received to serve others, as faithful stewards of God's grace in its various forms. If anyone speaks, they should do so as one who speaks the very words of God. If anyone serves, they should do so with the strength God provides, **so that in all things God may be praised through Jesus Christ.** *To him be the glory and the power for ever and ever. Amen."*

What you will find in the next few pages should not be used merely as an assessment, but as an exploration tool to allow the Holy Spirit to quicken His Grace and Gifts within your heart.

The following Scriptures explores the Spiritual Gifts of the Holy Spirit. These Scriptures exhorts us to pursue them and be eager for their assimilation and use in our lives.

1 Corinthians 12:1 (NIV) Spiritual Gifts
"[12:1] Now about spiritual gifts, brothers, I do not want you to be ignorant."

1 Corinthians 14:1 (NIV) Gifts of Prophecy and Tongues "[14:1] Follow the way of love and eagerly desire spiritual gifts, especially the gift of prophecy."

1 Corinthians 14:12 (NIV)
"[12] So it is with you. Since you are eager to have spiritual gifts, try to excel in gifts that build up the church."

1 Corinthians 14:39-40 (NIV)
"Therefore, my brothers, be eager to prophesy, and do not forbid speaking in tongues. [40] But everything should be done in a fitting and orderly way."

Historical re-emergence of the Holy Spirit.

Before we head into looking at the three Parts of the Spiritual Gifts, let us look at the contemporary historical re-emergence of the Holy Spirit.

One of the distinctives of the Church in Acts, and the New Testament Churches that was planted, is their emphasis on the supernatural gifts of the Spirit at work in the church. Throughout the evolving church history there remained a remnant who always embraced an openness to the work and ministry of the Holy Spirit.

During the latter half of the nineteenth century, many people from across the denominational spectrum experienced and embraced these workings of the Holy Spirit and the Gracious Gifts He blessed them with. The Pentecostal and Charismatic Churches evolved as the prominence of the Holy Spirit's work gained renewed acceptance.

The acceptance of the Person and work of the Holy Spirit has never been confined to these denominations only, but as we observe, His work is seen and appreciated by most Believers around the world, regardless of denominational affiliation. Unfortunately, there's been some diverse theories and practices, including some misuse and abuse, which accompanied this renewal of spiritual gifts. Regardless, the Holy Spirit is here with us, as Jesus promised, and He is surely working marvellously to build the Church through His people.

While experience must not be our authority, it serves a vital role in developing a practical understanding of this subject.

At the beginning of the twentieth century, the early Pentecostals discovered the biblical teaching about the baptism of the Holy Spirit, speaking in tongues, and the gifts of the Spirit, and they in earnest sought to receive and implement these truths. As God poured out His Spirit with signs following, what they once found obscure, mysterious, or merely theoretical, suddenly became a clear and living reality. As they followed the leading of the Spirit, they corrected misconceptions and abuses by referring back to the Bible and its explanation of the purpose and operation of spiritual gifts.

Spiritual Gifts are defined and explained in three parts:

There are primarily three main portions of Scripture that describe and define Spiritual Gifts. These portions help us see them in their specific assignment for our lives. Let us take a brief overview of these three differentiations.

Three passages in the New Testament—Romans 12, Ephesians 4, and I Corinthians 12—list some gifts that God has granted the church.

1. Romans 12 discusses abilities, talents, or functions that God gives to all believers. These are commonly known as Service Gifts.
2. Ephesians 4 identifies special offices of leadership and ministry that God has given to the church. These are known as Ministerial office gifts.
3. In I Corinthians 12 and 14 we find supernatural signs, wonders, and miracles that occur by the direct empowerment and operation of the Holy Spirit through His people. These are known as Supernatural Spiritual Gifts.

For the sake of clarity, we will label these three lists respectively as the service gifts, the ministerial office gifts, and the supernatural gifts.

"MINISTERIAL" OFFICE GIFTS (Ephesians 4:11)

The Ministerial Gifts are primarily found in Ephesians chapter 4 and is commonly known as the Five-fold Ministry Gifts.

> *Ephesians 4:11-12 (NIV)*
> *[11] It was he who gave some to be **apostles**, some to be **prophets**, some to be **evangelists**, and some to be **pastors** and **teachers**, [12] to prepare God's people for works of service, so that the body of Christ may be built up.*

- Apostle
- Prophet
- Evangelist
- Pastor
- Teacher

"SERVICE" GIFTS (Romans 12:3-8)

The Service Gifts are recorded primarily in Romans chapter 12 and is frequently referred to as the Service Gifts.

> *Romans 12:3-8 (NIV)*
> *"For I say, through **the grace given to me**, to **everyone** who is among you, not to think of himself more highly than he ought to think, but to think soberly, as God has dealt to each one a measure of faith. For as we have many members in one body, but all the members do not have the same function, so we, being many, are one body in Christ, and individually members of one another. Having then gifts differing according to the grace that is given to us, let us use them: if **prophecy**, let us prophesy in proportion to our faith; or **ministry**, let us use it in our ministering; he who **teaches**, in teaching; he who **exhorts**, in exhortation; he who **gives**, with liberality; he who **leads**, with diligence; he who shows **mercy**, with cheerfulness"*

- Prophecy
- Ministry (Serving)
- Teaching
- Exhortation
- Giving
- Leading (ruling in KJV)
- Showing mercy

SUPERNATURAL "SPIRITUAL" GIFTS (1 Corinthians 12:1-9)

The Supernatural Spiritual Gifts are specifically explored in the First Book to the Church in Corinth. The extensive use of these gifts is seen throughout the New Testament writings.

> *1 Corinthians 12:7-11 (NIV)*
> *[7] Now to each one the manifestation of the Spirit is given for the common good. [8] To one there is given through the Spirit the message of **wisdom**, to another the message of **knowledge** by means of the same Spirit, [9] to another **faith** by the same Spirit, to another **gifts of healing** by that one Spirit, [10] to another **miraculous powers**, to another **prophecy**, to another **distinguishing between spirits**, to another speaking in different kinds of **tongues**,* and to still another the **interpretation of tongues**.* [11] All these are the work of one and the same Spirit, and he gives them to each one, just as he determines.*

- Word of wisdom
- Word of knowledge
- Faith
- Gifts of healings
- Working of miracles
- Prophecy (Explored under Service Gifts)
- Discerning of spirits
- Different kinds of tongues
- Interpretation of tongues

In the following sessions we will look at each of these general groupings in a more detailed manner.

Assimilation Sheet for
Introduction to Spiritual Gifts

1. Complete the sentence. *God saved us to <u>serve</u>!*

2. What is a Spiritual Gift? *"<u>A Spiritual Gift is a distinguishing ability given to us, by the Holy Spirit, specifically to build the Body of Christ up for their edification.</u>"*

3. Complete the sentence. *Spiritual Gifts are <u>Supernatural</u> abilities, powers and operations.*

4. Complete the sentence. *Spiritual Gifts are <u>Gracious Gifts</u> for Believers.*

5. Complete the sentence. *Spiritual Gifts are to be <u>used</u> and not treated or treasured just like ordinary trophies.*

6. Complete the sentence. *Spiritual Gifts operate by <u>faith</u> and must be <u>developed</u> and nurtured.*

7. Complete the sentence. *Spiritual Gifts are given for the <u>upbuilding</u> of the Body of Christ.*

8. Name the three parts of the Spiritual Gifts. Give at least one Scriptural reference to substantiate.
   1. _____
   2. _____
   3. _____

9. Name the Ministerial Office Gifts.
   1. _____
   2. _____
   3. _____
   4. _____
   5. _____

10. Name two Service Gifts.
    1. _____
    2. _____

11. Name two Supernatural Spiritual Gifts.
    1. _____
    2. _____

2

THE MINISTERIAL OFFICE GIFTS
SESSION TWO

During this session we will be exploring the Ministerial Gifts.

Ephesians 4:11-12 (NIV)
*[11] It was he who gave some to be **apostles**, some to be **prophets**, some to be **evangelists**, and some to be **pastors** and **teachers**, [12] to prepare God's people for works of service, so that the body of Christ may be built up.*

Ephesians 4:8 (KJV) Therefore He says: 'When He ascended on high, He led captivity captive, and gave gifts to men.'

*Ephesians 4:11-16 (KJV) And He Himself gave some to be **apostles**, some **prophets**, some **evangelists**, and some **pastors** and **teachers**, for the equipping of the saints for the work of ministry, for the edifying of the body of Christ, till we all come to the unity of the faith and the knowledge of the Son of God, to a perfect man, to the measure of the stature of the fullness of Christ; that we should no longer be children, tossed to and fro and carried about with every wind of doctrine, by the trickery*

> *of men, in the cunning craftiness by which they lie in wait to deceive, but, speaking the truth in love, may grow up in all things into Him who is the head—Christ—from whom the whole body, joined and knit together by what every joint supplies, according to the effective working by which every part does its share, causes growth of the body for the edifying of itself in love"*

This passage introduces to us what is often called the fivefold ministry. The five ministries listed are not simply God's gifts to individuals within the church, but they are God's gifts (Greek, *dogmata*) to the church as a whole. While Romans 12 speaks of abilities or functions, using both nouns and verbs to describe the operation of the service gifts, Ephesians 4 speaks of offices, using nouns to designate them. The indication is that the gifts of Ephesians 4 are more formal or defined ministries in and for the whole church. When Jesus ascended to Heaven, He gave gifts to the church— the ministers of the gospel.

As the passage reveals, the people who hold these offices are recognized leaders in the church, responsible for equipping others and thereby helping the church to function effectively, grow into maturity, and become established in doctrinal truth. The nature of their work requires that they be preachers of the gospel. In modern terminology, we typically call them 'Pastor' or 'Priest,' using this designation in a special sense, even though in the KJV and NKJV the term *minister* is a general one signifying a servant or worker.

Let us now take a few moments to look at each of these Ministerial Office Gifts:

1. Apostle.

An **apostle** (Greek, *Apostolos*) is literally someone sent on a mission, a messenger, an ambassador, or as a commissioner. Although no one can take the place of the twelve apostles of the Lamb (Revelation 21:14), who were eyewitnesses of Christ, others fulfill an apostolic office by serving as pioneer missionaries and leaders of other ministers.

> *Revelation 21:14 (NIV)*
> *The wall of the city had twelve foundations, and on them were the names of **the twelve apostles** of the Lamb.*

During the Lord Jesus' earthly ministry, after first calling some to follow Him and to be His Disciples, He one day – after a night in prayer – appointed some of His Disciples to become the first Apostles, His Sent ones.

> *Luke 6:12-13 (NIV) The Twelve Apostles*
> *"12 One of those days **Jesus went out to a mountainside to pray, and spent the night praying to God. 13 When morning came, he called his disciples to him and chose twelve of them, whom he also designated apostles.**"*

> *Mark 3:13-19 (NIV) The Appointing of the Twelve Apostles*
> *13 Jesus went up on a mountainside and **called to him those he wanted**, and they came to him. 14 **He appointed twelve– designating them apostles–that they might be with him and that he might send them out to preach 15 and to have authority to drive out demons.** 16 These are the twelve he appointed: Simon (to whom he gave the name Peter); 17 James son of Zebedee and his brother John (to them he gave the name Boanerges, which means Sons of Thunder); 18 Andrew, Philip, Bartholomew, Matthew, Thomas, James son of Alphaeus, Thaddaeus, Simon the Zealot 19 and Judas Iscariot, who betrayed him.*

> *Matthew 10:7-8 (NIV)*
> *As you go, preach this message: 'The kingdom of heaven is near.' 8 Heal the sick, raise the dead, cleanse those who have leprosy, drive out demons. Freely you have received, freely give.*

From these two accounts we learn that Jesus chose twelve from among all His Disciples and appointed them as Apostles. The reference in the Gospel of Mark helps us understand the special designation, as Apostles. The Bible says: *"that they might be with him and that he might send them out to preach 15 and to have authority to drive out demons."* The designation – Apostle – indicates that they were appointed with an entrustment, like John the Baptist, to go ahead of the Lord Jesus to preach wherever He might send them, with His blessing and designated authority, and empowerment to *"heal the sick, raise the dead, and to drive out demons."*

Apostleship was not only confined to the twelve Apostles.

One of the amazing blessings the New Testament Church received was the continuation of the Lord to appoint Apostles, as Gifts to the Church.

Apostles Paul and Barnabas

In the church at Antioch, whilst fasting and praying, the Holy Spirit spoke and instructed that Paul and Barnabas be sent out for the work they were called for. After prayer and the laying on of hands, they sent Paul and Barnabas as pioneer missionaries, and they became known as apostles even though neither were part of the original Twelve.

> *Acts 13:2 (NIV)*
> *"While they were worshiping the Lord and fasting, the Holy Spirit said, "Set apart for me **Barnabas and Saul** for the work to which I have called them." 3 So after they had fasted and prayed, they placed their hands on them and sent them off. 4 The two of them, sent on their way by the Holy Spirit, went down to Seleucia and sailed from there to Cyprus."*

Later in the Book of Acts we read about *"the Apostles Barnabas and Paul."*

> *Acts 14:14 (NIV)*
> *But when **the apostles Barnabas and Paul** heard of this, they tore their clothes and rushed out into the crowd, shouting:*

On a few occasions we see how Paul defends His Apostleship.

> *1 Corinthians 9:2 (NIV)*
> *Even though I may not be an apostle to others, surely, I am to you!* ***For you are the seal of my apostleship in the Lord.***

The Apostle Paul open his pastoral letters with the words "Paul, an Apostle" often.

> *Galatians 1:1 (NIV)*
> ***"Paul, an apostle**–sent not from men nor by man, but by Jesus Christ and God the Father, who raised him from the dead–"*

In the Pastoral Letter to the church in Galatia Paul trumps the case for his Apostleship as an Apostle to the Gentiles just as Peter was an Apostle to the Jews.

> *Galatians 2:8-9 (NIV)*
> *"For God, who was at work in the ministry of **Peter as an apostle to the Jews**, was also at work in my ministry as **an apostle to the Gentiles.** 9 James, Peter and John, those reputed to be pillars, **gave me and Barnabas the right hand of fellowship** when they recognized the grace given to me. They agreed that we should go to the Gentiles, and they to the Jews."*

In the Pastoral Letter to the church in Corinth he defends the ministry of an Apostle.

1 Corinthians 4:1 (NIV) **Apostles of Christ**
So then, men ought to regard us as servants of Christ and as those entrusted with the secret things of God.

1 Corinthians 4:9 (NIV)
For it seems to me that **God has put us apostles** *on display at the end of the procession, like men condemned to die in the arena. We have been made a spectacle to the whole universe, to angels as well as to men.*

1 Corinthians 9:1-2 (NIV) **The Rights of an Apostle**
Am I not free? Am I not an apostle? Have I not seen Jesus our Lord? Are you not the result of my work in the Lord? 2 Even though I may not be an apostle to others, surely, I am to you! For you are the seal of my apostleship in the Lord.

The signs of an Apostle are clearly outlined in the second Book of Corinthians.

2 Corinthians 12:12 (NIV)
[12] The things that mark an apostle—signs, wonders and miracles — were done among you with great perseverance.

Likewise, James the Lord's brother, not one of the original twelve, was called an apostle.

Galatians 1:19 (NIV)
I saw none of **the other apostles—only James, the Lord's brother.** *Although he was not one of the Twelve, he was the leader of the church in Jerusalem.*

Acts 15:13 (NIV)
When they finished, **James** *spoke up: "Brothers, listen to me. "*

The term Apostle/s is found 22/71 times respectively in the NIV translation. It is translated **apostle most times;** *messenger or worker* on a couple of times (2 Corinthians. 8: 23; Phil 2: 25); and **once more as a messenger in John** (John. 13: 16).

> *2 Corinthians 8:23 (NIV)*
> As for Titus, he is my partner and **fellow worker** among you; as for our brothers, they are representatives of the churches and an honor to Christ.

> *Philippians 2:25 (NIV)*
> But I think it is necessary to send back to you Epaphroditus, my brother, **fellow worker** and fellow soldier, who is also your **messenger**, whom you sent to take care of my needs.

> *John 13:16 (NIV)*
> I tell you the truth, no servant is greater than his master, nor is a **messenger** greater than the one who sent him.

At least twenty-four Apostles are recorded in the New Testament:

- Simon Peter and his brother Andrew (Mt. 10: 2)
- James, son of Zebedee and John his brother (Mt. 10: 2)
- Philip and his brother Bartholomew (Mt. 10: 3)
- James, son of Alphaeus and Judas his brother (Luke 6: 16) and
- Matthew, son of Alphaeus, perhaps brother of James and Judas (Mk. 2: 14; Lk. 6: 15)
- Thomas (Mt. 10: 3)
- Simon Zelotes, brother of James and Judas, according to tradition (Lk. 6: 15)
- Judas Iscariot (Mt. 10: 4)
- Matthias (Acts 1: 26)
- Barnabas (1Cor. 9: 5-6 Acts 13: 1-3; 14: 4, 14; Gal. 2: 9)
- Andronicus (Rom. 16: 7)

- Junia (Rom. 16: 7)
- Apollos (1Cor. 4: 6- 9)
- James, the Lord's brother (Gal. 1: 19; 2: 6; Jas. 1: 1)
- Silas (1Thess. 1: 1; 2: 6)
- Timothy (1Thess. 1: 1; 2: 6)
- Titus (2Cor. 8: 23)
- Epaphroditus (Php. 2: 25)
- Paul (Gal. 1: 1; 2: 8)
- Jesus Christ (Heb. 3: 1)

The Apostle Paul says in Ephesians chapter 4 that the Lord gave gifts to the church, and these equipping gifts are: Apostles, Prophets, Evangelists, Pastors and Teachers.

> *Ephesians 4:11-13 (NIV)*
> *"[11] It was **he who gave some to be apostles**, some to be prophets, some to be evangelists, and some to be pastors and teachers, [12] to prepare God's people for works of service, so that the body of Christ may be built up [13] until we all reach unity in the faith and in the knowledge of the Son of God and become mature, attaining to the whole measure of the fullness of Christ."*

In conclusion of learning about the existence of Apostles, and what defines them and their work, let us answer a few discovery questions.

Discovery Questions.

The answers to the following few questions might be tell-tale signs that might help you to affirm your designation as an Apostle.

- Do you have a strong sense that God anointed you to be a leader, and do you find yourself often taking the lead among Believers?
- Do you have the confident faith that wherever God might

be sending you, that you will be able to lead people to Christ and Disciple them into maturity?
- Do you find that people often follow your instructions?
- Do you naturally dream and envision new churches planted?
- Do people often ask you to serve in leadership positions because of your ability to make things happen?
- Do you have a strong sense of God's Call on your life to pioneer new ministries?
- Have you been able to successfully pioneer new churches before?

If the answer to all of these statements is a strong *"YES"* then you most certainly have been anointed by God as an Apostolic Leader to advance His Church. If the answer is more *"YES, sometimes"* then you should certainly open yourself up to the possibility that the Lord desire to increasingly use you to pioneer new ministries for Him. If the answer is a *"NO, I have never sensed such an urge or prompting,"* then you might be one of those precious believers who has been blessed with some other prominent gift to serve the Body of Christ.

2. Prophet.

A **prophet** is one who imparts and delivers special, divinely inspired, messages and directions from God.

> *Acts 11:27-30 (NIV)*
> *27 During this time some prophets came down from Jerusalem to Antioch. 28 One of them, named **Agabus**, stood up and through **the Spirit predicted that a severe famine would spread over the entire Roman world**. (This happened during the reign of Claudius.) 29 The disciples, as each one was able, decided to provide help for the brothers and sisters living in Judea. 30 This they did, sending their gift to the elders by Barnabas and Saul.*

Acts 15:32 (NIV)
32 Judas and Silas, who themselves were prophets, *said much to encourage and strengthen the believers.*

Acts 21:10-14 (NIV)
10 After we had been there a number of days, ***a prophet named Agabus*** *came down from Judea. 11 Coming over to us, he took Paul's belt, tied his own hands and feet with it and said,* ***"The Holy Spirit says, 'In this way the Jewish leaders in Jerusalem will bind the owner of this belt and will hand him over to the Gentiles.'"***
12 When we heard this, we and the people there pleaded with Paul not to go up to Jerusalem. 13 Then Paul answered, "Why are you weeping and breaking my heart? I am ready not only to be bound, but also to die in Jerusalem for the name of the Lord Jesus." 14 When he would not be dissuaded, we gave up and said, ***"The Lord's will be done."***

While many people in the church may prophesy from time to time, the office of a prophet is filled by someone whom God consistently uses in this manner in his public ministry. All preachers should preach the Word of God and preach under the anointing of the Holy Spirit, but the prophet is specially called and enabled to proclaim the specific will, purpose, and counsel of God to His people. He will frequently communicate messages concerning God's plan for the future or the church's need to take action in God's plan.

Prophets are those who speak for God.

Hebrews 1: 1 (NIV)
"1 In the past God spoke to our ancestors through the prophets at many times and in various ways,"

Acts 3: 21 (NIV)
21 Heaven must receive him until the time comes for God to restore everything, as he promised long ago through his holy prophets.

Prophets are primarily preachers of righteousness, who bring messages of encouragement, strengthening and comfort.

Acts 15: 32-34 (NIV)
32 Judas and Silas, who themselves were prophets, said much to encourage and strengthen the believers. 33 After spending some time there, they were sent off by the believers with the blessing of peace to return to those who had sent them. [34] 35 But Paul and Barnabas remained in Antioch, where they and many others taught and preached the word of the Lord.

1Corinthians 14: 3-5 (NIV)
3 But the one who prophesies speaks to people for their strengthening, encouraging and comfort. 4 Anyone who speaks in a tongue edifies themselves, but the one who prophesies edifies the church. 5 I would like every one of you to speak in tongues, but I would rather have you prophesy. The one who prophesies is greater than the one who speaks in tongues, unless someone interprets, so that the church may be edified.

Sometimes Prophets foretell the future.

Luke 24: 44-49 (NIV)
He said to them, "This is what I told you while I was still with you: Everything must be fulfilled that is written about me in the Law of Moses, the Prophets and the Psalms." Then he opened their minds so they could understand the Scriptures. 46 He told them, "This is what is written: The Messiah will suffer and rise from the dead on the third day, 47 and repentance for the forgiveness of sins will be preached in his name to all nations, beginning at Jerusalem. 48 You are witnesses of these things. 49 I am going to send you what my Father has promised; but stay in the city until you have been clothed with power from on high."

Prophecy is one of the gifts of the Spirit.

1Corinthians 12:10 (NIV)
10 to another miraculous powers, to another prophecy, to another distinguishing between spirits, to another speaking in different kinds of tongues,"

The office of a Prophet is next in importance to apostles.

1 Corinthians 12:28-31 (NIV)
"28 And God has placed in the church first of all apostles, second prophets, third teachers, then miracles, then gifts of healing, of helping, of guidance, and of different kinds of tongues. 29 Are all apostles? Are all prophets? Are all teachers? Do all work miracles? 30 Do all have gifts of healing? Do all speak in tongues? Do all interpret? 31 Now eagerly desire the greater gifts."

Those who exercise this gift are known as prophets as well.

Acts 13:1-3 (NIV)
1 Now in the church at Antioch there were prophets and teachers: Barnabas, Simeon called Niger, Lucius of Cyrene, Manaen (who had been brought up with Herod the tetrarch) and Saul. 2 While they were worshiping the Lord and fasting, the Holy Spirit said, "Set apart for me Barnabas and Saul for the work to which I have called them." 3 So after they had fasted and prayed, they placed their hands on them and sent them off."

Directions for the exercise of this gift are found in 1Corinthians chapter 14.

1Samuel 19:18-24 (NIV)
18 When David had fled and made his escape, he went to Samuel at Ramah and told him all that Saul had done to him. Then he

and Samuel went to Naioth and stayed there. 19 Word came to Saul: "David is in Naioth at Ramah"; 20 so he sent men to capture him. But when they saw a group of prophets prophesying, with Samuel standing there as their leader, the Spirit of God came on Saul's men, and they also prophesied. 21 Saul was told about it, and he sent more men, and they prophesied too. Saul sent men a third time, and they also prophesied. 22 Finally, he himself left for Ramah and went to the great cistern at Seku. And he asked, "Where are Samuel and David?" "Over in Naioth at Ramah," they said. 23 So Saul went to Naioth at Ramah. But the Spirit of God came even on him, and he walked along prophesying until he came to Naioth. 24 He stripped off his garments, and he too prophesied in Samuel's presence. He lay naked all that day and all that night. This is why people say, "Is Saul also among the prophets?"

2 Chronicles 9: 29 (NIV)
29 *As for the other events of Solomon's reign, from beginning to end, are they not written in the records of* **Nathan the prophet**, *in* **the prophecy of Ahijah** *the Shilonite and in* **the visions of Iddo the seer** *concerning Jeroboam son of Nebat?*

In conclusion of learning about Prophets, and what defines them and their work, let us answer a few discovery questions.

Discovery Questions.

The answers to the following few questions might be telltale signs that God might have anointed you as a Prophet.

- Do you have a strong experience of seeing things, which God shows you, before they happen?
- Do you frequently see that the direct and special messages God gives you impact people greatly?

- Have you experienced that people were deeply offended when you brought them the message God gave you?
- Do you frequently find yourself praying for messages of God to deliver to His people?
- Do you often get asked to pray to God for direction about people's life situations?
- Do you have a strong sense and confidence that God reveals and speaks through you to others?
- Do you often find yourself seeing people's lives as open books before you?
- Do you often hear how things happened just as God said it would through messages you delivered to people?
- Do you find yourself naturally tuned in to hear what God is saying, or want to say, through you to people?

If the answer to all of these statements is a strong **"YES"** then you most certainly have been anointed by God as a Prophet to the Church. If the answer is more **"YES, sometimes"** then you should certainly open yourself up to the possibility that the Lord desire to increasingly use you to hear, receive and deliver His direct, personal messages to people. If the answer is a *"NO, I have never sensed such an urge or prompting,"* then you might be one of those precious believers who has been blessed with some other prominent gift to serve the Body of Christ.

3. Evangelist.

An **evangelist** is literally a preacher of the gospel. He proclaims the good news for the benefit of the unsaved. Greek – **euangelistes**, literally means **the bringer of glad tidings.**

> *Acts 21:8-9 (NIV)*
> *[8] Leaving the next day, we reached Caesarea and stayed at the house of **Philip the evangelist**, one of the Seven. [9] He had four unmarried daughters who prophesied.*

2 Timothy 4:5 (NIV)
[5] But you, keep your head in all situations, endure hardship, ***do the work of an evangelist,*** *discharge all the duties of your ministry.*

This biblical term is not limited to the modern usage of an itinerant preacher who holds special services. Rather, it connotes a minister who is **particularly effective in winning souls**, whether individually or in public preaching.

In conclusion of learning about Evangelists, and what defines them and their work, let us answer a few discovery questions.

Discovery Questions.

The answers to the following few questions might be telltale signs God anointed you as an Evangelist.

- Have you been able to lead people to Christ?
- Do you often find yourself sharing your faith with others in a way that move them to also accept Jesus as the Saviour and Lord?
- Do you often see people respond to the Gospel message when you deliver it?
- Do you find it naturally easy to share with people how to put their faith in Jesus?
- Do you often hear that people came to faith in Jesus Christ as a result of your sharing the Gospel Message?
- Do you find yourself daily looking for opportunities to share your faith and lead people to Christ?
- Do you have a strong sense that God anointed you with a special ability to lead people to salvation?
- Do people often ask you to come and share the Gospel Message with unbelievers?

If the answer to all of these statements is a strong **"YES"** then you probably have been anointed as an Evangelist. If the answer is more *"YES, sometimes"* then you should certainly open yourself up to the possibility that the Lord desire to increasingly use you to share your faith with others. If the answer is a *"NO, I have never sensed such an urge or prompting beyond the occasional opportunity for me to share my faith,"* then you might be one of those precious believers who has been blessed with some other prominent gift to serve the Body of Christ.

4. Pastor.

A **pastor** (literally, "**Shepherd**") is one who leads and takes care of God's people. The Greek word used, and only translated here as Pastor, is the Word "**poimen.**" The other 16 times it is translated as "shepherd." The Bible also speaks of him as a bishop (literally, "Overseer") and an elder.

I Peter 5:1-4 describes the pastor's role of leading, overseeing, and instructing the believers under his care:

> **I Peter 5:1-4** *(NIV)*
> *"The elders who are among you I exhort, I who am a fellow elder and a witness of the sufferings of Christ, and also a partaker of the glory that will be revealed:* **Shepherd the flock of God which is among you,** *serving as overseers, not by constraint, but willingly, not for dishonest gain but eagerly; nor as being lords over those entrusted to you, but being examples to the flock; and when the Chief Shepherd appears, you will receive the crown of glory that does not fade away."*

The New Testament always speaks of elders in the plural, indicating that in each city the church was led by a pastoral team. Scripture, history, and common sense all indicate that there was a senior pastor or presiding elder.

Today we may think of the elders of the church in a city as the senior pastor and pastoral staff of a local church, or as the pastors of various congregations in one city who cooperate as part of the same organization.

The functions of a Pastor are likened unto that of being a Shepherd. We can learn more about these characteristics in John 10 where we read about the Great Shepherd and the heart with which He Shepherded His Sheep. **Ezekiel 34** also gives us an insight into the heart and operation of a Shepherd.

In conclusion of learning about Pastors, and what defines them and their work, let us answer a few discovery questions.

Discovery Questions.

The answers to the following few questions might be telltale signs that might help you to know whether you have been called and anointed as a Shepherd.

- Do you have a sense that God called and anointed you specifically to care for His people?
- Do you enjoy taking care of the spiritual and welfare needs of people?
- Do you feel more comfortable to work with people with whom you have well established relationships?
- Do you find yourself intentionally building deep and meaningful relationships with others so that you can care for them better?
- Do you often hear that people appreciate you for being there for them, and for taking good care of them?
- Do you have a deep sense that God gifted you to walk alongside, and to take care of people?
- Are you most fulfilled when you care for people in their most difficult situations?
- Do you find yourself giving Holy Spirit inspired messages and help to people in their difficulties?

If the answer to all of these statements is a strong *"YES"* then you most certainly have been called and anointed as a Pastor. If the answer is more *"YES, sometimes"* then you should certainly open yourself up to the possibility that the Lord desire to increasingly use you to take care of the needs and welfare of others. If the answer is a *"NO, I have never sensed such an urge or prompting,"* then you might be one of those precious believers who has been blessed with some other prominent gift to serve the Body of Christ.

5. Teacher.

A **teacher** is one who has been anointed and have special giftedness in bringing instruction in the Word of God. (Acts 13:1)

> *Acts 13:1 (NIV)*
> *[13:1] In the church at Antioch there were prophets and **teachers**: Barnabas, Simeon called Niger, Lucius of Cyrene, Manaen (who had been brought up with Herod the tetrarch) and Saul.*

As we have seen, in this context, and specifically in relation to these Spiritual Gifts in the Bible, the preaching and teaching roles are assigned to the overseers in the local church. While many people in the church may have the gift of teaching and can teach effectively in various settings, such as Sunday school classes and home Bible studies, the office of pastor-teacher stands above them. The pastor-teacher is the leading preacher and teacher of the Word. God has not only given him the gift of teaching, but God has given him to the church as its teacher and overseer.

In conclusion of learning about Teachers, and what defines them and their work, let us answer a few discovery questions.

Discovery Questions.

The answers to the following few questions might be telltale signs that will most certainly affirm that God called and anointed you as a Teacher to the body of Christ.

- Do you believe that God called and anointed you to be a Teacher of the Word of God?
- Do you enjoy teaching people in a systematic and understandable way the Truths of God's Word?
- Do you enjoy studying the Word and discovering new truths that you might be able to share?
- Do you frequently find yourself looking for new and innovative ways to communicate more efficiently the truths of God's Word?
- Do you feel honored to be able to see that, through your sharing the truths of God's Word, that fellow Believers grow in their faith?
- Do you have a strong urge to bring the truth to people to displace false beliefs and doctrines?
- Do you take delight, both in knowing the doctrines of the Bible, and by sharing them with others?
- Do you often receive compliments that you are a good teacher of the WORD OF GOD?

If the answer to all of these statements is a strong **"YES"** then you most certainly have been blessed by God in being gifted with the teaching gift as well as being given as a Gift from God to the Church. If the answer is more **"YES, sometimes"** then you should certainly open yourself up to the possibility that the Lord desire to increasingly use you to teach others through you. If the answer is a **"NO, I have never sensed such an urge or prompting,"** then you might be one of those precious believers who has been blessed with some other prominent gift to serve the Body of Christ.

What is the Purpose of these fivefold Ministry Gifts?

The purpose of the Ministerial Gifts is to equip and activate the Gifts of God in Believers.

Ephesians 4:12-16 (NIV)

[12] to prepare God's people for works of service, so that the body of Christ may be built up [13] until we all reach unity in the faith and in the **knowledge of the Son of God** and become **mature,** *attaining to the whole measure of the fullness of Christ. [14] Then we will no longer be infants, tossed back and forth by the waves, and blown here and there by every wind of teaching and by the cunning and craftiness of men in their deceitful scheming. [15] Instead, speaking the truth in love, we will in all things grow up into him who is the Head, that is, Christ. [16] From him the whole body, joined and held together by every supporting ligament, grows and builds itself up in love, as each part does its work.*

The Amplified Version expounds beautifully on the role and function of these Gifts God gave to the church.

Ephesians 4:12-16 (AMP)

[12] His intention was the perfecting and the full equipping of the saints (His consecrated people), [that they should do] the work of ministering toward building up Christ's body (the church), [13] [That it might develop] until we all attain oneness in the faith and in the comprehension of the [full and accurate] knowledge of the Son of God, that [we might arrive] at really *mature manhood (the completeness of personality which is nothing less than the standard height of Christ's own perfection), the measure of the stature of the fullness of the Christ and the completeness found in Him. [14] So then, we may no longer be children, tossed [like ships] to and fro between chance gusts of teaching and wavering with every changing wind of doctrine, [the prey of] the cunning and cleverness of unscrupulous men, [gamblers engaged] in every shifting form of trickery in inventing errors to mislead. [15] Rather, let our lives lovingly express truth [in all things, speaking truly, dealing truly, living truly]. Enfolded in love, let us grow up in every* *way and in all things into Him Who is the Head, [even] Christ (the Messiah, the Anointed One). [16] For because of Him the whole body (the church, in all its various parts), closely joined and firmly knit together by the joints and ligaments with which it is supplied, when each part [with power adapted to its need] is working properly [in all its functions], grows to full maturity, building itself up in love.*

Verse 12 explains the purpose for which God gave apostles, prophets, evangelists, pastors and teachers to the church. The commas in this verse, in the KJV, could lead someone to interpret it as describing three separate tasks of these ministers, but punctuation was not part of the original text of Scripture. Translators added punctuation to aid in reading and for understanding. In this case, a study of the Greek text and various translations makes it clear that there is one purpose with a threefold progression, as follows:

- God gave the ministerial Gifts to the church for the "**perfecting**" (AMP) or "**equipping**" (NKJV) of the Believers.
- The Believers are equipped so they can do "**the work of ministry.**" Here, "**ministry**" means "**service**," or all the functions of the church. **Every believer should have a ministry**—not necessarily a public preaching ministry but a specific place of service in the body of Christ. **It is the task of the apostles, prophets, evangelists, pastors and teachers to help each Believer to find their work of ministry** and **train them to perform that task properly** within the body. Those who hold the five ministerial offices are to *inspire, motivate, disciple, instruct, and prepare the Believers* so that **everyone become an active, productive member of the body.**
- When each member of the body performs his proper function, the whole body will be edified, or built up. The goal is to attain maturity in Christ. **Beginning** with "*the*

unity of the Spirit in the bond of peace" (Ephesians 4:3), we are to pursue **"*the unity of the faith"*** and **"the knowledge of the Son of God,"** to a perfect man, to the measure of the stature of the fullness of Christ" (Ephesians 4:13).

According to Ephesians 4:14-16, each local body of believers should seek everything God enabled them to have, that will characterize them as mature Believers:

- Becoming established in the faith so that they are not swayed by false doctrine and false leaders.
- Speaking the truth in love. They should learn to minister to one another and to unbelievers with a balance of honesty and compassion, equally valuing and manifesting truth and love.
- Submitting to the lordship of Jesus Christ in all things and depending upon His divine supply for all things.
- Everyone learning to contribute his or her share to the work of the church, so that the body can grow and be built up in love, using their Spiritual Gifts to build the Church up.

Summary

The ministerial office gifts of Ephesians chapter 4 are God's endowment to the local and worldwide church for the purpose of equipping the members for their assigned tasks. During the next session we will look at the service gifts of Romans 12, especially as to how God gives each member of the church one or more special abilities to help the church function productively as a body.

3

THE SERVICE GIFTS
SESSION THREE

The Service Gifts are those Supernatural Gifts, given to Believers, to enable them to perform and serve in extra-ordinary ways, and with extra-ordinary authority and ability.

> *Romans 12:3-8 (NIV)*
> *"For I say, through **the grace given to me**, to **everyone** who is among you, not to think of himself more highly than he ought to think, but to think soberly, as God has dealt to each one a measure of faith. For as we have many members in one body, but all the members do not have the same function, so we, being many, are one body in Christ, and individually members of one another. Having then gifts differing according to the grace that is given to us, let us use them: **if prophecy**, let us prophesy in proportion to our faith; **or ministry**, let us use it in our ministering; **he who teaches**, in teaching; **he who exhorts**, in exhortation; **he who gives**, with liberality; **he who leads**, with diligence; **he who shows mercy**, with cheerfulness"*

The Greek word for "gifts" here is *charismata*, the plural of *charisma*. It is also used of the nine spiritual gifts of I Corinthians 12. This word is related to *charis*, or "grace," which refers to **the free, undeserved blessing and work of God**. The connotation is that these gifts are free, unmerited, miraculous endowments from God.

In this chapter, Paul cited seven avenues of his revelation of the service gifts. His manner of presentation reveals that the list of gifts here is **not exhaustive but representative or illustrative of the ways God uses individuals in His church**. There are many other aspects of Christian service that this passage does not specifically identify.

These are **truly giftings from God** and **not merely human attainments**. While there are some natural human abilities that correspond to this list, at least in part, even the talents we receive from birth, and those nurtured in us, have their ultimate source in the design, purpose, and grace of God.

In this session we will explore the following service gifts:

- Prophecy
- Serving
- Teaching
- Exhortation
- Giving
- Leading (ruling in KJV)
- Showing mercy

1. The Gift of Prophecy.

The first in the list is prophecy, and it refers to a divinely inspired utterance, or speaking under divine unction to edify others. It refers specifically to a supernatural public message in the language of the audience.

> Romans 12:6 (NIV)
> *We have different gifts, according to the grace given us. If a man's gift is prophesying, let him use it in proportion to his faith.*

It takes faith to prophecy, both since it requires faith to know that it was the voice of the Holy Spirit bringing the message to you, as well as speaking up to deliver the message in a way in which it will be heard and received with the right emphasis that the Holy Spirit delivered it to you.

The Greek word that is used is *"prophēteía"* and it describes the verb's meaning: *"to prophecy, prophesying; the gift of communicating and enforcing revealed truth."*

The Strong's Concordance defines it as:

"4394 prophēteía (from 4396 /prophētēs, "prophet," which is derived from 4253/pró, "before" and 5346 /phēmí, "make clear, assert as a priority") – properly, what is clarified beforehand; prophecy which involves divinely empowered forth-telling(asserting the mind of God) or foretelling (prediction) "[1]

The same word is used in the outlining of the 9 spiritual gifts and its subsequent use. I can only think that it has such prominence in the edification and upbuilding of the Body of Christ that Paul emphasised it in both of these compilations or summarizations of the Gifts.

From the Corinthians 14 text we are led to understand that we *"can all prophesy,"* or in my words *"bring encouraging and upbuilding messages,"* however, the further definition, that sets this use apart from the 1 Corinthians 12 reference is that here there is the injection of *"if someone comes with a revelation"* the other should retreat and allow preference to that kind of prophecy. I think that this later reference might refer to the *"level of faith"* that is required and applied in the use of the spiritual gift. In my understanding, at least for as far as what the same word is used, this service gift is the same spiritual gift of prophecy as explored in 1 Corinthians 12.

Some do explain, and even translate it, to reference more "the gift of preaching." I have to default to the Greek text. The Greek word for *"preaching"* is *"kérugma"* and there is no indication in the Greek that it is what Paul mentioned. He would have used *"kérugma"* instead of *"prophēteía"* if that is what he meant.

> *1 Corinthians 14:29-33 (NIV)*
> *[29]* **Two or three prophets should speak,** *and the others should weigh carefully what is said. [30] And if a revelation comes to someone who is sitting down, the first speaker should stop. [31] For* **you can all prophesy in turn so that everyone may be instructed and encouraged.** *[32] The spirits of prophets are subject to the control of prophets. [33] For God is not a God of disorder but of peace.*

As in this case it seems that these **"Prophets"** spoke **"without a revelation"** and would therefore be subject to those who truly bring a prophetic, forecasting message as a result of a divine revelation they received. It seems to indicate the more general prophetic use of anointed **"encouragement, godly instruction and guidance"** until someone has a **"revelation"** which should be regarded with greater respect.

> *Acts 2:17 (NIV)*
> *[17] "'In the last days, God says, I will pour out my Spirit on all people.* ***Your sons and daughters will prophesy,*** *your young men will see visions, your old men will dream dreams."*

> *1 Corinthians 14:3 (NIV)*
> *"[3] But* ***everyone who prophesies speaks to men for their strengthening, encouragement and comfort."***

If someone has this gift, he should exercise it in proportion to his faith—as much as his measure of faith will enable him. Speak the Word by faith, that it will change and transform those who hear and apply it in their lives. It requires faith to speak what you believe God is saying to you, and through you, to others.

Discover Questions.

In conclusion of learning about the Gift of Prophecy, and what defines it, let us answer a few discovery questions. The answers to the following few questions might be telltale signs that might help you to know whether you have received this gift.

- Do you delight in delivering encouraging messages from God to edify, exhort and comfort others?
- Do you often find encouraging messages, through your time in the Word and prayer, that you confidently share with others?
- Do you spontaneously sense that the Holy Spirit give you messages that will encourage and strengthen others?
- Do you often hear that prophetic messages you gave others, encouraged them, and brought great clarity and direction to what God wanted for them?
- Do you feel both blessed to be able to receive messages from God, as well as blessed to be able to confidently share them with others?

If the answer is a strong "**YES**" then you most certainly have been blessed by God in receiving the spiritual gift of prophecy to serve others. If the answer is more "**YES, sometimes**" then you should certainly open yourself up to the possibility that the Lord desire to increasingly use you to encourage and strengthen others through divinely inspired messages He delivers to you, and through you. If the answer is a "**NO, I have never sensed such an urge or prompting,**" then you might be one of those precious believers who has been blessed with some other prominent gift to serve the Body of Christ.

2. The Gift of Serving

Serving means service to others, particularly service in the church. Some people *are especially gifted with an attitude and ability of service in certain capacities.* The Greek word is *diakonia*, which is a broad word that covers a variety of services, work, or assistance. It can also refer specifically to the work of a deacon, who helps with the business and organizational matters in a local church.

> *Romans 12:7 (NIV)*
> ***If it is serving, let him serve;*** *if it is teaching, let him teach;*

> *Acts 6:1-6 (NIV)*
> *[6:1] In those days when the number of disciples was increasing, the Grecian Jews among them complained against the Hebraic Jews because their widows were being overlooked in* ***the daily distribution of food.*** *[2] So the Twelve gathered all the disciples together and said, "****It would not be right for us to neglect the ministry of the word of God in order to wait on tables.*** *[3] Brothers, choose seven men from among you who are known to be full of the Spirit and wisdom.* ***We will turn this responsibility over to them*** *[4] and will give our attention to prayer and the ministry of the word." [5] This proposal pleased the whole group. They chose Stephen, a man full of faith and of the Holy Spirit; also, Philip, Procorus, Nicanor, Timon, Parmenas, and Nicolas from Antioch, a convert to Judaism. [6] They presented these men to the apostles, who prayed and laid their hands on them.*

What we learned from the Letter to Timothy is that those who serve as deacons in the local church should prove themselves as trustworthy and faithful stewards. The organized church has long benefitted from the sacrificial service of those operating in this gift.

> *1 Timothy 3:8-13 (NIV)*
> *Deacons, likewise, are to be men worthy of respect, sincere, not indulging in much wine, and not pursuing dishonest gain. [9] They must keep hold of the deep truths of the faith with a clear conscience. [10] They must first be tested; and then if there is*

nothing against them, let them serve as deacons. In the same way, their wives are to be women worthy of respect, not malicious talkers but temperate and trustworthy in everything. A deacon must be the husband of but one wife and must manage his children and his household well. [13] Those who have served well gain an excellent standing and great assurance in their faith in Christ Jesus.

Discovery Questions.

In conclusion of learning about the Gift of Serving, and what defines it, let us answer a few discovery questions. The answers to the following few questions might be telltale signs that might help you to know whether you have received this gift.

- Do you delight in doing ordinary tasks that make things easier for others?
- Do you enjoy being part of the team that set up and pack equipment away before and after church services?
- Do you enjoy making sure that facilities and things like dishes are clean so that others can enjoy a clean and safe environment?
- Do you find yourself always looking to do the little things that makes things easier for others?
- Do you actually prefer to do those behind the scenes things that make things go smoothly for those who serve up front and in front of others?
- Do you feel privileged to be able to serve and to help others fulfill their purpose?

If the answer to all of these statements is a strong "YES" then you most certainly have been blessed by God in receiving this spiritual gift to serve others. If the answer is more "YES, sometimes" then you should certainly open yourself up to the possibility that the Lord desire to increasingly use you to serve others through you. If the answer is a "NO, I have never sensed such an urge or prompting, then you might be one of those precious believers who has been blessed with some other prominent gift to serve the Body of Christ.

3. The Gift of Teaching.

The gift of **teaching**, or the giving of instruction, is that gift of God by which others are taught in the truths of God's Word. House Group Leaders, Bible study group teachers, and Sunday school teachers are possible examples of people who operate in this gift. This is the gift of opening up something through teaching to someone, through the power of the Holy Spirit. This "opening up" is the gift in operation where you share some personal revelation or truth from the Word of God in a way that it is clearly understood, and where those receiving such teaching are inspired to put it into practice.

> *Romans 12:7 (NIV)*
> *If it is serving, let him serve; **if it is teaching, let him teach;***

Definition:

The Greek word for Teacher is "***didaskalos.***" The Greek word for Teaching is "***didasko***". The Bible study tools define it as:

- to teach
- to hold discourse with others in order to instruct them, deliver didactic discourses
- to be a teacher
- to discharge the office of a teacher, conduct oneself as a teacher
- to teach one
- to impart instruction
- instil doctrine into one
- the thing taught or enjoined
- to explain or expound a thing

- to teach one something[2]

Jesus taught the people in the Synagogues and on the streets. We learn a lot about this spiritual gift by the way Jesus operated with it.

Mark 6:34 (NIV)
*When Jesus landed and saw a large crowd, he had compassion on them, because they were like sheep without a shepherd. So, **he began teaching them many things.***

Jesus taught with authority and power. When someone flows in this gift, you will find that there is a level of authority and power on such teaching.

Luke 4:32 (NIV)
They were amazed at his teaching,** because his message **had authority.

Luke 4:36 (NIV)
*All the people were amazed and said to each other, **"What is this teaching? With authority and power,** he gives orders to evil spirits and they come out!"*

Jesus taught us that His teaching came from above. A true teaching will carry with it a heavenly anointing of revelation and the spiritual eyes and hearts will be opened.

John 7:16-17 (NIV)
*16 Jesus answered, **"My teaching is not my own.** It comes from him who sent me. 17 If anyone chooses to do God's will, he will find out whether **my teaching comes from God** or whether I speak on my own."*

The Apostles practiced this gift everywhere they went. The things they taught became known as the Apostle's Teachings.

> *Acts 2:42 (NIV)*
> They devoted themselves to the **apostles' teaching** and to the fellowship, to the breaking of bread and to prayer.

> *Acts 5:28 (NIV)*
> "We gave you strict orders not to teach in this name," he said. "Yet **you have filled Jerusalem with your teaching** and are determined to make us guilty of this man's blood."

You have not taught someone until they have learned, and they have not learnt until you have taught them. The onus is on the teacher to ensure that the students learn. The fruit of this gift is that people learn truths when you teach it to them. You are able to communicate complex things in a simple and easy to understand way.

Acts 13 tells us that there were Teachers and Prophets fasting and praying together when the Holy Spirit spoke.

> *Acts 13:1 (NIV)*
> In the church at Antioch there were prophets and **teachers:** Barnabas, Simeon called Niger, Lucius of Cyrene, Manaen (who had been brought up with Herod the tetrarch) and Saul.

The Gracious intervention in making this gift active in our lives is the empowering that comes from the Holy Spirit, in allowing you to share His Instruction and Teaching in a way that allows others to be taught and be instructed. You know that God anointed you to teach His Word when you sense a strong willingness to be used by God to teach the truths of God's Word to others, and when you see how people assimilate the truths you share.

Discovery Questions.

In conclusion of learning about the Gift of Teaching, and what defines it, let us answer a few discovery questions. The answers to the following few questions might be telltale signs that might help you to know whether you have received this gift.

- Have you recently heard from Believers that they were greatly helped by the truths that you shared with them?
- Do you enjoy seeing people gain new insights when you share with them?
- Do you enjoy studying the Word and discovering new truths that you might be able to share?
- Do you frequently find yourself looking for new and innovative ways to communicate more efficiently the truths of God's Word?
- Do you feel honored to be able to see that, through your sharing the truths of God's Word, that fellow Believers grow in their faith?

If the answer to all of these statements is a strong "YES" then you most certainly have been blessed by God in receiving this spiritual gift to teach others. If the answer is more "YES, sometimes" then you should certainly open yourself up to the possibility that the Lord desire to increasingly use you to teach others through you. If the answer is a "NO, I have never sensed such an urge or prompting," then you might be one of those precious believers who has been blessed with some other prominent gift to serve the Body of Christ.

4. The Gift of Exhortation.

Exhortation means to give encouragement or comfort. Some translations actually use encouraging and encourage instead of exhortation. *To exhort is to encourage.* Some people exercise this gift by public testimony, while others do so primarily by personal contact. Those who exercise this Gift often do so spontaneously with strangers, their friends or people they know who needs some cheering up. They exercise it in a variety of ways including naturally talking with people, telephone calls, letters, and cards.

> *Romans 12:8 (NIV)*
> "8 *if it is encouraging, let him encourage; if it is contributing to the needs of others, let him give generously; if it is leadership, let him govern diligently; if it is showing mercy, let him do it cheerfully."*

The Greek word is from the root word "**parakaleō**" which means "**to call to a person, to call to the side.**" To "**exhort**" is to come alongside someone.

Joseph was well-known for this gift that the apostles gave him the surname Barnabas, meaning "***Son of Encouragement.***"

> *Acts 4:36-37 (NIV)*
> *[36] Joseph, a Levite from Cyprus, whom the apostles called* **Barnabas (which means Son of Encouragement)**, *[37] sold a field he owned and brought the money and put it at the apostles' feet.*

Barnabas practiced this gift when he brought Paul to the Apostles. He walked alongside Paul until Paul was well established in his calling. Mentors often operate in this gifting as they pour courage and hope into protégés.

> *Acts 9:26-27 (NIV)*
> *[26] When he came to Jerusalem, he tried to join the disciples, but they were all afraid of him, not believing that he really was a disciple. [27] But Barnabas took him and brought him to the apostles. He told them how Saul on his journey had seen the Lord and that the Lord had spoken to him, and how in Damascus he had preached fearlessly in the name of Jesus.*

The Apostle operated in this gift when he spoke in the synagogue in Antioch on one of his visits.

> *Acts 13:15 (NIV)*
> *After the reading from the Law and the Prophets, the synagogue rulers sent word to them, saying, "Brothers, if you have a message of encouragement for the people, please speak."*

Paul seemed to operate in this gift quite a bit when he visited the region of Macedonia and Greece.

> *Acts 20:1-2 (NIV) Through Macedonia and Greece*
> *"1 When the uproar had ended, Paul sent for the disciples and, **after encouraging them**, said good-by and set out for Macedonia. 2 He traveled through that area, **speaking many words of encouragement to the people**, and finally arrived in Greece,"*

When we live united with Christ then we will always find ourselves encouraged.

> *Philippians 2:1 (NIV)*
> *"1 **If you have any encouragement from being united with Christ**, if any comfort from his love, if any fellowship with the Spirit, if any tenderness and compassion,"*

Sometimes we find a brother or sister who just bring encouragement when they are with you.

> *Philemon 1:7 (NIV)*
> *"7 Your love has given me great joy and **encouragement**, because you, brother, have refreshed the hearts of the saints."*

Discovery Questions.

In conclusion of learning about the Gift of Exhortation, and what defines it, let us answer a few discovery questions. The answers to the following few questions might be telltale signs that might help you to know whether you have received this gift.

- Do you naturally and spontaneously see the positive side of sometimes difficult situations?
- Do you normally find some uplifting and positive thing to say to others?
- Do you daily make the effort to compliment people?
- Do you frequently hear that your positive attitude and words encourage others?
- Do you generally feel privileged that you have this positive ability to point people to the good and blessed things in life?

If the answer to all of these statements is a strong "**YES**" then you most certainly have been blessed by God in receiving this spiritual gift to bring encouragement and hope to others. If the answer is more "**YES, sometimes**" then you should certainly open yourself up to the possibility that the Lord desire to increasingly use you to exhort others through you. If the answer is a "**NO, I have never sensed such an urge or prompting**," then you might be one of those precious believers who has been blessed with some other prominent gift to serve the Body of Christ.

5. The Gift of Giving.

The **gift of giving** is sharing material blessings with the church and with others.

> *Romans 12:8 AMP*
> *"He who exhorts (encourages), to his exhortation;* **he who**

contributes, let him do it in simplicity and liberality; he who gives aid and superintends, with zeal and singleness of mind; he who does acts of mercy, with genuine cheerfulness and joyful eagerness."

The Amplified Bible (**AMP**) says to give with "**simplicity**," but most commentators understand the underlying Greek word to mean "**liberally, and generously.**" It can also mean "**singleness of heart, sincere concern.**" Some people are blessed significantly more than others with the means and opportunity to give to God's cause.

> 1 Timothy 6:17-20 (NIV) 17 Command those who are rich in this present world not to be arrogant nor to put their hope in wealth, which is so uncertain, but to put their hope in God, who richly provides us with everything for our enjoyment. 18 Command them to do good, to be rich in good deeds, and to be generous and willing to share. 19 In this way they will lay up treasure for themselves as a firm foundation for the coming age, so that they may take hold of the life that is truly life.

They **should not consider** their material blessings to be **a sign of superiority** but **a gift of God for the purpose of assisting His kingdom in a special way.** They should not be selfish but generous, recognizing that in God's plan they have greater ability and responsibility to give than most others.

> 2 Corinthians 9:10-11 (NIV) 10 Now he who supplies seed to the sower and bread for food will also supply and increase your store of seed and will enlarge the harvest of your righteousness. 11 You will be enriched in every way so that you can be generous on every occasion, and through us your generosity will result in thanksgiving to God.

Discovery Questions.

In conclusion of learning about the Gift of Giving, and what defines it, let us answer a few discovery questions. The answers to the following few questions might be telltale signs that might help you to know whether you have received this gift.

- Are you quite disciplined in managing your finances?
- Are your finances in a state where you generally are able to give generously to the Lord's work?
- Do your financial records show that you are able to give more than just your tithe?
- Are you often approached to give to some Kingdom advancing cause?
- Are you able to give generously when requests are made to give?
- Do you often find yourself, even when you are stretched, giving, just because you believe in a cause, and because you love to see God's work advance?
- Do often revisit your budget to see where you are able to reduce expenses to enable you to do more for the advance of the Kingdom of God?

If the answer to all of these statements is a strong "**YES**" then you most certainly have been blessed by God in receiving this spiritual gift to be a generous giver. If the answer is more "**YES, sometimes**" then you should certainly open yourself up to the possibility that the Lord desire to increasingly use you to give so that others may be blessed through your giving and support. If the answer is a "**NO, I have never sensed such an urge or prompting,**" then you might be one of those precious believers who has been blessed with some other prominent gift to serve the Body of Christ.

6. The Gift of Leadership.

Leading, or ruling in the KJV, speaks of direction, guidance, and influence within the church. Leaders are to exercise their role with diligence, carefulness, and earnestness. God has ordained rulers or leaders in His church.

The Greek word gives beautiful expression of it meaning. The Greek word is **"proistēmi"** and means *"to put before, to set over and to rule."* With diligence which is the word *"spoudē"* and where we get our English word *"expedient"* from (***to be diligent and earnest in effort.***)

> *Romans 12:8 (NIV)*
> *8 if it is encouraging, let him encourage; if it is contributing to the needs of others, let him give generously;* ***if it is leadership, let him govern diligently;*** *if it is showing mercy, let him do it cheerfully.*

It is important to submit to human authority in the church, as long as human leaders exercise their authority under God according to the guidelines of His Word.

> *Hebrews 13:17 (NIV)*
> *17 Have confidence in your leaders and submit to their authority, because they keep watch over you as those who must give an account. Do this so that their work will be a joy, not a burden, for that would be of no benefit to you.*

The church needs various people with leadership and administrative ability. In addition to the pastor and pastoral staff, the successful congregation will have capable leaders over various departments and activities as well as influential opinion makers and role models who may or may not have an official position.

Discovery Questions.

In conclusion of learning about the Gift of Leadership, and what defines it, let us answer a few discovery questions. The answers to the following few questions might be telltale signs that might help you to know whether you have received this gift.

- Do you find that others easily follow the decisions you make?
- Do you find that people often look to you for guidance and direction in what to do?
- Do people often ask you what to do next?
- Do you find that people naturally follow the ideas and suggestions you propose?
- Do you feel that you have been blessed to make thought-through decisions?

If the answer to all of these statements is a strong "**YES**" then you most certainly have been blessed by God in receiving this spiritual gift to lead others. If the answer is more "**YES, sometimes**" then you should certainly open yourself up to the possibility that the Lord desire to increasingly use you to lead others. If the answer is a "**NO, I have never sensed such an urge or prompting,**" then you might be one of those precious believers who has been blessed with some other prominent gift to serve the Body of Christ.

7. The Gift of Showing Mercy.

Showing mercy means **being merciful and kind to others.** It can include visiting the sick, helping the poor, and assisting widows and orphans.

> *Romans 12:8 (NIV)*
> *if it is encouraging, let him encourage; if it is contributing to the needs of others, let him give generously; if it is leadership, let*

*him govern diligently; **if it is showing mercy, let him do it cheerfully.***

Matthew 25:31-40 (NIV) The Sheep and the Goats
[31] "When the Son of Man comes in his glory, and all the angels with him, he will sit on his throne in heavenly glory. [32] All the nations will be gathered before him, and he will separate the people one from another as a shepherd separates the sheep from the goats. [33] He will put the sheep on his right and the goats on his left. [34] "Then the King will say to those on his right, 'Come, you who are blessed by my Father; take your inheritance, the kingdom prepared for you since the creation of the world. [35] For I was hungry and you gave me something to eat, I was thirsty and you gave me something to drink, I was a stranger and you invited me in, [36] I needed clothes and you clothed me, I was sick and you looked after me, I was in prison and you came to visit me.' [37] "Then the righteous will answer him, 'Lord, when did we see you hungry and feed you, or thirsty and give you something to drink? [38] When did we see you a stranger and invite you in, or needing clothes and clothe you? [39] When did we see you sick or in prison and go to visit you?' [40] "The King will reply, 'I tell you the truth, whatever you did for one of the least of these brothers of mine, you did for me.'

Galatians 2:10 (NIV)
[10] All they asked was that we should continue to remember the poor, the very thing I was eager to do.

James 1:27 (NIV)
[27] Religion that God our Father accepts as pure and faultless is this: to look after orphans and widows in their distress and to keep oneself from being polluted by the world.

James 2:15-17 (NIV)
[15] Suppose a brother or sister is without clothes and daily food. [16] If one of you says to him, "Go, I wish you well; keep warm and well fed," but does nothing about his physical needs, what good is it? [17] In the same way, faith by itself, if it is not accompanied by action, is dead.

A person who fills this role should do it cheerfully, not in a begrudging, mournful, or patronizing way. To some extent, every mature Christian should be able to function in the seven areas just listed. **All Christians are to be** *an effective witness,* **to serve, to encourage, to give,** and **to show mercy.** All should have **some basic ability to instruct unbelievers in the plan of salvation and to lead new converts in the ways of the Lord.**

This passage tells us, however, that each Christian has some area of special strength, given by God. While we should always "**be ready for every good work**" (Titus 3:1), we need to discern what our strong points are and use them effectively.

Discovery Questions.

In conclusion of learning about the Gift of Mercy, and what defines it, let us answer a few discovery questions. The answers to the following few questions might be telltale signs that might help you to know whether you have received this gift.

- Do you prefer working and assisting people who find themselves physically and mentally challenged?
- Do you often and naturally find yourself taking care of those with material and physical needs?
- People often call on me to make hospital visits.
- Do you frequently get asked to visit those in troublesome circumstances?
- Do you love walking alongside people to help them find solutions to their problems?

- Do you feel blessed to be able to have the temperament to help those in physical, mental and material challenging situations?

If the answer to all of these statements is a strong "**YES**" then you most certainly have been blessed by God in receiving this spiritual gift to show Mercy others. If the answer is more "**YES, sometimes**" then you should certainly open yourself up to the possibility that the Lord desire to increasingly use you to extend and show Mercy to others. If the answer is a "**NO, I have never sensed such an urge or prompting,**" then you might be one of those precious believers who has been blessed with some other prominent gift to serve the Body of Christ.

Afterword

To summarize, each Christian is part of the Body, the Body of Christ that is, and has a particular gift, role, or function in the church, or possibly several of them. Whatever God has given him to do; he should exercise it to his full capacity but always with humility.

Being a Christian means being a part of a body. Understanding where God, the creator and developer of the Body placed you, will bring you to a place of understanding your purpose, and finding fulfillment.

4

THE SUPERNATURAL SPIRITUAL GIFTS
SESSION FOUR

In this session we will look, and explore, the Supernatural Spiritual Gifts.

The Supernatural Spiritual Gifts are primarily defined in 1 Corinthians chapter 12.

> *1 Corinthians 12:7-11 (NIV)*
>
> *[7] Now to each one the manifestation of the Spirit is given for the common good. [8] To one there is given through the Spirit the message of wisdom, to another the message of knowledge by means of the same Spirit, [9] to another faith by the same Spirit, to another gifts of healing by that one Spirit, [10] to another miraculous powers, to another prophecy, to another distinguishing between spirits, to another speaking in different kinds of tongues,* and to still another the interpretation of tongues.* [11] All these are the work of one and the same Spirit, and he gives them to each one, just as he determines.*

The Supernatural Spiritual Gifts are:

We recognize nine Gifts in this portion of Scripture. They are:

- Word of Wisdom
- Word of Knowledge
- Faith
- Gifts of healings
- Working of miracles
- Prophecy
- Discerning of spirits
- Different kinds of tongues
- Interpretation of tongues

1. Words of Wisdom

A Word of Wisdom is characterized by it being wise counsel and guidance within a specified situation. The Wisdom that the Holy Spirit will reveal, will bring clarity, soundness and practical application within a known situation. It will answer the "How to" and "what must I do" in a given circumstance that you are facing.

> *1 Corinthians 2:6-8 (NIV)*
> *6 **We do, however, speak a message of wisdom** among the mature, but not the wisdom of this age or of the rulers of this age, who are coming to nothing. 7. No, **we declare God's wisdom, a mystery that has been hidden and that God destined for our glory before time began.** 8. None of the rulers of this age understood it, for if they had, they would not have crucified the Lord of glory.*

In this Scripture reference we see this Gift of Words of Wisdom in operation. We bring messages that in essence brings Supernatural Wisdom, not naturally known. As we see in another example in Acts chapter six, that when this Gift is in operation, it is hard to stand up against its soundness and clarity.

> Acts 6:3,10 (NIV)
> 3 Brothers and sisters, choose seven men from among you who are **known to be full of the Spirit and wisdom.** We will turn this responsibility over to them. 10 But they could not stand up against **the wisdom the Spirit gave** him as he spoke.

The Apostle Paul expounds on How this Gift brings revelation of things not previously known.

> I Corinthians 2:1-13 (NIV)
> 'And so it was with me, brothers and sisters. When I came to you, I did not come with eloquence or human wisdom as I proclaimed to you the testimony about God. I came to you in weakness with great fear and trembling. My message and my preaching were not with wise and persuasive words, but with a demonstration of the Spirit's power, so that your faith might not rest on human wisdom, but on God's power. We do, however, speak a message of wisdom among the mature, but not the wisdom of this age or of the rulers of this age, who are coming to nothing. No, we declare God's wisdom, a mystery that has been hidden and that God destined for our glory before time began. None of the rulers of this age understood it, for if they had, they would not have crucified the Lord of glory. However, as it is written: "What no eye has seen, what no ear has heard, and what no human mind has conceived" — the things God has prepared for those who love him— these are the things God has revealed to us by his Spirit. The Spirit searches all things, even the deep things of God. What we have received is not the spirit of the world, but the Spirit who is from God, so that we may understand what God has freely given us. This is what we speak, not in words taught us by human wisdom but in words taught by the Spirit, explaining spiritual realities with Spirit-

taught words. For who knows a person's thoughts except their own spirit within them? In the same way no one knows the thoughts of God except the Spirit of God. For I resolved to know nothing while I was with you except Jesus Christ and him crucified.'

We receive these Words of Wisdom by the Holy Spirit. This Wisdom is not acquired in natural ways, we receive it by divine revelation from the Holy Spirit.

I Corinthians 12:8 (NIV)
'To one there is given through the Spirit a message of wisdom, to another a message of knowledge by means of the same Spirit,'

One way in which we can receive this Gift is to ask God for it. The Apostle James exhorts us who lack wisdom to go to God and to ask Him for wisdom.

James 1:5,6 (NIV)
'If any of you lacks wisdom, you should ask God, who gives generously to all without finding fault, and it will be given to you. But when you ask, you must believe and not doubt, because the one who doubts is like a wave of the sea, blown and tossed by the wind.'

It is clear from the Apostle Peter's second letter that the Apostle Paul wrote Words of Wisdom that He received from God.

2 Peter 3:15,16 (NIV)
15 Bear in mind that our Lord's patience means salvation, just as our dear brother Paul also wrote you with the wisdom that God gave him. He writes the same way in all his letters, speaking in them of these matters. 16 His letters contain some things that are hard to understand, which ignorant and unstable people distort, as they do the other Scriptures, to their own destruction.

Discovery Questions.

The answers to the following few questions might be tell-tale signs that might help you to know whether you have received this gift.

- Do you find it easy to apply biblical principles, in context, in your life?
- Do you often find yourself coming up with solutions to fairly complicated situations?
- Do you frequently find yourself helping believers find solutions and answers through biblical examples and stories?
- Do you often hear that the Biblical Truth you share is most relevant and specific to felt needs?
- Do you have a sense of deep peace and personal confidence when you need to make important decisions?

If the answer to all of these statements is a strong "**YES**" then you most certainly have been blessed by God in receiving the spiritual gift of Wisdom to help and guide others. If the answer is more "**YES, sometimes**" then you should certainly open yourself up to the possibility that the Lord desire to increasingly use you to help and guide others through the wisdom He gave to you. If the answer is a "**NO, I have never sensed such an urge or prompting,**" then you might be one of those precious believers who has been blessed with some other prominent gift to serve the Body of Christ.

2. Words of Knowledge

A Word of Knowledge is characterized by knowledge being Supernaturally revealed to a Believer who had no prior knowledge or insight into the revealed details. Jesus and many Believers subsequently experienced the operation of this extra-ordinary gift.

We read of one prominent example, of this Gift in operation, in Acts chapter five where the Holy Spirit reveals knowledge about a transaction that took place, and a devised scheme, to lie about the proceeds of the sale.

> *Acts 5:1-11(NIV) Ananias and Sapphira*
> *'Now a man named Ananias, together with his wife Sapphira, also sold a piece of property. With his wife's full knowledge, he kept back part of the money for himself, but brought the rest and put it at the apostles' feet. Then Peter said, "Ananias, how is it that Satan has so filled your heart that you have lied to the Holy Spirit and have kept for yourself some of the money you received for the land? Didn't it belong to you before it was sold? And after it was sold, wasn't the money at your disposal? What made you think of doing such a thing? You have not lied just to human beings but to God." When Ananias heard this, he fell down and died. And great fear seized all who heard what had happened. Then some young men came forward, wrapped up his body, and carried him out and buried him. About three hours later his wife came in, not knowing what had happened. Peter asked her, "Tell me, is this the price you and Ananias got for the land?" "Yes," she said, "that is the price." Peter said to her, "How could you conspire to test the Spirit of the Lord? Listen! The feet of the men who buried your husband are at the door, and they will carry you out also." At that moment she fell down at his feet and died. Then the young men came in and, finding her dead, carried her out and buried her beside her husband. Great fear seized the whole church and all who heard about these events.'*

A few Gifts of the Holy Spirit was in operation here. The result of their scheming was disastrous.

It is mind-blowing how the Holy Spirit is able to bring knowledge to a person. This can only be understood, and received, by those who enjoy the indwelling of the Holy Spirit.

> *I Corinthians 2:14 (NIV)*
> *'The person without the Spirit does not accept the things that come from the Spirit of God but considers them foolishness and cannot understand them because they are discerned only through the Spirit.'*

We receive this Gift from the Holy Spirit.

> *1 Corinthians 12:8 (NIV)*
> *'To one there is given through the Spirit a message of wisdom, to another **a message of knowledge** by means of the same Spirit,'*

The "Knowledge" Paul refers to, in his second letter to the church in Corinthians, as well as his address to the church in Colossae, is this Gift of Knowledge.

> *2 Corinthians 11:6 (NIV)*
> *'I may indeed be untrained as a speaker, but **I do have knowledge.** We have made this perfectly clear to you in every way.'*

> *Colossians 2:2,3 (NIV)*
> *'My goal is that they may be encouraged in heart and united in love, so that they may have the full riches of complete understanding, in order that they may know the mystery of God, namely, Christ, in whom are hidden all the treasures of wisdom and knowledge.'*

I pray that many of you will be filled with this kind of Supernatural Knowledge, and that through its operation and use in our lives that the wisdom of God will be shared and many give praises to God.

Discovery Questions.

The answers to the following few questions might be tell-tale signs that might help you to know whether you have received this gift.

- Do you frequently find that the Holy Spirit give you insight into people's lives without any prior knowledge of them and their circumstances?
- Do you often find that you have knowledge about people, their children, their work, their personality, their present circumstances, without having any prior knowledge of them?
- Do you find yourself at times knowing people's names, place names, conditions in people, without ever learning it or being introduced to them?
- Do you often receive and share insight into the spiritual situations of people, and then consequently see how it brought them closer to God?
- Do you often find new strategies and techniques from studying the Scriptures that you eventually see help further the Kingdom of God?
- Do you frequently find yourself praying to understand what God desires to say to His people, that lines up with the Word?
- Do you often find that the Holy Spirit gives you first-hand knowledge and insight about situations?

If the answer to all of these statements is a strong "**YES**" then you most certainly have been blessed by God in receiving this spiritual gift of Knowledge. If the answer is more "**YES, sometimes**" then you should certainly open yourself up to the possibility that the Lord desire to increasingly use you to encourage others, or to bring insight into specific situations and circumstances. If the answer is a "**NO, I have never sensed such an urge or prompting,**" then you might be one of those precious believers who has been blessed with some other prominent gift to serve the Body of Christ.

3. Faith

The Gift of Faith is seen in operation when extra-ordinary faith is demonstrated as to show the Power and Greatness of God.

> *Acts 11:22-24 (NIV)*
> *'News of this reached the church in Jerusalem, and they sent Barnabas to Antioch. When he arrived and saw what the grace of God had done, he was glad and encouraged them all to remain true to the Lord with all their hearts. He was a good man, full of the Holy Spirit and faith, and a great number of people were brought to the Lord.'*

The Apostles constantly walked in this Gift of Faith.

> *Acts 27:21-25(NIV)*
> *'After they had gone a long time without food, Paul stood up before them and said: "Men, you should have taken my advice not to sail from Crete; then you would have spared yourselves this damage and loss. But now I urge you to keep up your courage, because not one of you will be lost; only the ship will be destroyed. Last night an angel of the God to whom I belong and whom I serve stood beside me and said, 'Do not be afraid, Paul. You must stand trial before Caesar; and God has graciously given you the lives of all who sail with you.' So keep up your courage, men, for I have faith in God that it will happen just as he told me.'*

As we can see here again, a number of Gifts operate together. Faith rises in our hearts and God fills us with courage to accomplish the almost impossible when we act on His Words.

Abraham - the Father of Faith

Father Abraham was such a Man of Faith. He was known as the Father of Faith due to him walking in this kind of Supernatural Faith.

> *Romans 4:18-21 (NIV)*
> *'Against all hope, Abraham in hope believed and so became the father of many nations, just as it had been said to him, "So shall your offspring be." Without weakening in his faith, he faced the fact that his body was as good as dead—since he was about a hundred years old—and that Sarah's womb was also dead. Yet he did not waver through unbelief regarding the promise of God, but was strengthened in his faith and gave glory to God, being fully persuaded that God had power to do what he had promised.'*

We receive this Faith from the Holy Spirit.

> *I Corinthians 12:9 (NIV) 'to another faith by the same Spirit, to another gifts of healing by that one Spirit,'*

Hebrews 11 is an entire chapter devoted to people who practiced their Faith.

Discovery Questions.

The answers to the following few questions might be telltale signs that might help you to know whether you have received this gift.

- Do you find it easy to trust God when He gives you new assignments?
- Do you often find yourself doing things and taking on things that has not been attempted or done before, simply since you sensed the leading of the Holy Spirit in it?

- Do you frequently find yourself stepping out in faith to do things?
- Do you frequently hear how people admire you for the boldness they observe, which you apply, to advance the Kingdom of God?
- Do you feel confident to do things when you have a strong sense of personal conviction?

If the answer to all of these statements is a strong "**YES**" then you most certainly have been blessed by God in receiving the spiritual gift of Faith. If the answer is more "**YES, sometimes**" then you should certainly open yourself up to the possibility that the Lord desire to increasingly use you to advance His work by applying the Gift of Faith. If the answer is a "**NO, I have never sensed such an urge or prompting**," then you might be one of those precious believers who has been blessed with some other prominent gift to serve the Body of Christ.

4. Gifts of Healing

The Gift of Healing is seen in operation when Believers are moved to lay their hands on sick people, and they receive their healing in a supernatural way.

The Apostles operated in this Gift quite frequently. One such occasion was when Peter and John healed the Cripple man at the Gate Beautiful.

> *Acts 3:1-10 (NIV)*
> *'One day Peter and John were going up to the temple at the time of prayer—at three in the afternoon. Now a man who was lame from birth was being carried to the temple gate called Beautiful, where he was put every day to beg from those going into the temple courts. When he saw Peter and John about to enter, he asked them for money. Peter looked straight at him, as did John. Then Peter said, "Look at us!" So the man gave them his*

> *attention, expecting to get something from them. Then Peter said, "Silver or gold I do not have, but what I do have I give you. In the name of Jesus Christ of Nazareth, walk." Taking him by the right hand, he helped him up, and instantly the man's feet and ankles became strong. He jumped to his feet and began to walk. Then he went with them into the temple courts, walking and jumping, and praising God. When all the people saw him walking and praising God, they recognized him as the same man who used to sit begging at the temple gate called Beautiful, and they were filled with wonder and amazement at what had happened to him.'*

It is so much easier to simply to just highlight the one or two verse that jump out at us, however, I pray that by going through the whole portions we catch the Spirit of it to its fullest extent.

Another example of How these Apostles walked in this Gift on a daily basis is seen in Acts chapter five. The Bible says that the Apostles "performed many signs and wonders."

Acts 5:12-16 (NIV)
> *'The apostles performed many signs and wonders among the people. And all the believers used to meet together in Solomon's Colonnade. No one else dared join them, even though they were highly regarded by the people. Nevertheless, more and more men and women believed in the Lord and were added to their number. As a result, people brought the sick into the streets and laid them on beds and mats so that at least Peter's shadow might fall on some of them as he passed by. Crowds gathered also from the towns around Jerusalem, bringing their sick and those tormented by impure spirits, and all of them were healed.'*

The result of these signs and wonders and miraculous Healing was that many came to the Lord.

Acts 9:32-35 (NIV)

> *'As Peter traveled about the country, he went to visit the Lord's people who lived in Lydda. There he found a man named Aeneas, who was paralyzed and had been bedridden for eight years. "Aeneas," Peter said to him, "Jesus Christ heals you. Get up and roll up your mat." Immediately Aeneas got up. All those who lived in Lydda and Sharon saw him and turned to the Lord.'*

> *Acts 28:7-10 (NIV) 'There was an estate nearby that belonged to Publius, the chief official of the island. He welcomed us to his home and showed us generous hospitality for three days. His father was sick in bed, suffering from fever and dysentery. Paul went in to see him and, after prayer, placed his hands on him and healed him. When this had happened, the rest of the sick on the island came and were cured. They honored us in many ways; and when we were ready to sail, they furnished us with the supplies we needed.'*

We receive this Gift to Heal the sick and to perform miracles from the Holy Spirit.

> *I Corinthians 12:9,28 (NIV)*
> *'9 to another faith by the same Spirit, to another gifts of healing by that one Spirit, 28 And God has placed in the church first of all apostles, second prophets, third teachers, then miracles, then gifts of healing, of helping, of guidance, and of different kinds of tongues.'*

Discovery Questions.

The answers to the following few questions might be tell-tale signs that might help you to know whether you have received this gift.

- I have been used by God to pray for the sick and they received their healing?

- Do you see people who suffer from spiritual and mental unwellness healed under your prayers?
- Do you often see instantaneous healings under your ministry?
- Do you frequently find people giving praise to God for healing them when you prayed for them?
- Do you frequently have a sense that the Lord want to heal people in your ministry, and then, when you pray for them, they receive their healing?

If the answer to all of these statements is a strong "**YES**" then you most certainly have been blessed by God in receiving this spiritual gift of Healing. If the answer is more "**YES, sometimes**" then you should certainly open yourself up to the possibility that the Lord desire to increasingly use you to Heal others. If the answer is a "**NO, I have never sensed such an urge or prompting,**" then you might be one of those precious believers who has been blessed with some other prominent gift to serve the Body of Christ.

5. Working of Miracles

The Working of Miracles is seen in operation when Believers perform miracles in an extra-ordinary way under the influence of the Holy Spirit.

Raising someone from the dead is impossible in the natural unless God performs such a miracle, such as was the case with Tabitha.

> *Acts 9:36-42 (NIV) In Joppa there was a disciple named Tabitha (in Greek her name is Dorcas); she was always doing good and helping the poor. About that time, she became sick and died, and her body was washed and placed in an upstairs room. Lydda was near Joppa; so, when the disciples heard that Peter was in Lydda, they sent two men to him and urged him, "Please come at once!" Peter went with them, and when he arrived, he was*

taken upstairs to the room. All the widows stood around him, crying and showing him the robes and other clothing that Dorcas had made while she was still with them. Peter sent them all out of the room; then he got down on his knees and prayed. Turning toward the dead woman, he said, "Tabitha, get up." She opened her eyes and seeing Peter she sat up. He took her by the hand and helped her to her feet. Then he called for the believers, especially the widows, and presented her to them alive. This became known all over Joppa, and many people believed in the Lord.

We see the most incredible miracles take place when we open ourselves up to the powerful work of the Holy Spirit. Paul experienced this "extraordinary miracles" wherever he went to preach the Gospel.

Acts 19:11-12 (NIV)
'God did extraordinary miracles through Paul, so that even handkerchiefs and aprons that had touched him were taken to the sick, and their illnesses were cured, and the evil spirits left them.'

Paul raised a young boy to life in Acts chapter twenty.

Acts 20:7-12 (NIV)
'On the first day of the week we came together to break bread. Paul spoke to the people and, because he intended to leave the next day, kept on talking until midnight. There were many lamps in the upstairs room where we were meeting. Seated in a window was a young man named Eutychus, who was sinking into a deep sleep as Paul talked on and on. When he was sound asleep, he fell to the ground from the third story and was picked up dead. Paul went down, threw himself on the young man and put his arms around him. "Don't be alarmed," he said. "He's alive!" Then he went upstairs again and broke bread and ate.

After talking until daylight, he left. The people took the young man home alive and were greatly comforted.'

Paul declared that is was by the Power of the Holy Spirit that he was able to perform all the miracles.

Romans 15:18-19 (NIV)
"18 I will not venture to speak of anything except what Christ has accomplished through me in leading the Gentiles to obey God by what I have said and done—19 by the power of signs and wonders, through the power of the Spirit of God. So from Jerusalem all the way around to Illyricum, I have fully proclaimed the gospel of Christ."

1 Corinthians 12:10,28 (NIV)
"10 to another miraculous powers, to another prophecy, to another distinguishing between spirits, to another speaking in different kinds of tongues, and to still another the interpretation of tongues. 28 And God has placed in the church first of all apostles, second prophets, third teachers, then miracles, then gifts of healing, of helping, of guidance, and of different kinds of tongues."

One of the distinctive signs of an Apostle is that flow in this Gift of the Working of Miracles.

2 Corinthians 12:12 (NIV)
"12 I persevered in demonstrating among you the marks of a true apostle, including signs, wonders and miracles."

Discovery Questions.

The answers to the following few questions might be tell-tale signs that might help you to know whether you have received this gift.

- Do you see extra-ordinary miracles take place when you pray?
- Do you often see demon spirits come out of people when you minister to them?
- Do you frequently find yourself pray for impossible things to become possible, and then it happens just as you prayed?
- Do you frequently find that things you declared and prayed for, come true just as you declared?
- Do you often see blind eyes open and deaf ears open when you pray for them?

If the answer to all of these statements is a strong **"YES"** then you most certainly have been blessed by God in receiving the spiritual gift of working Miracles. If the answer is more **"YES, sometimes"** then you should certainly open yourself up to the possibility that the Lord desire to increasingly use you to perform mighty miracles through you. If the answer is a **"NO, I have never sensed such an urge or prompting,"** then you might be one of those precious believers who has been blessed with some other prominent gift to serve the Body of Christ.

6. Prophecy

The Gift of Prophecy, as is often only explored here, was explained in the previous session. This gift is experienced when a Believer bring a revelation of some future activity, event or happening through the enablement of the Holy Spirit, and it consistently happens just as it was prophesied.

7. Discerning of Spirits

The Gift of Discerning of spirits is experienced when a Believer come to accurately discern differing spirits. This proves especially helpful in discerning opposing spirits.

Luke 4:33-35 (NIV)

33 In the synagogue there was a man possessed by a demon, an impure spirit. He cried out at the top of his voice, 34 Go away! What do you want with us, Jesus of Nazareth? Have you come to destroy us? I know who you are —the Holy One of God! 35 Be quiet!" Jesus said sternly. "Come out of him!" Then the demon threw the man down before them all and came out without injuring him."

Acts 16:16-18 (NIV) Paul and Silas in Prison

"16 Once when we were going to the place of prayer, we were met by a female slave who had a spirit by which she predicted the future. She earned a great deal of money for her owners by fortune-telling. 17 She followed Paul and the rest of us, shouting, "These men are servants of the Most High God, who are telling you the way to be saved." 18 She kept this up for many days. Finally, Paul became so annoyed that he turned around and said to the spirit, "In the name of Jesus Christ I command you to come out of her!" At that moment the spirit left her."

We need the discerning of spirits so much more in the day that we are living in. For a powerful ministry we need to discern the spirit within a man, and if needed, cast it out. I believe that there are more people tormented by evil spirits than what we give attention to. Jesus amounted us to have power over all the power of the evil one, and to cast out demons.

I Corinthians 12:10 (NIV)

"10 to another miraculous powers, to another prophecy, to another distinguishing between spirits, to another speaking in different kinds of tongues, and to still another the interpretation of tongues."

May we walk in this discernment daily. I pray that we will have a zeal and desire to have this Gift, to see the captives set free around us.

I John 4:1-6 (NIV)

"1 Dear friends, do not believe every spirit, but test the spirits to see whether they are from God, because many false prophets have gone out into the world. 2 This is how you can recognize the Spirit of God: Every spirit that acknowledges that Jesus Christ has come in the flesh is from God, 3 but every spirit that does not acknowledge Jesus is not from God. This is the spirit of the antichrist, which you have heard is coming and even now is already in the world. 4 You, dear children, are from God and have overcome them, because the one who is in you is greater than the one who is in the world. 5 They are from the world and therefore speak from the viewpoint of the world, and the world listens to them. 6 We are from God, and whoever knows God listens to us; but whoever is not from God does not listen to us. This is how we recognize the Spirit of truth and the spirit of falsehood."

Discovery Questions.

The answers to the following few questions might be tell-tale signs that might help you to know whether you have received this gift.

- Do you often find yourself seeing through the pretences of people, especially before it is evident to other people?
- Do you often see the specific Call and Purpose of God on people?
- Do you have a strong sense of assurance to discern when a person is afflicted by an evil spirit?
- Do you quickly discern whether a teaching is from God, Satan or from a person himself?
- Do you easily tell whether a person speaking in tongues is bringing a divine message, merely praying in the Spirit, or faking it?

If the answer to all of these statements is a strong "**YES**" then you most certainly have been blessed by God in receiving this spiritual gift of Discerning of Spirits. If the answer is more "**YES, sometimes**" then you should certainly open yourself up to the possibility that the Lord desire to increasingly use you to discern the spirits in a place and in people. If the answer is a "**NO, I have never sensed such an urge or prompting,**" then you might be one of those precious believers who has been blessed with some other prominent gift to serve the Body of Christ.

8. The Gift of Tongues

The Gift of Tongues is the ability to speak in a language, not learned, but received from the Holy Spirit when you received the baptism of the Holy Spirit. The Gift of tongues is a supernatural ability to bring messages from God to His people in a language that is not necessarily understood in the natural. We can use the gift of tongues to communicate, with the help of the Holy Spirit within us, to the Father in an inexplicable way.

> *Mark 16:17 (NIV)*
> *"17 And these signs will accompany those who believe: In my name they will drive out demons; they will speak in new tongues;"*

> *Acts 2:1-13 (NIV)*
> *"1 When the day of Pentecost came, they were all together in one place. 2 Suddenly a sound like the blowing of a violent wind came from heaven and filled the whole house where they were sitting. 3 They saw what seemed to be tongues of fire that separated and came to rest on each of them. 4 All of them were filled with the Holy Spirit and began to speak in other tongues as the Spirit enabled them. 5 Now there were staying in Jerusalem God-fearing Jews from every nation under heaven. 6 When they heard this sound, a crowd came together in bewilderment, because each one heard their own language*

> being spoken. 7 Utterly amazed, they asked: "Aren't all these who are speaking Galileans? 8 Then how is it that each of us hears them in our native language? 9 Parthians, Medes and Elamites; residents of Mesopotamia, Judea and Cappadocia, Pontus and Asia, 10 Phrygia and Pamphylia, Egypt and the parts of Libya near Cyrene; visitors from Rome 11 (both Jews and converts to Judaism); Cretans and Arabs—we hear them declaring the wonders of God in our own tongues!" 12 Amazed and perplexed, they asked one another, "What does this mean?" 13 Some, however, made fun of them and said, "They have had too much wine."'"

Peter stood up in their midst and remanded them that none of them were drunk from wine, but that it was the effect of the Holy Spirit's Baptism that caused them to behave and act in the way they did. It was the Holy Spirit's influence that enabled them to speak in languages, other than their own know language. It was the Gift of Tongues in full operation.

> Acts 10:44-46 (NIV)
> "44 While Peter was still speaking these words, the Holy Spirit came on all who heard the message. 45 The circumcised believers who had come with Peter were astonished that the gift of the Holy Spirit had been poured out even on Gentiles. 46 For they heard them speaking in tongues and praising God."

> Acts 19:1-7 (NIV)
> "1 While Apollos was at Corinth, Paul took the road through the interior and arrived at Ephesus. There he found some disciples 2 and asked them, "Did you receive the Holy Spirit when you believed?" They answered, "No, we have not even heard that there is a Holy Spirit." 3 So Paul asked, "Then what baptism did you receive?" "John's baptism," they replied. 4 Paul said, "John's baptism was a baptism of repentance. He told the people to believe in the one coming after him, that is, in Jesus." 5 On

hearing this, they were baptized in the name of the Lord Jesus. 6 When Paul placed his hands on them, the Holy Spirit came on them, and they spoke in tongues and prophesied. 7 There were about twelve men in all."

1 Corinthians 12:10,28 (NIV)
"*10 to another miraculous powers, to another prophecy, to another distinguishing between spirits, to another speaking in different kinds of tongues, and to still another the interpretation of tongues. 28 And God has placed in the church first of all apostles, second prophets, third teachers, then miracles, then gifts of healing, of helping, of guidance, and of different kinds of tongues.*"

1 Corinthians 14:13-19 (NIV)
"*13 For this reason the one who speaks in a tongue should pray that they may interpret what they say. 14 For if I pray in a tongue, my spirit prays, but my mind is unfruitful. 15 So what shall I do? I will pray with my spirit, but I will also pray with my understanding; I will sing with my spirit, but I will also sing with my understanding. 16 Otherwise when you are praising God in the Spirit, how can someone else, who is now put in the position of an inquirer, say "Amen" to your thanksgiving, since they do not know what you are saying? 17 You are giving thanks well enough, but no one else is edified. 18 I thank God that I speak in tongues more than all of you. 19 But in the church, I would rather speak five intelligible words to instruct others than ten thousand words in a tongue.*"

Discovery Questions.

The answers to the following few questions might be tell-tale signs that might help you to know whether you have received this gift.

- Have you received the gift of speaking in a language, you

have never learnt, but received this amazing ability when you received the Baptism in the Holy Spirit?
- Do you often sense, apart from your private prayer times, that God might bring a specific message to you and through you when you pray in the Spirit?
- Do you have a strong sense that God sometimes gives you a discernible message for His people while you speak in tongues?
- Have People told you that when you spoke in tongues, they felt how God spoke through you, and that the interpretation of the tongues confirmed it?
- Do you have a clear sense when you speak in tongues, whether it is a divine message, or merely yourself praying in the Spirit?

If the answer to all of these statements is a strong "**YES**" then you most certainly have been blessed by God in receiving this spiritual gift of speaking in tongues. If the answer is more "**YES, sometimes**" then you should certainly open yourself up to the possibility that the Lord desire to increasingly use you to bring divine message in tongues, that will ultimately bless and encourage others through it and its interpretation. If the answer is a "NO, I have never sensed such an urge or prompting, then you might be one of those precious believers who has been blessed with some other prominent gift to serve the Body of Christ.

9. Interpretation of Tongues

The Gift of Interpretation of Tongues is often experienced among Believers where someone, or the speaker self, receive a divinely inspired message in Tongues, and then understand a specific message through it to be delivered for the encouragement, exhortation or edification of the fellow Believers.

1 Corinthians 14:13 (NIV)
"13 For this reason the one who speaks in a tongue should pray that they may interpret what they say."

1 Corinthians 14:5 (NIV)
"5 I would like every one of you to speak in tongues, but I would rather have you prophesy. The one who prophesies is greater than the one who speaks in tongues, unless someone interprets, so that the church may be edified."

1 Corinthians 14:26-28 (NIV)
"26 What then shall we say, brothers and sisters? When you come together, each of you has a hymn, or a word of instruction, a revelation, a tongue or an interpretation. Everything must be done so that the church may be built up. 27 If anyone speaks in a tongue, two—or at the most three—should speak, one at a time, and someone must interpret. 28 If there is no interpreter, the speaker should keep quiet in the church and speak to himself and to God."

Discovery Questions.

The answers to the following few questions might be tell-tale signs that might help you to know whether you have received this gift.

- Do you often find yourself knowing what God wants to say to His people when someone brings a message in tongues?
- Do you often, instantaneously, receive the interpretation of tongues when someone bring a message in tongues?
- Do you find yourself knowing what people are saying even though you have no learnt knowledge of a language?
- Do you find yourself praying for the interpretation of tongues so that you might be used by God to bring messages of hope, through the interpretation, to build people up?

- Have you heard people say to you that the messages you brought in response to someone bring a message in tongues, spoke to them and encouraged them?

If the answer to all of these statements is a strong "YES" then you most certainly have been blessed by God in receiving this spiritual gift to teach others. If the answer is more "YES, sometimes" then you should certainly open yourself up to the possibility that the Lord desire to increasingly use you to teach others through you. If the answer is a "NO, I have never sensed such an urge or prompting," then you might be one of those precious believers who has been blessed with some other prominent gift to serve the Body of Christ.

Afterword

This concludes our brief journey to understanding the Supernatural Spiritual Gifts. During the concluding sessions of this encounter, we will complete a questionnaire to learn and know our Spiritual Gifts. We will also take this time to affirm the spiritual gifts in the lives of those who are here with us. I pray that the concluding parts of this weekend encounter will serve as great encouragement to you.

5

DISCOVERING YOUR SPIRITUAL GIFTS
SESSION FIVE

This guide has been developed to assist you in discovering your spiritual gifts, and it should not be viewed as a test. The only right answers here are honest and sincere answers. The answers you provide will help you find the areas where the Holy Spirit' enablement might be best applied to building the church up.

Before You Start

Follow These Six Steps:

Step 1 - Print out the answer sheet from the following pages.

Go through the list of 100 statements on the questionnaire. For each one, mark on the answer sheet to what extent the statement is true of your life:
    3 = **MOSTLY**, or
    2 = **SOMETIMES**, or
    1 = **LITTLE**, or
    0 = **NOT AT ALL**

Be Careful! Do not score according to what you think should be true or hope might be true in the future. Be honest and score on the basis of present and recent experiences. If you are a young Christian or new in the faith, the results will need extra care in interpretation.

Step 2 - Score your questionnaire.

When you are finished, score the questionnaire according to the instructions on the scoring sheet.

Step 3 – Identify your top 3 Gifts.

Identify the top 3 to 5 gifts where you scored 10 or more.

Step 4 – Affirm each others top 3 Gifts.

Ask a close friend within the group, or even your Pastor, to score you by identifying your top 3 gifts as they see them. See whether this confirms your scoring. In most cases, unless the person assessing you does not know you at all, the assessor will probably affirm 80 to 100% the most prominent gifts of God on your life.

Step 5 - Study your gifts.

Specifically Study the gift definitions and Scripture references of those gifts where you had a 10 or above score. Look for ways in which you can develop them more, or where you can open yourself up to be used by the Holy Spirit to use you more within those identified areas.

Step 6 – Use your gifts.

Use these gifts in your ministry to build the Body of Christ up, and always be on the quest to eagerly desire more spiritual gifts to use.

VORSTER SPIRITUAL GIFTS QUESTIONAIRE.

For each statement, mark to what extent it is true in your life:
   3 = MOSTLY, or
   2 = SOMETIMES, or
   1 = LITTLE, or
   0 = NOT AT ALL

Now, turn over to the **VORSTER SPIRITUAL GIFTS DISCOVERY QUESTION SHEET**

6

VORSTER SPIRITUAL GIFTS QUESTIONNAIRE

SESSION SIX

For each of the 100 statements, mark to what extent it is true in your life:

- MOSTLY = 3,
- SOMETIMES = 2,
- LITTLE = 1, or
- NOT AT ALL = 0

Mark the 100 statements in the Vorster Questionnaire in the following few pages!

No.	Gifts discovery questions	Score
\multicolumn{3}{|c|}{**VORSTER SPIRITUAL GIFTS DISCOVERY QUESTION SHEET**}	
1	I often receive and deliver direct messages from God that edify, exhort or comfort others.	
2	I enjoy helping to do ordinary tasks that will make things easier for others.	
3	I have heard that I have helped Believers learn truths from the Bible through my sharing.	
4	I quite naturally and spontaneous see the positive side of sometimes difficult situations.	
5	I am quite disciplined in managing my finances well, as to enable me to give generously to the Lord's work.	
6	I find it easy to make decisions that others are willing to follow.	
7	I have a strong preference to help those who are physically and mentally challenged, and to help alleviate their suffering.	
8	I find it easy to apply biblical principles, in context, in my own life.	
9	I often find that the Holy Spirit gives me insight about people I have no prior knowledge about.	

Vorster Spiritual Gifts Questionnaire Q 1-9

10	I find it fairly easy to take on new assignments I sense the Lord instructs me to do.	
11	I have been used by God to pray for the sick and they received their healing.	
12	I often see extra-ordinary miracles take place when I pray in the Name of the Lord Jesus.	
13	I often find myself being able to see through the pretenses of people, even before it was evident to other people.	
14	I have received the gift of speaking in a language I have never learnt but received this amazing ability when I received the Holy Spirit.	
15	I often find myself being able to instantly know what the Lord wants to say to His people when someone brings a message in tongues.	
16	I feel like God anointed me as a leader, especially when I am with other Believers.	
17	I feel like God anointed me as someone who sees things, before they happen.	
18	I have been able to lead people to accept Jesus as their Lord and Saviour.	
19	I feel like God anointed me as someone to take care of other Believers.	
20	I feel like God anointed me to teach other Believers the deep things of God.	

Vorster Spiritual Gifts Questionnaire Q 10-20

21	I have received from the Holy Spirit and proclaimed specific things that will happen in the future, and it happened just as I saw it.
22	I always find joy in cleaning, setting things up, or packing things up after ministry opportunities.
23	I love seeing people gain new insights in God's Word from my sharing with them.
24	I always find some uplifting and positive thing to say to others.
25	I give considerably more than a tithe of my income to the Lord's work, and this is reflected in my monthly budget records.
26	I find that people generally look to me for guidance in what needs to be done.
27	I have cared for others when they have had material or physical needs.
28	I often find myself coming up with solutions to fairly complicated situations.
29	I often receive and share insights of spiritual situations with people that help bring them closer to God.
30	I often do things that's not been done or attempted before, purely because I sense the leading of the Holy Spirit in doing it.
31	I often see spiritually troubled people healed through my prayers and ministry.
32	I often see demon spirits come out of people when I minister to them.

Vorster Spiritual Gifts Questionnaire Q 21-32

33	I often see the specific Call and Purpose of God on certain people.	
34	I often sense, apart from my private prayer times, that God might bring a specific message through me when I pray in the Spirit.	
35	I often pray and receive the interpretation when someone speaks in tongues.	
36	I have an assurance that wherever God might call me to a new place, or assignment, that I will be able to lead people to Christ and care for them.	
37	I have delivered messages, at the right time, that impacted people's lives greatly.	
38	I often share my testimony to others of how the Lord saved me, and then see them put their faith in Jesus Christ as well.	
39	I love taking care of the spiritual needs and welfare of Believers.	
40	I love teaching Believers the word of God in a systematic and logically understandable way.	
41	I have been told that specific personal messages I brought to people, under the inspiration of the Holy Spirit, must have come from the Lord, since it happened just as the Lord said	
42	I always look for opportunities to help with menial tasks to make things easier for others.	

Vorster Spiritual Gifts Questionnaire Q 33-42

43	I love to study God's Word and look for things not seen or understood before.	
44	I daily take time to compliment others.	
45	I am often asked to give to some Kingdom Advancing causes, and by the Grace of God I am able to find the funds to give towards such causes.	
46	I am often asked to give directives in what needs to happen next.	
47	I am often asked to visit people in hospitals and in troublesome circumstances.	
48	I frequently find myself guiding Believers to finding solutions from Biblical examples and stories.	
49	I often find divine strategies and techniques, through my time in the Bible and prayer, that God seem to use in furthering His kingdom.	
50	I frequently find myself stepping out in faith to do things.	
51	I frequently find myself in ministry situations where I pray for unwell people and where they receive instant healing.	
52	I frequently find myself in ministry situations where I pray for the impossible to become possible and then it happens just as I prayed.	
53	I have a strong sense of assurance to discern when a person is afflicted by an evil spirit.	

Vorster Spiritual Gifts Questionnaire Q 43-53

54	I have a strong sense that God sometimes gives me a discernable message for His people while I speak in tongues.	
55	I have a strong sense to discern what people say even though I do not know the language.	
56	I often see that people do what I ask them to do without questioning me.	
57	I have deeply upset people when I brought them the Message God gave me to give to them.	
58	I often see how people respond positively to the gospel message when I deliver it.	
59	I feel much more comfortable to work with people with whom I developed a relationship over a long period of time, and to share in their daily wellbeing.	
60	I feel comfortable to defend the truths of God's Word against false beliefs.	
61	I often have a strong sense of what God wants to say to people in relation to their particular situations.	
62	I prefer to do the hard work behind the scenes to help the work of God go smoothly.	
63	I often take time to think about ways in which to share the truths of God's Word more effectively to help Believers in their walk with God.	

Vorster Spiritual Gifts Questionnaire Q 54-63

64	I often hear that my positive attitude and words encourage people.	
65	I often give sacrificially and commit to give consistently, even though it stretches me at times beyond what I have in hand, just because of my faith in a matter, and because of my love to sow into God's work.	
66	My ideas and suggestions are usually accepted by most as the way to move forward.	
67	I love to give my time to help people find solutions and outcomes to their problems.	
68	I often hear that the biblical truth I share is most relevant and specific to the felt needs of fellow believers.	
69	I daily seek to understand what God desires to say to His People, that lines up with the Bible	
70	I often hear that people admire me for the bold steps I take to advance the work of God.	
71	I often hear that people bring honour to God for healing them through my prayers and ministry.	
72	I often find myself in situations where supernatural provisions and breakthroughs occur after my prayers and declarations.	
73	I quickly recognize whether a person is teaching something he received from God, from Satan, or of himself.	

74	People have told me that when I spoke in tongues, they felt how God spoke through me, and that the interpretation of the tongues confirmed it.	
75	I always pray that God will give me understanding when people speak in tongues that I might encourage and bring messages of hope that will build people up.	
76	I always have a burning desire to be sent out to start a new church.	
77	I always have a burning desire to hear from God and bring messages of hope and encouragement to His People.	
78	It gives me great satisfaction to tell people how to put their faith in Jesus Christ to be their Lord and Saviour.	
79	I have this notion to want to build deep and meaningful relationships with people, and through that interaction, to serve them better.	
80	I know the doctrines of the Bible and love sharing them with Believers.	
81	I often feel that I know exactly what God wants to say and do in a meeting and what specific ministry is needed at a specific point in time.	
82	I feel privileged to be able to serve others by doing the unthankful tasks.	

Vorster Spiritual Gifts Questionnaire Q 74-82

83	I feel honored to see people grow in their faith as a result of my sharing the truths of God's Word with them.	
84	I feel privileged to have a naturally positive outlook and that I am able to show people the good and blessed things in their lives.	
85	I have consistently lowered my standard of living in order to advance God's work.	
86	I find it easy to make thought-through decisions.	
87	I feel blessed and called to help those in less fortunate physical, mental or material circumstances.	
88	I often sense great peace and personal confidence when important decisions need to be made.	
89	I often find that the Holy Spirit gives me knowledge and insight about situations firsthand.	
90	I often do things when I have a sense of great personal conviction.	
91	I often have a sense to pray for the sick in my ministry, and then see amazing healings take place.	
92	I often pray for the blind, deaf and cripple, and then see amazing miracles take place.	
93	I can usually tell immediately whether a person speaking in tongues is bringing a divine message, or merely praying in the Spirit, or faking it.	

Vorster Spiritual Gifts Questionnaire Q 83-93

94	I have a clear sense when I speak in tongues, whether it is a divine message, or me merely praying in the Spirit.	
95	I have heard others say to me that the words I spoke after someone spoke in tongues really spoke to them and built them up and encourage them.	
96	I often get asked to serve in leadership positions because of my ability to make things happen.	
97	I often get asked to pray about situations and hear what God says to do in those situations.	
98	I often hear people say that it was through my sharing the gospel message, that they were saved.	
99	I often hear people say that I am a good friend, especially since I am always there for them, understand them, and care for them.	
100	I often hear people say that I am a good Teacher of the Word of God.	

Vorster Spiritual Gifts Questionnaire Q 94-100

In Conclusion

In the next session we will add the results to determine the specific gifts God gave you already.

7

VORSTER GIFTS SCORE SHEET
SESSION SEVEN

In this session we will tally up the scores we gave each of the questions in the Vorster Spiritual Gifts Discovery Questionnaire.

Instructions for Scoring

1. Turn to your Score Sheet, towards the back of the book, after reading these instructions.
2. Add your Score Sheet answers together, from left to right, and write that total in the Totals box next to each gift.

Example: Add together the number you wrote in box 1, plus the number in box 21, plus the number in box 41, plus the number in box 61 and the number in box 81. Those five numbers, added together, become your total score to be written in the **TOTAL** box.

VORSTER GIFTS SCORE SHEET

Write down scores from questionnaire here.					Total score	Rank results	GIFTS
1	21	41	61	81			Prophecy
2	22	42	62	82			Serving
3	23	43	63	83			Teaching
4	24	44	64	84			Exhortation
5	25	45	65	85			Giving
6	26	46	66	86			Leading
7	27	47	67	87			Mercy
8	28	48	68	88			Words of Wisdom
9	29	49	69	89			Words of Knowledge
10	30	50	70	90			Faith
11	31	51	71	91			Gifts of Healing
12	32	52	72	92			Working of Miracles
13	33	53	73	93			Discerning of Spirits
14	34	54	74	94			Tongues
15	35	55	75	95			Interpretation of Tongues
16	36	56	76	96			Apostle
17	37	57	77	97			Prophet
18	38	58	78	98			Evangelist
19	39	59	79	99			Pastor
20	40	60	80	100			Teacher

Vorster Gifts Score Sheet

Directions

When you have finished responding to all 100 statements and scored your test, follow the instructions listed below for better understanding.

STEP 1

After adding up your points, you should have several notably high scores. These are your probable spiritual gifts. Please indicate them below, starting with your highest score. Any score below 9, however, is probably not a positive indicator of a gift. If you had other high scores, or if you feel sure you have certain gifts even though they didn't receive high marks, put them down as well. You have just taken the first step toward discovering your spiritual gifts. Please understand that this exercise only indicates your probable gifts. Over the next few weeks you should use the following five steps to more clearly determine your spiritual gifts.

STEP 2

Pray, believing that God will continue to reveal to you what gifts He has given you. Don't forget 1 Cor. 12:11: Gifts have been distributed "to each individual." Pray also for the wisdom and desire to use your gifts with the greatest efficiency for Him.

STEP 3

Study the Bible passages that deal specifically with this topic: Romans 12, 1 Corinthians 12-14, Ephesians 3, 4 and 1 Peter 4. And take time to reflect on the contexts of the many Bible stories of men and women who used their gifts for God. Such accounts serve as examples and as inspiration.

STEP 4

Experiment by using your new-found gifts. This may be a new experience, and you may not know where to start. See the next page for some suggestions. As you begin to work for God, your gifts will develop in an exciting way.

STEP 5

Confirm the gifts of others. When you see another person using his gift effectively, say so. This isn't flattery, it's a vital step in the ongoing process of spiritual gift development.

Let's begin this process right away. Please mark down the spiritual gifts you've observed in three fellow Christians in your congregation. Your keen observations will be appreciated by each of them and your pastor.

This is a good opportunity to let your friends know what their gifts are, simply by listing them here. It's also a good time to let them know, in a very gracious (and anonymous) way, what their gifts aren't by leaving those gifts off the list. Make this an honest appraisal.

The summary of gifts beginning on the next page may help you in your evaluation.

STEP 6

Expect confirmation of your gifts by other church members. Following your handing in this inventory to your pastor, your inventory will be returned with a listing of some of the gifts your fellow believers have observed in you. Everyone who hands in his inventory should receive an evaluation. You may not agree with this evaluation! But instead of dismissing these opinions, explore them. Look for ways to develop the abilities others believe you possess.

. . .

Take a moment now to write down the scores from questionnaire here.

Write down the Top three Gifts according to your score results.
YOUR SPIRITUAL GIFTS
1.
2.
3.
Do the result surprise you? _____
What did you think they were before you started?
1.
2.
3.

Take a moment to score at least two friends.
FRIENDS SPIRITUAL GIFTS
FRIEND: _____
1.
2.
3.
FRIEND: _____
1.
2.
3.

Ask your Pastor or Spiritual Leader for their assessment:
PASTOR'S SPIRITUAL GIFT ASSESSMENT OF YOU:
1.
2.
3.

Spiritual Gifts List:

Prophecy
  Serving
  Teaching
  Exhortation
  Giving
  Leading
  Mercy
  Words of Wisdom
  Words of Knowledge
  Faith
  Gifts of Healing
  Working of Miracles
  Discerning of Spirits
  Tongues
  Interpretation of Tongues
  Apostle
  Prophet
  Evangelist
  Pastor
  Teacher

IN CLOSING

I pray that you too found this very inspirational, as many thousands of other Believers had in the past. I pray that you will pursue Spiritual Gifts that will build and encourage the Body of Christ, especially the Gift of Prophecy.

> *1 Peter 4:10 (NIV)* **"Each of you should use whatever gift you have received to serve others**, *as faithful stewards of God's grace in its various forms.* **If anyone speaks**, *they should do so as one who speaks the very words of God.* **If anyone serves**, *they*

should do so with the strength God provides, so that in all things God may be praised through Jesus Christ. To him be the glory and the power for ever and ever. Amen."

Use the Gifts God gave you to build the Church up. May Jesus be glorified through the way you use the Gifts of the Holy Spirit.

PART II

SURVEY OF THE BIBLE WEEKEND ENCOUNTER

WEEKEND TWO

ENCOUNTER SCHEDULE

- Session 1 – Introduction
- Session 2 - The Authority of the Bible
- Session 3 – Making the most of my time in the Word
- Session 4 - Further Study

INTRODUCTION
SESSION ONE

Jesus taught us *the Spiritual Discipline of having an intake of the Word of God* on a Daily Basis. During His days of Testing, Jesus used the Word to defend and persevere through the temptations Satan tried on Him. Jesus quoted Deuteronomy 8 verse 3 that: *"Man shall not live by bread alone, but by every Word that proceeds from the mouth of God."* On another occasion Jesus presented Himself as the Bread of Life.

Every New Testament Book endorses and encourages us to embrace the Words of the Lord on a daily basis.

> *Luke 4:4 (NKJV) 4 But Jesus answered him, saying, "It is written, 'Man shall not live by bread alone, but by every word of God.'"*

This is what Jesus taught through His example when He faced the Temptation of Satan. Throughout the various aspects of How Satan attempted to seduce and entice Jesus, His defence was consistent: He stood on the Word and used it like a sword and shield.

The Psalmist also tells us of the incredible blessing and impact, meditating and delighting in the Word of God brings.

> *Psalms 1:1-3 NIV "1 Blessed is the one who does not walk in step with the wicked or stand in the way that sinners take or sit in the company of mockers, 2 but whose delight is in the law of the Lord, and who meditates on his Law Day and night. 3 That person is like a tree planted by streams of water, which yields its fruit in season and whose leaf does not wither— whatever they do prospers"*

The Apostle Paul exhorts the church in Colossea to allow the Word of God to dwell richly in them.

> *Colossians 3:16 NIV "16 Let the Word of Christ dwell among you richly as you teach and admonish one another with all wisdom through psalms, hymns, and songs from the Spirit, singing to God with gratitude in your hearts."*

The entrance of the Word of God into our lives, activates the faith we so desperately needs for wholesome and godly living.

> *Romans 10:17 ESV "17 So faith comes from hearing, and hearing through the word of Christ."*

The effectiveness in assimilating and treasuring the Word of God is determined by the heart attitude with which we take time in the Word of God, as well as our willingness and determination to put it into practice.

The Fruitfulness and success of our growth in the Lord, and our Faith in Him, firmly relies on our embracing of the Bible as God's irrevocable Word to us, and the Foundation upon which we will build our Faith and life.

In the following sessions we will briefly explore the Authority of the Word of God, as well as How we may extract the most out of our time in the Word of God. I pray that it will be a huge activator in your life.

9

THE AUTHORITY OF THE BIBLE
SESSION TWO

The Authority of the Bible can be argued from an Archaeological, **Historical**, and Prophetic dimension. It is more than coincidence that people without Internet, social media or postal services could speak so accurately into future events, which was fulfilled, unless it was Divinely inspired.

One of the outstanding things Paul taught Timothy was How irrefutable and central the Word of God stands in our lives, and for our well-being.

> *2 Timothy 3:16*
> *All Scripture is God-breathed and is useful for teaching, rebuking, correcting and training in righteousness,*

The Apostle Peter also emphasised this essential aspect in his Pastoral letter.

> *2 Peter 1:20-21*
> *Above all, you must understand that no prophecy of Scripture came about by the prophet's own interpretation of things. For prophecy never had its origin in the human will, but prophets,*

though human, spoke from God as they were carried along by the Holy Spirit.

The Dead Sea **Scrolls**, amongst other historical manuscripts, support the accuracy of the writings and the inerrancy of the Scriptures. One of the aspects to confirm and validate the Authority of the Scriptures is the **consistency** of its Message through so many writers, over so many years, from so many varied backgrounds. They all wrote the same consistent message without ever crossing paths to collaborate their perceptions.

Psalm 19:7-9
The law of the Lord is perfect, refreshing the soul. The statutes of the Lord are trustworthy, making wise the simple. The precepts of the Lord are right, giving joy to the heart. The commands of the Lord are radiant, giving light to the eyes. The fear of the Lord is pure, enduring forever. The decrees of the Lord are firm, and all of them are righteous.

They all had the same message and as "their" messages came into fulfillment, their cohesive and divinely ordered origin was affirmed. We often speak about the best Wisdom coming from seeing things in hindsight. The more manuscripts are discovered the more it affirms the miracle of having the "Words of God" in written memory.

We therefor build our lives on the Bible as the inerrant Word of God. I encourage you to hold your Bible in high regard. Treasure its contents as it holds the keys to life eternal. On one occasion Jesus pointed people to the fact that they will remain in error as long as what they do not know the Scriptures.

Matthew 22:29
Jesus replied, "You are in error because you do not know the Scriptures or the power of God."

The Bible is the inerrant Word of God.

The Bible is the most reputable book ever written. The Bible was written over a **1500-year** period by over 40 Authors who wrote Messages from God down as the Holy Spirit inspired them.

- **It can be trusted as the most reliable manuscript ever written**

The many manuscripts confirm its accuracy. *Firstly*, we have the **number** of manuscripts that proof to be exactly the same, and then *secondly*, we have the **consistency** in the manuscripts, proving beyond doubt their reliability. No other historical document has as many consistent manuscripts.

- **It consists of a compilation from over 40 writers**

The Authority of the Bible, as the Word of God, is further reinforced by the strong consistent message regardless of being written by over **40** writers, many of whom lived in different time periods and circumstances. The only conclusion can be that the messages were all authored by the Holy Spirit, and reduced to writing by this variety of men and woman. Barely do you find one writer being consistent over his or her own lifetime, yet for these, more than 40 writers, they spoke from one heart and mouth.

- **Written over a 1500-year period**

The period over which these writers wrote spans more than **1500** years. To put that in perspective, just think How much life and humanity evolved over the recent 1500 year period, yet, their messages transcended beyond primitivism, class distinctions, education and communicating contextually. The message continues to speak to us regardless of How developed and evolved life might be.

- **More than 5 Billion Bibles printed**

The Bible remains the most printed book of any kind on the planet. No other single book has been reproduced as much as the Bible. This is a remarkable feat since it was outlawed and burned in many riotous revolutions. Many tried to diminish its influence and message throughout its history, yet, regardless of the many attempts to have it destroyed, it remains to be the most printed book year after year.

- **Over 100 million Bibles sold every year**

It is reported, and widely known, that the Bible continues to sell more than a 100 million copies a year.

- **First written book ever printed**

The introduction of the <u>Gutenberg</u> Press also saw the mass production of the Bible as the first book to be reproduced, en-mass in printed form. The Gutenberg Press produced the first ever printed form of any book or manuscripts. It was appropriate that it launched its production lineage with the Bible.

- **Most verifiable and oldest manuscripts of any document on the planet**

It remains one of the remarkable testimonies of the Greatness of God, that God was able to sustain and contain such consistency and meticulous care of each and every manuscript that was ever reproduced of the various writings of the parts of the Bible.

The make-up of the Bible.

The Bible was compiled over a period of time and eventually determined to be the Holy Scriptures as we enjoy it today. The First Canon of Scriptures was the **Hebrew** Bible and it consisted of the Old Testament writings as we know it today.

The Hebrew Bible

The Hebrew Bible is historically known as the **Tanakh**[1], which consist of three parts or compilations.

The **First Part** consist of a compilation of the first five Books of the Bible and was known as the **Torah.**

The **Second compilation** is known as the **Nevi'im**[2] and consist of the "*Former Prophets*", the books of *Joshua, Judges, Samuel and Kings,* and the Prophetic books of *Isaiah, Jeremiah and Ezekiel and the Twelve Minor Prophets.*

The **third part** consist of the **Ketuvim**[3] which consisted of *Psalms, Proverbs and Job, then also the "Hamesh Migillot" which consisted of Lamentations, Esther, Song of Songs, Ruth, Ecclesiastes* and the remaining Books of *Daniel, Ezra-Nehemiah and the Chronicles.*[4]

This three-part compilation became known as the **Tanakh** and was accepted as "Holy Scriptures" by the 2 BC[5]

The Septuagint

The Septuagint is the first **translation** of the **Tanakh** into **Greek** and is widely used as the standard against which translations are measured. The Septuagint consisted of the Pentateuch, the Historical Books, The Poetic Books and both the Minor and the Major Prophetic Books.

- **The Pentateuch**

The Pentateuch consists of the **first five books** of the Bible. These are the books known to be written by Moses. The Pentateuch consists of *Genesis, Exodus, Leviticus, Numbers and Deuteronomy.*

The Pentateuch gives us a historical account of the first family and how they grew and developed, under the purpose of God into the Israelite family.

The Pentateuch also provides us with a sound biblical framework for godly living through the observance of the laws of Moses, as well as understanding the significance of the Tabernacle as it relates to our daily time with God.

The Pentateuch helps us to understand the Nature of God and His dealing with His people. We learn to know God is the Provider, the Guide, the Great Shepherd, the Miracle Worker, the Deliverer, The Holy God, and the Upper Ruler of the Nations of the World.

The Pentateuch provides us with a solid foundation to build our understanding of God, His Power and Authority. These books will become a constant referencing point in your daily life as it was used and applied in the lives of the Prophets, Jesus, and New Testament Believers.

I pray that your life will be deeply enriched through your journey in the Pentateuch.

- **The Historic Books**

The Historic Books are made up of the all the books that gives us a historic account of the Israelite Nation, their conquest of the Promised Land and how they developed into a Nation operating within Canaan. The Historic Books consists of *Joshua, Judges, Ruth, 1 and 2 Samuel, 1 and 2 Kings, 1 and 2 Chronicles, Ezra, Nehemiah, Esther and Job.*

The Historic Books teaches us on how they won and lost battles as they grew in their faith, as well as bearing the consequences of not walking with God.

The Historic Books give us the Journey of how God led Israel. He first led them through His obedient Servants Moses, Joshua, the Judges, the Priests until they demanded a King.

The Historic Books gives us that account of the Kings and how they led Israel and later the divided Kingdom.

- **The Poetic Books**

The Poetic Books consists of the *Psalms, Proverbs, Ecclesiastes, Lamentations and Song of Songs.*

The Poetic Books provides us with an incredible guidance for godly wisdom and living, as well as great guidance in encapsulating words to express and present our deepest and most earnest thoughts and prayers to God.

- **Prophetic Books**

The Prophetic Books provide us with prophetic utterances which both addressed the people of Israel, Judah as well as Nations and their Leaders through these Prophets.

The Prophetic Books consists of two parts, namely: Major and Minor Prophets. **The Minor Prophets** consists of those Prophets whose personal life and story became a prophetic utterance, as well as God used them to speak to the Kings and people of their time. They are Hosea, Joel, Amos, Obadiah, Jonah, Micah, Nahum, Habakkuk, Zephaniah, Haggai, Zechariah, and Malachi.

The Major Prophets include Isaiah, Jeremiah, Lamentations, Ezekiel, and Daniel. These books were declared "major" because of the amount of text, and not because they were considered more important than the "minor" prophetic books. The Old Testament prophet tended to come into prominence especially during times of crisis. God used the prophets to provide direction and wisdom during times of crisis. They were also used by God to remind the people of their covenantal promises.

The relevance of biblical prophecy is not only the information revealed to the people about the circumstances being faced in their time or in a time to come, but also what the message reveals about the nature of God. Prophecy in the Bible is part of God's self-revelation, by which we come to know God through what he has done in the past and what He plans to do in the future.

Many of these Prophetic Books, not only spoke into their contemporary circumstances, but more specifically spoke to future events still to be experienced. Examples of this is found in Daniel, Jeremiah, Isaiah, Joel and Haggai. In fact, almost every one of these Prophets spoke words relevant to the day that we live in.

The Bible

From the Septuagint the Bible was compiled as we have it today. The Septuagint was translated into Greek from the Hebraic text from about 200BC, and then the New Testament Books were written and compiled to make up what is known today as the Bible. This compilation and writing of the New Testament part took until about **100AD**.

The oldest surviving full text of the New Testament is the "**Codex Sinaiticus**", which was "**discovered**" at the St Catherine monastery at the base of Mt Sinai in Egypt in the 1840s and 1850s.[6] Dating from circa 325-360 CE, it is not known where it was scribed, however it is quite possible that it was done in Rome or even Egypt.

Much has been written over the years of various Councils who, under the Guidance of God, determined which letters and Gospels to add to make up the final Canon of Scripture as we know it today. Those books included in the Bible are called canonical, indicating that the group who met together determined that the collection reflect the true representation of God's word and will.

The Bible consists of an **Old Testament** and the **New Testament**. The Old Testament compilations was explored previously.

- **The New Testament**

The New Testament is a collection of 27 books consisting of 4 parts; namely the Four Gospels, the Acts of the Apostles, the Pastoral Epistles and an Apocalyptic Prophetic Book - Revelation.[7] These books were canonized as Sacred Writings and was all written between 50 – 120 AD,[8] and affirmed through the determination at various gatherings of Church Leaders. As early as **382 AD** at the Council of Rome[9] the incorporation of these 27 books was accepted as part of the complete Bible.

- **Gospels**

The Gospels consists of the Gospel accounts of four of the Apostles namely: *Matthew, Mark, Luke and John.* These four books explore the life of Jesus' earthly life and ministry and includes His Teaching to His Disciples. The Gospels also gives us a graphic account of the high prize Christ paid for our redemption. As Believers, we also embrace the instructions given to the Apostles as instructions to us as Believers.

- **The Acts of the Apostles**

The Acts of the Apostles is the account of the Apostle Luke of the ministry and work of the Apostles. It also gives us an insight into the growth and development of the early church. In many ways it is a handbook for those who desire to lead disciple-making churches. It encapsulates the essentials of prayer, witnessing, discipleship, stewardship, study and application of the Word of God and enduring and standing for one's faith in the midst of much persecution.

- **Pastoral Epistles**

The Pastoral Epistles consists of the various letter from Apostles to a variety of churches and individuals with great Christian living teaching and guidance for us today.

- **Revelation.**

The Book of Revelation comprises of a Vision John, the Apostle, had on the Island of Patmos, and prepares us for what lies ahead for the church and the world. It also gives us a correlated outline of things to come in this life and eternity.

Translations of the Bible

The first translation of the Bible, as we know it today, was first available in <u>Greek</u>, and then subsequently translated through the years into a number of languages. Nowadays there are many translations, some more closely and accurately translated than others. I recommend a translation that is easier to understand, especially as English is my second language, but also one that will present the truths of God's Words in a responsible and as close as possible to the original way to me.

Through the years I have heard many arguments about the specific translation that should be read. As I contemplated those who more arduously argued on this, I observed very little of the values of the Bible translated in their lives. I believe that we need to embrace God's Word with an openness to hear His voice and a congruent heart attitude to apply and putting it into practice.

I also believe that it is of paramount importance to embrace the Author and what we have in our hands, more than what we lambaste the medium in which His message was brought to us. In the end we have to embrace, whichever translation we use, as the final authority in our lives. SO, whichever translation you use has to bring within you a sense that you believe that this closely resemble the heart and intention of what God wanted to communicate.

The promulgation of Scriptures

- **The Tables of Stone**

The only written instruction God Himself wrote, and gave, was that given to Moses on the Mountain.

Exodus 24:12
The Lord said to Moses, "Come up to me on the mountain and stay

here, and ***I will give you the tablets of stone*** *with the law and commandments* ***I have written for their instruction.***"

We have one other account of where the Finger of God wrote a message on the wall in the Book of Daniel. Apart from these two accounts, the rest of the Words of the Lord was reduced to writing under the instruction of the Lord.

- **The writings on Scrolls**

Jeremiah 30:2-3
This is the word that came to Jeremiah from the Lord: "This is what the Lord, the God of Israel, says: 'Write in a book all the words I have spoken to you.'"

I thank God for those obedient Servants of His who wrote down the Words He gave them. It is our responsibility to keep His Words and to ensure that we neither add nor diminish what He said.

- **The Gutenberg Bible**

The 1450 Gutenberg Bible was one of the first known printed books in the world. Printing revolutionized the multiplication of writings. Apart from the origins of the Bible being among the oldest and most reputed among records in the world, the Gutenberg Bible provided the world with the first printed Bible from the original Latin Vulgate. Since its early successes, the Bible continued to be printed and today remains the most sold book in the world year after year.

In Conclusion

During the next session we will explore ways in which we can make the most of our time in the Word.

Assimilation Sheet for
The Authority of the Bible

1. Complete the sentence. *The authority of the Bible can be argued from an Archeological, <u>Historical</u>, and Prophetic dimension.*

2. Complete the sentence. *The Dead Sea <u>Scrolls</u>, amongst other historical manuscripts, support the accuracy of the writings and the inerrancy of the Scriptures.*

3. Complete the sentence. *One of the aspects to confirm and validate the Authority of the Scriptures is the <u>consistency</u> of its message through so many writers, over so many years, from such varied backgrounds.*

4. Complete the sentence. *The Bible was written over a <u>1500-year</u> period by over 40 Authors who wrote Messages from God down as the Holy Spirit inspired them.*

5. Complete the sentence. *Firstly, we have the <u>Number</u> of Manuscripts that proof to be exactly the same, and then secondly, we have the <u>consistency</u> in the manuscripts, proving beyond doubt their reliability.*

6. Complete the sentence. *The Authority of the Bible, as the Word of God, is further reinforced by the strong consistent message regardless of being written by over <u>40</u> writers, many of whom lived in different time periods and circumstances.*

7. Complete the sentence. *The period over which the writers wrote, spans more than <u>1500</u> years.*

8. Complete the sentence. *The introduction of the <u>Gutenberg</u> Press also saw the mass production of the Bible as the first book to be reproduced, en-mass in printed form.*

9. Complete the sentence. *The first Canon of Scriptures was the <u>Hebrew</u> Bible and it consisted of the Old Testament writings as we know it today.*

10. What was the Hebrew Bible historically known as? <u>*The Tanakh.*</u>

11. The Tanakh consisted of three parts. Name the three parts of the Tanakh:

- <u>*Torah*</u>

- *Nevi'im*
- *Ketuvim*

12. What was the first translation of the Hebrew Bible called, and into what language was it translated? <u>*The Septuagint, and it was a translation into Greek.*</u>

13. The Torah was also known by what name? <u>*It was also known as the Pentateuch.*</u>

14. Complete the sentence. *The Pentateuch consists of the first <u>five</u> books of the Bible.*

15. Complete the sentence. *As early as <u>382</u> AD at the Council of Rome[10] the incorporation of these 27 books was accepted as part of the complete Bible.*

16. Name the three main ways in which the Word of God was passed down to us in written?

- <u>*Tables of Stone*</u>
- <u>*The writings on Scrolls*</u>
- <u>*Manuscripts*</u>
- <u>*The Gutenberg Press*</u>

10

MAKING THE MOST OF MY TIME IN THE WORD
SESSION THREE

How can I make the most of my time in the Word of God? During this session we will explore ways in which we can benefit most from our time in the Word, as well as How this time in the Word can help us grow and mature best.

1. A Good discipline in assimilating the Word of God is to:

- **Make a commitment to do it <u>daily</u>.**

Nothing impacts our lives as consistently practicing spiritual disciplines. The best way to grow in our faith is by staying connected to the Vine. Sundays are not the only, or best times to have an intake of the Word of God, no, we need a daily intake of the Word.

As much as we know the value of eating daily to nourish and maintain a healthy physical body, we know that a commitment to daily take and receive the Word of the Lord will sustain and maintain a healthy connectedness to the source of all we need.

John 15:7 (NIV)
7 If you remain in me and my words remain in you, ask whatever you wish, and it will be done for you.

- **Set aside a specific and dedicated time to be alone with God and in His <u>Word</u>.**

We usually enjoy breakfast, lunch and dinner around set times. In the same way schedule a time or times in the Word. Set aside a time and place where you can be alone with God and His Word.

- **Find and follow a Bible <u>Reading</u> plan.**

A Reading plan will help you read through the entire Bible on a yearly basis. It also helps us stay on track to consistently have a balanced intake of the Word. Good Bible Reading Plans consist of a portion in the Old Testament, a portion from the New Testament, and often a Psalm or two and perhaps a portion from the Proverbs.

Get a One Year Bible.

These could be found in One-Year Bibles like the Zondervan NIV One-Year Bible. I have seen this being used by my wife for over 30 years. It can be a huge resource and it works!

You could also find Bible Reading Plans on the YouVersion Bible App. The most important thing is that you start one today.

2. The SOAP method

Whilst reading the Bible daily, apply the SOAP method to ensure that you don't just read the Bible as if it is another book, but as it really is: God's Word to you and me to live by.

Make a commitment to put it into practice.

The SOAP method stands for:

- S – <u>Scripture</u> (The specific reading of the day),
- O – <u>Observation</u> (What is God saying to me through the reading of today?),
- A – <u>Application</u> (How can I put this into practice today? How can I do this? And make a commitment to do it), and
- P – <u>Prayer</u> (Take a few moments to pray the application and commitment into your life.) E.g. *"Heavenly Father, today you spoke to me about forgiveness through Your Word. I choose to forgive like you want me to. I commit to forgive those who are going to do things that I don't like. I forgive them. I forgive those who are harmful and hurtful towards me. Help me to be quick to forgive. Thank you for your forgiveness. Amen"*

3. Listen and do!

Encounter God through your daily reading of the Bible. God speaks, and desires to speak to us as His children. Listen and do! You will always be encouraged and strengthened through the reading and meditation of the Word.

4. Meditate on the Word

Meditate on the Word of God. Pause, while reading, and think about it. Learn the Word of God.

5. Study the Bible.

Take those Scriptures that stand out to you, and those that you sense God is speaking to you about, and learn them of by heart, meditate on them and remind God about His promises to you regularly.

6. Be a man and woman of the Word of God.

Where do you start?

A good place to start is to start by reading the Gospel of John. Read at least three chapters of the New and Old Testament a day. Also read 5 Psalms and 1 chapter in Proverbs. This will put you on a good and healthy spiritual discipline diet. It will take you between 15-45 minutes to complete such a regime of reading the Word.

The average reading from a Bible Reading Plans takes about 20 minutes. Combined with meditating and prayer it will require around 60 minutes to give any kind of credence to your effort.

A Good strategy to follow!

You might want to consider the following guidelines when you spend time in the Word:

- **The message of the Books**

Each Book has a message. It sometimes helps when you read the Introduction to a Bible Book to ascertain the historical and political background, and contextual time in which the Book was written. It also helps to understand the biblical contemporaries of the time. Many times, there is strong link between some of the Prophets and the time in which a certain Book plays out. This helps to find context as well as build a unified understanding of how God communicates and how our Faithful God works with those who obey and follow Him.

- **God speaks to us through His Word.**

Allow the Holy Spirit to speak to you every time you pick up His Word. He wants to speak. Open your heart to hear Him speak to you as you read and contemplate the Word. The Reason He spoke to His people in the Bible is still the same reason He speaks to us today. The very things He addressed with His people in the Bible are still the same things He addresses in us about today.

- **How God spoke to His Servants through the <u>Word</u>.**

What often helps is when we make the connection between how God spoke to His Servants throughout the Old Testament, and how He continues to speak to us today. Live with an expectation in your heart that God will speak to you too like He spoke to His Servants throughout the Bible. God spoke in the Old Testament times, Gospel times, and throughout New Testament times.

- **Hear God speak to us <u>today</u>**

It is essential to know that God speaks to us through the written Word. God also speaks to us through the Holy Spirit while we read and meditate the Word of God. Listen to the Voice of the Holy Spirit. God speaks to us through His Servants who bring the Word of God to us. At some point in your walk with God, God will not only speak to you through His Word, but He will also give you Words to deliver and bring to others. While you read and pray, always keep an openness to understand whether the Lord is speaking to you or wants you to bring encouragement to someone else.

- **It is essential that we <u>live</u> by every Word that proceeds from the mouth of God.**

Make a commitment to put the Word into practice. Act on His Word to you, just like the men and woman of God acted and responded to the Words God spoke to them. They constantly sought the Lord for His guidance in every life decision that they made.

- **We need to be <u>guided</u> by the Word of God.**

In the Old Testament we learn about the Urim and Thummim, the two stones being used to determine outcomes and answers from the Lord.

> Exodus 28:30 (NIV) 30 Also put the Urim and the Thummim in the breastpiece, so they may be over Aaron's heart whenever he enters the presence of the LORD. Thus Aaron will always bear the means of making decisions for the Israelites over his heart before the LORD.

The priest was to establish, beforehand, How the answer of the Lord will be determined. One such occasion was when Saul enquired of the Lord to determine why He never answered him.

> 1 Samuel 14:41-42 (NIV) 41 Then Saul prayed to the LORD, the God of Israel, "Why have you not answered your servant today? If the fault is in me or my son Jonathan, respond with Urim, but if the men of Israel are at fault, respond with Thummim." Jonathan and Saul were taken by lot, and the men were cleared. 42 Saul said, "Cast the lot between me and Jonathan my son." And Jonathan was taken.

We have a number occasions where the Leaders would not proceed before enquiring of the LORD.

> Ezra 2:63 (NIV) 63 The governor ordered them not to eat any of the most sacred food until there was a priest ministering with the Urim and Thummim.

In the same way we need to enquire of the Lord before we make decisions. Let the Word of God guide and direct our footsteps.

> Psalms 119:105 (NIV) 105 Your word is a lamp for my feet, and a light on my path.

> Proverbs 3:5-6 (NIV) 5 Trust in the LORD with all your heart and lean not on your own understanding; 6 in all your ways submit to him, and he will make your paths straight.

We need to build our lives against the advice gained from the Word of God. Allow God to speak to you on a daily basis, through His Word.

- **Do not <u>add</u> or diminish any of the Words of God**

It is essential that we neither read into the Word what it does not say, nor add to what it said. Some people are in the habit of stretching the truth of the Word to such extents that it does not even look like what the Word actually said. Read and apply it like a child. Take it as it was given to us.

> *Deuteronomy 4:2 (NIV) Do not add to what I command you and do not subtract from it but keep the commands of the Lord your God that I give you.*

> *Revelation 22:18-19 (NIV) I warn everyone who hears the words of the prophecy of this scroll: If anyone adds anything to them, God will add to that person the plagues described in this scroll. And if anyone takes words away from this scroll of prophecy, God will take away from that person any share in the tree of life and in the Holy City, which are described in this scroll.*

In Conclusion

The Word of God is living and active. The Word of God enlightens us by guiding and directing us in the right paths. Every moment we spend in the Word of God, we activate its transformative power to direct us, renew us, strengthen us, guide us and build us up. If His Word remains in us we will bear much fruit.

Assimilation Sheet for
Making the most of my time in the Word

1. Complete the sentence on practicing good disciplines. *Make a commitment to do it <u>daily</u>.*

2. Complete the sentence. *Set aside a specific and dedicated time to be alone with God and His <u>Word</u>.*

3. Complete the sentence. *Find and follow a Bible <u>Reading</u> Plan.*

4. Name the four words in the acronym SOAP.

- S - <u>Scripture</u>
- O - <u>Observation</u>
- A - <u>Application</u>
- P - <u>Prayer</u>

5. In becoming a Man and woman of the Word there are a few strategies to follow. Complete the following statements.

- *The <u>message</u> of the Books*
- *God <u>speaks</u> to us through His Word*
- *How God spoke to His Servants through the <u>Word</u>*
- *Hear God speak to us <u>today</u>*
- *It is essential that we <u>live</u> by every Word that proceeds from the mouth of God*
- *We need to be <u>guided</u> by the Word of God*
- *Do not <u>add</u> or diminish any of the Words of God*

11

FURTHER STUDY

Since most of our disciples may be new to the faith, we need to help them understand, The Bible, its Message, and how to receive and live by it daily. The best way to do this is through an intensive weekend encounter like this one.

To make this Encounter an enhanced experience we recommend that you also complete the "Survey of the Bible" course of Bruce Wilkinson from Teach every Nation. Dr. Bruce Wilkinson is a prolific Teacher and this encounter will enrich your understanding and appreciation of the Word of God.

His "Survey of the Bible" course will help you to:

- See the Big Picture. You'll be introduced to the structure of your Bible so you can manage its content, purposes and applications throughout your life.
- Discover Your Story in *His*. You will see the plan of God in creation and His desire to redeem His people from the consequences of sin and to offer redemption to all of mankind.
- Find Learning Fun. Utilizing memory pegs, animation and

creative staging, difficult content is made mind-easy and memorization become effortless.

- Understand the Historical Timeline. We've broken the historical timeline into 20 different periods – 10 in the Old Testament and 10 in the New Testament.
- Find Out Who, Why and When. You will be able to match 10 key Bible characters with each of those Old and New Testament historical periods.
- Finally, Pinpoint What and Where. You'll explore maps that make sense, to discover where the Garden of Eden was, where Abraham came from, where Jesus walked, Paul was imprisoned and much more.
- Discover Life Change over the Course of Your Lifetime. Consistent review is a crucial element in making this big-picture tool your own. After just a few sessions, you'll be building on this tool for a lifetime of spiritual growth and ministry.

Small Group Curriculum
(Also Great for Classes,
Family & Personal Devotions)

Survey of the Bible Course

You can purchase this material from www.brucewilkinsoncourses.org

PART III

SHARING YOUR FAITH WEEKEND ENCOUNTER

WEEKEND THREE

ENCOUNTER SCHEDULE

- Session 1 – INTRODUCTION TO SHARING OUR FAITH
- Session 2 - SHARING OUR FAITH IN A PRACTICAL WAY
- Session 3 – THE PRACTICAL GOSPEL MESSAGE

INTRODUCTION TO SHARING OUR FAITH
SESSION ONE

We are all witnesses of what God has done in our lives. Our call is to testify and share this with others.

Jesus taught His Disciples *the Spiritual Discipline of Witnessing* when He first taught them on the mountain. He said to them that they were **Light** and **Salt** and that they should let their **"light so shine before others that they may see your good deeds and glorify your Father in Heaven."** This is a clear directive to be a witness, to be a Light to the World.

Witnessing requires a commitment to both be a "light" and "Salt."

> *Matthew 5:13-16 (NIV)* [13] ***"You are the salt of the earth.*** *But if the salt loses its saltiness, how can it be made salty again? It is no longer good for anything, except to be thrown out and trampled underfoot.* [14] ***"You are the light of the world.*** *A town built on a hill cannot be hidden.* [15] *Neither do people light a lamp and put it under a bowl. Instead they put it on its stand, and it gives light to everyone in the house.* [16] *In the same way, let your light*

shine before others, that they may see your good deeds and glorify your Father in heaven.""

To be a "*light*" means that we commit to go on public display as an example for others to see the *Light* of Christ shining brightly in our lives through the **good deeds** they observe in and through our lives.

To be "*Salt*" requires us to live worthily, upholding the values of the Kingdom of God through our high-principled conduct. On the other hand, to be a witness also requires us to share the Word of God by mouth.

Witnessing requires a commitment to "preach" the Good News.

During the parting moments before Jesus Ascended to Heaven, He gave His Disciples the "**Great Commission**." The Great Commission requires us to **go** out into the whole world and **preach** the Good News about Jesus Christ and **Disciple** them into obedient Followers of Jesus Christ.

> *Mark 16:15 (NIV) "15 He said to them, "Go into all the world and preach the gospel to all creation."*

> *Mark 16:20 (NIV) "20 Then the disciples went out and preached everywhere, and the Lord worked with them and confirmed his word by the signs that accompanied it."*

Witnessing requires a commitment to both "preach" and "disciple."

Jesus not only requires His Followers to "*go into all the world and preach the gospel*," but He also requires them to ***disciple*** those whose hearts are opened and who respond to the Gospel message that is preached.

> *Matthew 28:19-20 (NIV) "19 Therefore go and make disciples of all nations, baptizing them in the name of the Father and of the Son and of the Holy Spirit, 20 and teaching them to obey everything I have commanded you. And surely, I am with you always, to the very end of the age."*

The church in Acts did exactly that; they preached and made disciples. Jesus instructed us to **preach** the gospel and to **teach** our disciples what He taught us. The early church did just that. It was this broader embracing of the Final Instruction the Lord gave His Disciples that gave precedence to it becoming the "**Great Commission.**"

> *Acts 11:19-21 (NIV) "19 Now those who had been scattered by the persecution that broke out when Stephen was killed traveled as far as Phoenicia, Cyprus and Antioch, spreading the word only among Jews. 20 Some of them, however, men from Cyprus and Cyrene, went to Antioch and began to speak to Greeks also, telling them the good news about the Lord Jesus. 21 The Lord's hand was with them, and a great number of people believed and turned to the Lord."*

> *Acts 11:25-26 (NIV) 25 Then Barnabas went to Tarsus to look for Saul, 26 and when he found him, he brought him to Antioch. So for a whole year Barnabas and Saul met with the church and taught great numbers of people. The disciples were called Christians first at Antioch.*

We see this pattern replicated on many accounts in the Acts of the Apostles. It is no wonder that the early church grew exponentially. I believe, and see, that we will experience the same impact and transformation of nations as what the Apostles and the early church experienced when we embrace again, as the body of Christ, as Believers, the "**Great Commission**" as our mission. We will cover the earth with the Good News of Jesus Christ.

How will they believe without someone telling them?

Periodically we need to ask ourselves: ***How will they believe unless we tell them?*** The answer to this question should always move us to a commitment to act and share our faith.

> *Romans 10:14-15 (NIV) 14 How, then, can they call on the one they have not believed in? And how can they believe in the one of whom they have not heard? And how can they hear without someone preaching to them? 15 And how can they preach unless they are sent? As it is written, "How beautiful are the feet of those who bring good news!"*

Jesus modelled preaching and discipling

Jesus started His earthly ministry by doing exactly that; He preached a Message of Repentance everywhere he went. John the Baptist also started His ministry by preaching. The Apostles did the same. It is no wonder that they were able to reach their entire world with the Gospel since they went out, preached, and bore witness, and discipled the new Believers.

> *Matthew 3:1-2 (NIV) "1 In those days John the Baptist came, preaching in the wilderness of Judea 2 and saying, 'Repent, for the kingdom of heaven has come near.'"*

> *Matthew 4:17 (NIV) "17 From that time on Jesus began to preach, 'Repent, for the kingdom of heaven has come near.'"*

As a result of this preaching Jesus found His first Disciples. We see this process modelled by Jesus in the Gospel of Luke. First Jesus preached, and then performed a miracle, and then Peter bowed his knees to Jesus and followed Him to be His Disciple.

> *Luke 5:1 (NIV) "1 One day as Jesus was standing by the Lake of Gennesaret, the people were crowding around him and listening to the word of God."*

Jesus preached the Word of God next to the Lake of Gennesaret. It is here that He met Peter, Andrew, James and John, the owners of two fishing trawlers.

> *Luke 5:4-6 (NIV) "4 When he had finished speaking, he said to Simon, 'Put out into deep water, and let down the nets for a catch.' 5 Simon answered, 'Master, we've worked hard all night and haven't caught anything. But because you say so, I will let down the nets.' 6 When they had done so, they caught such a large number of fish that their nets began to break."*

Jesus performed a miracle that astounded them. One of the consistent elements we witness in the work of the early church was their passionate obedience to **preach** Jesus, **"perform miracles, signs and wonders,"** and **disciple**. In the midst of severe persecution, the church advanced and even won the hostile Roman Empire.

> *Luke 5:8-9 (NIV) "8 When Simon Peter saw this, he fell at Jesus' knees and said, 'Go away from me, Lord; I am a sinful man!' 9 For he and all his companions were astonished at the catch of fish they had taken."*

On a number of occasions, we see this same pattern of ministry replicated as well; Preach, miracles, repentance and people becoming Followers.

> *Luke 5:10-11 (NIV) 10 "...Then Jesus said to Simon, 'Don't be afraid; from now on you will fish for people.' 11 So they pulled their boats up on shore, left everything and followed him."*

These first Disciples of the Lord witnesses firsthand a miracle, the impact of which impacted them so much that Peter fell to his knees and **_confessed_** that he was a sinner. The impact of us **_preaching_** or speaking the Word of God should result in people putting their faith in Jesus.

Peter preached, performed miracles and discipled wherever he went

The Apostle Peter was such an example of practicing this Spiritual Discipline right from the onset of the Church's Foundation. He is the one who stood up in the Day of Pentecost and preached that message that saw 3000 people coming to Christ.

> *Acts 2:14 (NIV) Peter Addresses the Crowd "14 Then Peter stood up with the Eleven, raised his voice and addressed the crowd: 'Fellow Jews and all of you who live in Jerusalem, let me explain this to you; listen carefully to what I say.'"*

Peter preached Jesus.

> *Acts 2:22 (NIV) "22 'Fellow Israelites, listen to this: Jesus of Nazareth was a man accredited by God to you by miracles, wonders and signs, which God did among you through him, as you yourselves know.'"*

His message included the death and resurrection of Jesus.

> *Acts 2:31-33 (NIV) 31 Seeing what was to come, he spoke of the resurrection of the Messiah, that he was not abandoned to the realm of the dead, nor did his body see decay. 32 God has raised this Jesus to life, and we are all witnesses of it. 33 Exalted to the right hand of God, he has received from the Father the promised Holy Spirit and has poured out what you now see and hear."*

No preaching is complete unless it culminates in an opportunity or a call to **repentance** and to **accept** Christ as Lord. The Lord's Hand will be upon the hearers to bring the conviction, but we have to follow through by leading them to Salvation.

This is exactly what transpired when Peter preached that incredible message on the Day of Pentecost. The people came under such a conviction that they actually asked Peter: "What shall we do?" They wanted to be saved. They wanted to be reconciled with God. They wanted to receive this Jesus into their lives.

> *Acts 2:36-41 (NIV) 36 "Therefore let all Israel be assured of this: God has made this Jesus, whom you crucified, both Lord and Messiah." 37 When the people heard this, they were cut to the heart and said to Peter and the other apostles, "Brothers, what shall we do?" 38 Peter replied, "Repent and be baptized, every one of you, in the name of Jesus Christ for the forgiveness of your sins. And you will receive the gift of the Holy Spirit. 39 The promise is for you and your children and for all who are far off—for all whom the Lord our God will call." 40 With many other words he warned them; and he pleaded with them, "Save yourselves from this corrupt generation." 41 Those who accepted his message were baptized, and about three thousand were added to their number that day"*

On many other occasions we see the same pattern of witnessing being followed; miracles, preaching and people putting their faith in Jesus Christ.

In the Acts of the Apostles, chapter three, we read about the Lame Beggar being healed, which was followed with an opportunity to share about Jesus of Nazareth. 5000 people came to the Lord as a result of that witnessing about the Lord Jesus being the Resurrected Christ and Messiah.

> *Acts 3:9-10 (NIV) "9 When all the people saw him walking and praising God, 10 they recognized him as the same man who*

used to sit begging at the temple gate called Beautiful, and they were filled with wonder and amazement at what had happened to him."

The focus of his message was clear: repent, that your sins might be wiped out, and that times of refreshing might come.

> Acts 3:19 (NIV) "19 Repent, then, and turn to God, so that your sins may be wiped out, that times of refreshing may come from the Lord,"

The impact of the Lord working with Peter as He brought witness of the Lord Jesus was incredible. First the Sadducees and Teachers of the Law was infuriated by Peter and John's message on the Resurrection of Jesus Christ that they imprisoned them, but the impact of the message was so powerful that 5000 people believed the message. Secondly, Peter and John, after imprisonment, came out even stronger and continued in the work of the Lord.

> Acts 4:2 (NIV) "2 They were greatly disturbed because the apostles were teaching the people, proclaiming in Jesus the resurrection of the dead."

> Acts 4:4 (NIV) "4 But many who heard the message believed; so the number of men who believed grew to about five thousand."

The undeniable impact was clear to everyone in Jerusalem and beyond. More and more people believed in the Lord, both as a result of them seeing the demonstration of the Power of God, as well as hearing the Message that was delivered by the Apostles.

> Acts 5:12 (NIV) The Apostles Heal Many "12 The apostles performed many signs and wonders among the people. And all the believers used to meet together in Solomon's Colonnade."

> *Acts 5:14-15 (NIV) 14 Nevertheless, more and more men and women believed in the Lord and were added to their number. 15 As a result, people brought the sick into the streets and laid them on beds and mats so that at least Peter's shadow might fall on some of them as he passed by.*

The early Believers also preached everywhere

The early Believers spread the Word of God everywhere they went. The Gospel was preached everywhere. Preaching is bringing the message that Jesus is the Son of God, and by faith in Him as your Lord and Saviour, He can save you.

> *Acts 8:4 (NIV) "4 Those who had been scattered preached the word wherever they went."*

As these Believers went, they preached, both to Jews and Gentiles.

> *Acts 11:19-21 (NIV) "19 Now those who had been scattered by the persecution that broke out when Stephen was killed traveled as far as Phoenicia, Cyprus and Antioch, spreading the word only among Jews. 20 Some of them, however, men from Cyprus and Cyrene, went to Antioch and began to speak to Greeks also, telling them the good news about the Lord Jesus. 21 The Lord's hand was with them, and a great number of people believed and turned to the Lord."*

We see how the Words of Jesus came into fulfillment through these Believers, as they became witnesses in Judea, Samaria and into the ends of the earth. Here we have an account of them preaching to Greeks and later on to Samaritans as well.

Philip preached to the Samaritans.

Philip was one of the Believers who got scattered through the persecution that broke out in Jerusalem. Instead of shrinking back, they went and spread the Gospel everywhere, even to the Samaritans, which was totally cross-cultural for them at that time.

> Acts 8:5 (NIV) "5 Philip went down to a city in Samaria and proclaimed the Messiah there."

> Acts 8:12 (NIV) "12 But when they believed Philip as he proclaimed the good news of the kingdom of God and the name of Jesus Christ, they were baptized, both men and women."

> Acts 8:25 (NIV) "25 After they had further proclaimed the word of the Lord and testified about Jesus, Peter and John returned to Jerusalem, preaching the gospel in many Samaritan villages."

Paul immediately started preaching when he got saved

The Apostle Paul, when He came to the Lord, immediately started preaching and proving that Jesus was the Messiah.

> Acts 9:20 (NIV) "20 At once he began to preach in the synagogues that Jesus is the Son of God."

It is this obedient acting on the "***Great Commission***" that changed the entire world for Jesus.

In Acts Chapter 16 we see another example of the impact of ***preaching*** the Gospel and ***Witnessing*** for the Lord Jesus. After Paul had his ***Macedonian Vision*** him and his companions set out for Macedonia to preach the Good News of Jesus.

Acts 16:10 (NIV) "10 After Paul had seen the vision, we got ready at once to leave for Macedonia, concluding that God had called us to preach the gospel to them."

The result of Paul sharing the message of Christ was that, *"**The Lord opened her heart to respond to Paul's message.**"*

Acts 16:13-14 (NIV) "13 On the Sabbath we went outside the city gate to the river, where we expected to find a place of prayer. We sat down and began to speak to the women who had gathered there. 14 One of those listening was a woman from the city of Thyatira named Lydia, a dealer in purple cloth. She was a worshiper of God. The Lord opened her heart to respond to Paul's message."

What we learn from the *"**Witnessing**"* through the lives of the Apostles, and the Believers in Acts, are that they *"**preached**"* everywhere and that, *"the Lord"* truly *"worked with them to confirm the Word"*.

Conclusion

We are therefore required to make a commitment to witness by sharing our faith, preach and testify to what God did for us.

Assimilation Sheet for
INTRODUCTION TO SHARING OUR FAITH

1. Complete the statement. *Witnessing requires a commitment to both be a "light" and "Salt."*

2. Which Scripture teaches us this principle? *Matthew 5:13-16*

3. Complete the statement. *Witnessing requires a commitment to "preach" the Good News.*

4. Which Scripture teaches us this principle? *Mark 16:15*

5. Complete the statement. *Witnessing requires a commitment to both "preach" and "disciple."*

6. Which Scripture teaches us this principle? Matthew 28:19-20

7. How will the Gospel spread? *By someone preaching the gospel.*

8. What Scripture encourages us in this? *Romans 10:14-15*

9. What did Jesus model to us regarding how to minister? *He was preaching and discipling.*

10. Which Scripture teaches us this principle? *Matthew 4:17*

11. What was one of the outcomes of Jesus' preaching in Luke chapter five? *He found His Disciples.*

12. What was the key things that happened when Jesus preached in Luke 5 verses 1-11? *He performed a miracle, Peter confessed his sins, and they became His Followers.*

13. What did Peter do on the Day of Pentecost? *He preached.*

14. How many people came to the Lord as a result of this preaching? *3000 people were saved.*

15. What did Peter do in Acts chapter 3 verses 9 and onwards? *He healed a cripple man, preached and 5000 people came to the Lord.*

16. What was His main message? Give a verse. *Acts 3:19*

17. Where did the early Believers preach? Substantiate with Scriptures. *They preached everywhere. Acts 8:4, Acts 11:19-21.*

18. Which Believer preached to the Samaritans? Substantiate with Scriptures. *Philip. Acts 8:5, 12.*

19. What did Paul do when he got saved? Substantiate with Scriptures. *He preached. Acts 9:20*

20. Paul delivered a message in Acts chapter sixteen in Macedonia. What was the impact of their sharing? Substantiate with Scripture. *Lydia and her household came to the Lord. Acts 16:13-14*

21. What did the Lord do when they preached the Word? *The Lord worked with them and confirmed the Word.*

13

SHARING OUR FAITH IN A PRACTICAL WAY
SESSION TWO

In this session we will look at ways in which we can share our faith in a practical way.

How can we share our faith in a practical way?

1. Make the "Great Commission" your life's mission.

This means that you commit to embrace all the different aspects of the Great Commission and fulfill it daily. It is the most natural thing for new Believers to share their newfound faith in Jesus. I encourage you to make this a lifelong mission and discipline of yours to share your faith with others.

Make a commitment to this Mission. It requires:

- A commitment to "go."
- That we "preach" the Gospel.
- That we "baptise" those who accept Christ.
- That we "teach" the new Believers to obey everything Jesus taught us.

2. Make a commitment to put on the "shoes of preparedness" to share your faith.

We are encouraged to put on the "**Full Armour of God**" daily. One of the essential parts of the "**Armour of God**" is the "*Shoes of preparedness*". Being prepared brings within us an expectation to keep our eyes open for when the opportunity arises.

Being prepared also makes us less anxious when we have an opportunity to share. Being prepared also makes us also bolder and more confident since we expect to see how the Lord will open their hearts to receive Him as their Lord and Savior.

> *Ephesians 6:15 (NIV) "15 and with your feet fitted with the readiness that comes from the gospel of peace."*

> *Ephesians 6:15 (BBE) "15 Be ready with the good news of peace as shoes on your feet;"*

Our preparation for each day should include a readiness to share the Hope we have in Jesus, whilst attending to keep our good behavior.

> *1 Peter 3:15-16 (NIV 1984) "15 But in your hearts set apart Christ as Lord. Always be prepared to give an answer to everyone who asks you to give the reason for the hope that you have. But do this with gentleness and respect, 16 keeping a clear conscience, so that those who speak maliciously against your good behavior in Christ may be ashamed of their slander."*

3. Learn how to share the Gospel like the Apostles did?

One of the top reasons why people do not share their faith, according to research by Lesli White from Beliefnet.com[1], is that people "***don't feel that they are knowledgeable***" to share the Gospel.

During our next session we will learn the Gospel message clearly.

THE GOSPEL

The strategy and content that the Apostles, and first Believers, used to share the Gospel is well noted in the New Testament. It was Biblically founded and intentionally pursued under the Power of the Holy Spirit. They used the Word of God in almost every account of witnessing about Jesus, and strongly depended on the Holy Spirit to bring conviction, and on the Lord to confirm His Word through Signs and Wonders. They pleaded with the listeners to be reconciled with God, to repent of their sins, and to accept Jesus Christ as Lord.

The Apostle Paul, in his address to the Church in Corinth, reminds them of the Gospel message by which they were saved:

> *1 Corinthians 15:1-8 (NIV) 1 Now, brothers, I want to remind you of the gospel I preached to you, which you received and on which you have taken your stand. 2 By this gospel you are saved, if you hold firmly to the word, I preached to you. Otherwise, you have believed in vain. 3 For what I received I passed on to you as of first importance : that Christ died for our sins according to the Scriptures,4 that he was buried, that he was raised on the third day according to the Scriptures, 5 and that he appeared to Peter, and then to the Twelve. 6 After that, he appeared to more than five hundred of the brothers at the same time, most of whom are still living, though some have fallen asleep. 7 Then he appeared to James, then to all the apostles, 8 and last of all he appeared to me also, as to one abnormally born."*

The Gospel is about Jesus Christ, who <u>died</u> for our sins, in our place, to save us, but then <u>rose</u> from the dead and is <u>alive</u>. We now serve the living God! The validation of the Scriptures is remarkable throughout this message and throughout the preaching of Jesus, His Disciples and the numerous accounts of where we read of the Believers preaching.

1. Christ died for our sins, according to the Scriptures.

Christ died for our sins when we were still dead in our sins. We all sinned and need a Savior. Christ is our Savior.

> *Isaiah 53:5 (NIV) "5 But he was pierced for our transgressions, he was crushed for our iniquities; the punishment that brought us peace was upon him, and by his wounds we are healed."*

He was wounded for our transgressions. He is also the Lamb of God who took away our sins by becoming the sacrificial Lamb to satisfy the requirement of God for the remission of sins.

> *John 1:29 (NIV) "29 The next day John saw Jesus coming toward him and said, "Look, the Lamb of God, who takes away the sin of the world!"*

Christ, the Righteous, died in our place. We deserved to die, but Christ took our place on the Cross.

> *1 Peter 2:24 (NIV) "24 He himself bore our sins in his body on the tree, so that we might die to sins and live for righteousness; by his wounds you have been healed."*

2. Christ rose from the dead to offer us a living hope and eternal life.

We believe that Christ was buried, and then rose from the dead. He is alive and offers eternal life to all who believe in Him. We live this life for Him so that we will live with Him for eternity.

> *1 Corinthians 15:19-20, 22 (NIV) 19 If only for this life we have hope in Christ, we are to be pitied more than all men. 20 But Christ has indeed been raised from the dead, the firstfruits of those*

who have fallen asleep. 22 For as in Adam all die, so in Christ all will be made alive.

Eternal life can only be offered by One who rose from the dead. Christ rose from the dead and therefore He offers eternal life to all who believe in Him.

John 3:16 (NIV) 16 "For God so loved the world that he gave his one and only Son, that whoever believes in him shall not perish but have eternal life."

John 6:40 (NIV) "40 For my Father's will is that everyone who looks to the Son and believes in him shall have eternal life, and I will raise him up at the last day."

3. Christ is coming back again to take us to be with Him forever.

Jesus is coming back! He is coming back to bring us to be with Him forever. He is also coming to reward us for our walk in Him. We will all stand before Him, some to receive their eternal reward and some to be sent into eternal damnation.

Matthew 16:27 (NIV) "27 For the Son of Man is going to come in his Father's glory with his angels, and then he will reward each person according to what he has done."

Jesus Himself said that He is coming back again. In this Scripture He says that He is returning as the "Rewarder." Jesus also taught that when He returns, He will take us back with Him to be with Him forever. We live with this hope in our hearts always. We have a living Hope.

John 14:3 (NIV) "3 And if I go and prepare a place for you, I will come back and take you to be with me that you also may be where I am."

The Apostle Paul said in his letter, to the church in Thessalonica, that when Jesus returns, that we who are still alive will meet Him in the air, and be with Him forever. This is something to look forward to.

> *1 Thessalonians 4:16-17 (NIV)* "*16 For the Lord himself will come down from heaven, with a loud command, with the voice of the archangel and with the trumpet call of God, and the dead in Christ will rise first. 17 After that, we who are still alive and are left will be caught up together with them in the clouds to meet the Lord in the air. And so we will be with the Lord forever.*"

4. We receive Him as Lord by confessing our sins and ask Him to be our Lord.

The Bible teaches us that His blood washes and cleanses us. We are saved when we confess our sins and confess Jesus as the Lord of our lives. The Bible teaches us in 1 John chapter one that we receive forgiveness when we repent and confess our sins. The Lord purifies us from all our wrongdoings.

> *1 John 1:9 (NIV) 9 If we confess our sins, he is faithful and just and will forgive us our sins and purify us from all unrighteousness.*

The Bible also teaches that when we openly *"confess Jesus as the Lord"* of our lives and simultaneously believe in our hearts that God raised Him from the dead, that we will be saved.

> *Romans 10:9 (NIV)* "*9 That if you confess with your mouth, 'Jesus is Lord,' and believe in your heart that God raised him from the dead, you will be saved.*"

Peter concluded his message on the Day of Pentecost with a Call to Repentance.

Acts 2:38 (NIV) "38 Peter replied, 'Repent and be baptized, every one of you, in the name of Jesus Christ for the forgiveness of your sins. And you will receive the gift of the Holy Spirit.'"

Jesus Himself taught this Gospel message to His Disciples.

Luke 24:46-47 (NIV) 46 He told them, "This is what is written: The Christ will suffer and rise from the dead on the third day, 47 and repentance and forgiveness of sins will be preached in his name to all nations, beginning at Jerusalem."

A Note to remember when we present the Gospel Message:

The Gospel Message should be encased by the <u>Word</u> of God

Whenever Jesus preached, He referenced the Word of God. When Peter stood up on the Day of Pentecost and delivered that first Gospel Message, it was encased in Scriptural references. Twice in the first message he referenced the Scriptures.

Acts 2:14, 16 (NIV) "14 Then Peter stood up with the Eleven, raised his voice and addressed the crowd: 'Fellow Jews and all of you who live in Jerusalem, let me explain this to you; listen carefully to what I say. 16 No, this is what was spoken by the prophet Joel:'"

Acts 2:25 (NIV) "25 David said about him: 'I saw the Lord always before me. Because he is at my right hand, I will not be shaken.'"

When Peter and John spoke in the Colonnade of Solomon when Peter healed the cripple man, he encased it in references to Moses and the Prophets.

Acts 3:22-23 (NIV) "22 For Moses said, 'The Lord your God will

> raise up for you a prophet like me from among your own people; you must listen to everything he tells you. 23 Anyone who does not listen to him will be completely cut off from among his people.'"

> Acts 3:24-25 (NIV) 24 "Indeed, all the prophets from Samuel on, as many as have spoken, have foretold these days. 25 And you are heirs of the prophets and of the covenant God made with your fathers. He said to Abraham, 'Through your offspring all peoples on earth will be blessed.'"

When Peter and John were brought before the Sanhedrin because of their preaching and the healing miracle of the cripple man, Peter referenced the Scriptures

> Acts 4:10-12 (NIV) "10 then know this, you and all the people of Israel: It is by the name of Jesus Christ of Nazareth, whom you crucified but whom God raised from the dead, that this man stands before you healed. 11 He is "'the stone you builders rejected, which has become the capstone.' 12 Salvation is found in no one else, for there is no other name under heaven given to men by which we must be saved.'"

When Stephen spoke in Acts 7, he referenced the Word of God throughout his message. When Philip spoke to the Eunuch when the Holy Spirit directed him to go there, the Message was encased in Scripture.

The word of God is truly "**_Living_**" and "**_Active_**" and able to work Powerfully in us. The more we allow it on our lips we unlock its Power to bring change and transformation in the lives of people around us.

The Gospel should be centered on Jesus Christ as the <u>Son</u> of God.

Whenever the Apostles and first Believers preached and shared the Gospel it was always centered on Jesus Christ. The whole Gospel centers on the Salvatory Work of Jesus Christ on the cross of Calvary. It's not about you or me; it's about Jesus, and us putting our faith in Him.

> *Acts 2:22-24 (NIV) "22 "Men of Israel, listen to this: Jesus of Nazareth was a man accredited by God to you by miracles, wonders and signs, which God did among you through him, as you yourselves know.23 This man was handed over to you by God's set purpose and foreknowledge; and you, with the help of wicked men, put him to death by nailing him to the cross. 24 But God raised him from the dead, freeing him from the agony of death, because it was impossible for death to keep its hold on him."*

> *Acts 2:32-33 (NIV) "32 God has raised this Jesus to life, and we are all witnesses of the fact. 33 Exalted to the right hand of God, he has received from the Father the promised Holy Spirit and has poured out what you now see and hear."*

At every juncture Peter, and the other Believers, witnessed about Jesus as the Resurrected Christ.

> *Acts 3:16 (NIV) "16 By faith in the name of Jesus, this man whom you see and know was made strong. It is Jesus' name and the faith that comes through him that has given this complete healing to him, as you can all see."*

> *Acts 3:18-20 (NIV) "18 But this is how God fulfilled what he had foretold through all the prophets, saying that his Christ would suffer. 19 Repent, then, and turn to God, so that your sins may be wiped out, that times of refreshing may come from the Lord, 20 and that he may send the Christ, who has been appointed for you–even Jesus."*

The Gospel message is received by putting our <u>faith</u> in Jesus as Lord

The Gospel is received by confession, and by faith, in receiving Christ as Lord.

Romans 10:9-10 (NIV) 9 That if you confess with your mouth, "Jesus is Lord," and believe in your heart that God raised him from the dead, you will be saved. 10 For it is with your heart that you believe and are justified, and it is with your mouth that you confess and are saved.

Romans 10:13 (NIV) "13 for, "Everyone who calls on the name of the Lord will be saved."

The preaching of the Gospel was always, and should always be accompanied by a strong sense of <u>conviction</u> on the hearers.

When Peter stood up in the midst of the Twelve and preached on the Day of Pentecost, a deep conviction came on all those who heard the Word of God. It was this same strong conviction that accompanied their messages in the Synagogue and wherever they preached the Word. The Word of God is Living and active. The Gospel is the Power of God to change lives.

Acts 2:37-40 (NIV) 37 When the people heard this, they were cut to the heart and said to Peter and the other apostles, "Brothers, what shall we do?" 38 Peter replied, "Repent and be baptized, every one of you, in the name of Jesus Christ for the forgiveness of your sins. And you will receive the gift of the Holy Spirit. 39 The promise is for you and your children and for all who are far off—for all whom the Lord our God will call." 40 With many other words he warned them; and he pleaded with them, "Save yourselves from this corrupt generation.""

> *Acts 11:21 (NIV) "21 The Lord's hand was with them, and a great number of people believed and turned to the Lord."*

When Paul wrote to the Church in Thessalonica, he reminded them of how they received the Gospel. They received it; **"with deep conviction"**.

> *1 Thessalonians 1:4-5 (NIV) "4 For we know, brothers loved by God, that he has chosen you, 5 because our gospel came to you not simply with words, but also with power, with the Holy Spirit and with deep conviction. You know how we lived among you for your sake."*

Conclusion

When we keep these essentials of the Gospel message in the forefront of our hearts, we will see tremendous results, since the Gospel is the Power of God to change lives.

> Romans 1:16 (NIV) 16 For I am not ashamed of the gospel, because it is the power of God that brings salvation to everyone who believes: first to the Jew, then to the Gentile.

We will do well to encase the Gospel message with the Truth of the Word. We will do well to always focus our message on the work of Christ on the Cross, and that He is the returning Resurrected Christ.

Assimilation Sheet for
Sharing our faith in a Practical way.

1. **Complete the sentence.** *Make the "Great Commission" your life's mission.*

2. **Complete the sentence and provide a Scripture.** *Make a commitment to put on the "shoes of preparedness" to share your faith. Ephesians 6:15*

3. **Provide a Scriptural basis for sharing the Gospel.** *1 Corinthians 15:1-8*

4. **Share the Gospel Message briefly, and provide substantiating Scriptures for each point:**

- 1. Christ died for our sins, according to the Scriptures. *Isaiah 53:5, John 1:29, 1 Peter 2:24.*
- 2. Christ rose from the dead to offer us a living hope and eternal life. *1 Corinthians 15:19-20, 22, John 3:16, John 6:40.*
- 3. Christ is coming back again to take us to be with Him forever. *Matthew 16:27, John 14:3, 1 Thessalonians 4:16-17.*
- 4. We receive Him as Lord by confessing our sins and ask Him to be our Lord. *1 John 1:9, Romans 10:9, Acts 2:38, Luke 24:46-47.*

5. **Complete the sentence.** *The Gospel Message should be encased by the Word of God.* **Why do we do this? Give at least one example.** *Because of the example Christ gave us, as well as, following the example of Christ. Acts 2:14, 16, Acts 2:25, Acts 3:22-23, Acts 3:24-25, Acts 4:10-12.*

6. **Give at least one other reason for using the Word of God in presenting the Gospel Message.** *The word of God is "Living" and "Active" and able to work Powerfully in us.*

7. **Complete the sentence.** *The Gospel should be centered on Jesus Christ as the Son of God.*

8. **Which Scripture exhorts you most to present the gospel in this way?** *Acts 2:22-24, Acts 2:32-33, Acts 3:16, Acts 3:18-20.*

. . .

9. How do we receive Christ in our hearts? Provide a Scripture. *We receive Christ by confessing Him as Lord and by putting our faith in Jesus as Lord. Romans 10:9-10.*

10. Complete the sentence and provide at least one Scriptural reference. *The preaching of the Gospel was always, and should always be, accompanied by a strong sense of* conviction *on the hearers. Acts 2:37-40, Acts 11:21, 1 Thessalonians 1:4-5.*

11. What does the message in Romans 1 verse 16 encourage in? *The Gospel is the power of God that brings salvation to everyone who believes.*

14

THE PRACTICAL GOSPEL MESSAGE
SESSION THREE

Here is an easy to remember way of sharing the Gospel:

"Every conversation starts with an opener. We say: "Hi, How are you?" Or "How's your day going?" Or, we make statements on the weather or current affairs to engage in a conversation. It is no different for us when we start the actual presentation of the Gospel message, it starts with an opener, assuming of course that you established a platform from which you already engaged the person and are now ready to share Christ with them."

1. Opener

How are you? How are things going nowadays? Do you know Jesus Christ? Can I tell you about Him?

"Remember, the Gospel is all about people putting their faith in Jesus Christ. It's not about them, or about you, it's about Jesus. You desire to

reconcile them to God through faith in Jesus. The moment we start witnessing about Christ, the Power of God, to save people, is activated, and God starts working with you to open their hearts to save them. God needs a Messenger and the moment you become His Messenger, the Holy Spirit and Jesus start doing their part to bring conviction to save the hearers. You are delivering this message to implore people on Christ behalf to be reconciled to God."

2 Corinthians 5:18-20 (NIV) *18 All this is from God, who reconciled us to himself through Christ and* **gave us the ministry of reconciliation:** *19 that God was reconciling the world to himself in Christ, not counting people's sins against them. And* **he has committed to us the message of reconciliation.** *20 We are therefore Christ's ambassadors, as though God were making his appeal through us.* **We implore you on Christ's behalf: Be reconciled to God.**

The Bible message is clear: **Be reconciled to God!**

How can we be <u>reconciled</u> to God?

We have to be reconciled to come into a relationship with Jesus, but we need to first understand our standing and relationship with God. Most of us did not even know that we were lost without Him.

2. Man

Mankind is like sheep without a Shepherd. Mankind finds themselves caught in their sins. Many pursue things that make them have a sense of feeling alive, but truly trying to deal with the sense of being empty and looking to find the purpose for existence.

It is like loving someone: until they find a place in your heart, the relationship remains without meaning or purpose. We were created to live in fellowship with God, however, our sins separated us from God.

*Isaiah 59:1-4 (NIV) 1 Surely the arm of the LORD is not too short to save, nor his ear too dull to hear. 2 But **your iniquities have separated you from your God**; your sins have hidden his face from you, so that he will not hear. 3 For your hands are stained with blood, your fingers with guilt. Your lips have spoken falsely, and your tongue mutters wicked things. 4 No one calls for justice; no one pleads a case with integrity. They rely on empty arguments, they utter lies; they conceive trouble and give birth to evil.*

Many people live unfulfilled lives, having a sense of feeling empty on the inside, even though they might seem successful and fulfilled to others. The reason for this is found in the Bible: ***Our sinful lives deprive us of the glorious in-dwelt presence and Glory of God.*** Until we give Jesus His rightful place in our lives, we will always have a void that could only be filled by Him. Every person on the planet lives with this void and separation within them.

Romans 3:23 (NIV) "^{23} for all have sinned and fall short of the glory of God"

All of us sinned and are dead in our sins. Adam and Eve sinned in Eden. Through their sin, sin and spiritual death came to all mankind. We are all Sinners and are in need of a Saviour who can save us from our sin and give us eternal life.

1 Corinthians 15:22 (NIV 1984) "22 For as in Adam all die, so in Christ all will be made alive."

Until we accept the gracious work of Christ, who already made provision in dealing with our sins, the void remains in us. This can change when we acknowledge God and His love for us.

3. God

God loves us so much that he sent His Son to pay the price to redeem us of our sins. He now offers Salvation to all who accept and believe in His Son.

> *John 3:16 (NIV) "16 For God so loved the world that he gave his one and only Son, that whoever believes in him shall not perish but have eternal life."*

God is a loving God who does not want to see anyone lost, or to perish in their sin. He desires to have a restored relationship with us.

> 1 Timothy 2:3-4 (NIV) 3 This is good, and pleases God our Savior, 4 who wants all people to be saved and to come to a knowledge of the truth.

God does not want to see anyone die in their sins. He would rather have us repent, turn to him, and live.

> Ezekiel 18:32 (NIV) 32 For I take no pleasure in the death of anyone, declares the Sovereign LORD. Repent and live!

> Ezekiel 33:11 (NIV) 11 Say to them, 'As surely as I live, declares the Sovereign LORD, I take no pleasure in the death of the wicked, but rather that they turn from their ways and live. Turn! Turn from your evil ways! Why will you die, people of Israel?'

What our loving God wants is for all mankind to come to repentance of their sins and be saved by the blood of Jesus.

> 2 Peter 3:9 (NIV) 9 The Lord is not slow in keeping his promise, as some understand slowness. Instead, he is

patient with you, not wanting anyone to perish, but everyone to come to repentance.

This is only possible through His Son, Jesus Christ.

4. Jesus Christ

Who is Jesus Christ?

Jesus Christ is the Son of God, who was conceived by the Holy Spirit, and born of the Virgin Mary. He was crucified, and died for our sins, and was buried. On the third day He rose again, as victor over death, to give eternal life to all who would believe in Him.

> *Isaiah 53:5 (NIV) "5 But he was pierced for our transgressions, he was crushed for our iniquities; the punishment that brought us peace was upon him, and by his wounds we are healed."*

> *John 1:29 (NIV) "29 The next day John saw Jesus coming toward him and said, "Look, the Lamb of God, who takes away the sin of the world!"*

We appropriate this gracious work of Christ by putting our Faith in Jesus Christ to save us.

5. What we Believe

> *" Remember, we are asking them to put their faith in Jesus by the way we are presenting the Gospel. For this to remain authentic, we need to share with them why we have placed our faith in Jesus as well as declare what we believe. We need to make a confession of what believe."*

We believe that:

- Jesus is the Son of God
- He died on the Cross for our sins
- He rose again on the third day and is alive
- Forgiveness for our sins is only found in Him
- Only Jesus can save us and bring us back to a restored relationship with the Father.

"It is valuable that we declare our faith and what we believe. We are sharing our faith by declaring what we believe. We are witnessing when we declare our faith."

Here is a version of the Apostles' Creed to which we subscribe. Learn this off by heart and simply state your faith:

Apostles' Creed

I believe in God, the Father Almighty,
Creator of heaven and earth.
I believe in Jesus Christ, God's only Son, our Lord,
who was conceived by the Holy Spirit,
born of the Virgin Mary,
suffered under Pontius Pilate,
was crucified, died, and was buried;
He descended to the dead.
On the third day He rose again;
He ascended into heaven,
He is seated at the right hand of God, our Father,
And He will come to judge the living and the dead.
I believe in the Holy Spirit,
And I believe in one holy Christian and apostolic Church,
the communion of saints,
the forgiveness of sins,
the resurrection of the body,
and life everlasting, Amen.[1]

*"They might ask you: **What must I do to believe in Jesus? How can I be saved from my sins?** Or, we might ask them: **Do you believe in Jesus?** Either way, if they don't ask, you can ask them and then move on to the next point."*

6. Confession and Faith

We are saved when we confess our sins and confess our faith in Jesus Christ as Lord and Savior. God offered eternal life to all who would believe in His Son, Jesus Christ. When we repent of our sins, He forgives us and restores into a right relationship with God.

> *Romans 10:9-10 (NIV) "9 That if you confess with your mouth, 'Jesus is Lord,' and believe in your heart that God raised him from the dead, you will be saved. 10 For it is with your heart that you believe and are justified, and it is with your mouth that you confess and are saved."*

This verse in the Bible really sums it up beautifully: "**if we confess Jesus as Lord, and believe in our hearts that God raised Him from the dead**," we will be saved. This promise is available for everyone who calls on Jesus to be their Lord.

> *Romans 10:13 (NIV) 13 for, "Everyone who calls on the name of the Lord will be saved."*

The only thing that we need to do is repent of our sins, ask Him to be our Lord, and put our faith in Him.

> *Acts 2:38 (NIV) "38 Peter replied, 'Repent and be baptized, every one of you, in the name of Jesus Christ for the forgiveness of your sins. And you will receive the gift of the Holy Spirit.'"*

Jesus gave His Life to save us. He is standing at the door of our hearts, knocking. He wants to come into our lives.

> Revelation 3:20 (NIV) 20 Here I am! I stand at the door and knock. If anyone hears my voice and opens the door, I will come in and eat with that person, and they with me.

I believe He is here right now, knocking at the door of your heart.

"Once you shared with people on how to receive Jesus as their Lord and Savior, you can ask if they want to accept Jesus, and then you can ask them if you could lead them in a prayer for Salvation."

We have this amazing promise from the Bible in John chapter one, and it says that: We can become children of God when we receive Jesus into our lives.

> John 1:12-13 (NIV) 12 Yet to all who did receive him, to those who believed in his name, he gave the right to become children of God — 13 children born not of natural descent, nor of human decision or a husband's will, but born of God.

7. Ask

"After sharing your faith, you need to give and opportunity for them to respond to what you shared with them. This opportunity is presented by asking a question or two. Sometimes, like in the Book of Acts when Peter witnessed, the people will pause you to enquire as to How they may receive Jesus. If they don't ask on their own, then give them an opportunity to receive Jesus following their response to these questions. You need to ask them:"

Do you want to open the door of your heart and ask Jesus into your life?
May I lead you in a Prayer of confession, and to accept Jesus as your Lord and Savior?

"Now lead them in the following prayer of confession. Ask them to repeat the prayer after you. Pray the prayer, sentence by sentence, and let them repeat it after you."

8. Prayer

Father God in Heaven, I confess that I am a Sinner. I repent of my sins and ask for Your Forgiveness. Please forgive me, save me from my sin, and make me Your Child today. Wash me with Your Blood, Cleanse me by the Power of Your Holy Spirit. I ask You now to be my Lord and Savior. I ask you into my life. I ask this in the Name of Jesus. Amen

9. Congratulations

"Congratulate them on their decision to receive Jesus as the Lord of their lives."

- Affirm that Jesus accepted their confession of sins, according to 1 John 1 verse 9, and that
- He forgave them their sins.
- He washed them with His Blood.
- Affirm that they are now children of God.

"The essential concluding part of when people receive Jesus as their Lord and Saviour is the assurance that we need to give them that they are not alone, but that you will continue this journey with them, to help them as Followers of Jesus. This is what we have been praying for and trusting for: souls to be saved. Now that we see our prayers answered we can start phase two by getting them baptised and discipled."

Assimilation Sheet for
The Practical Gospel Message.

1. **What do we use at the Beginning of our presentation? Give an example.** <u>A. We use an opener. B. How are you? Do you know Jesus Christ? Can I tell you about Him?</u>

2. **What is the second point in our practical Gospel Message?** <u>We start discussing Mankind.</u>

3. **What message do we wish to convey about mankind? What Scripture can you use to substantiate your point?** <u>Mankind is like sheep without a Shepherd. Mankind find themselves caught in their sins. All of us sinned and are dead in our sins. Romans 3:23, 1 Corinthians 15:22.</u>

4. **What is the third point of our practical Gospel Message? Provide a Scripture.** <u>We talk about the love of God. John 3:16.</u>

5. **What is the fourth point of our practical Gospel Message? Provide a Scripture.** <u>We share about the work of Jesus Christ. He was crucified, and died for our sins, and was buried. On the third day He rose again, as victor over death, to give eternal life to all who would believe in Him. Isaiah 53:5, John 1:29.</u>

6. **What is the fifth point of our practical Gospel Message?** <u>We share what we Believe. We also share our statement of faith.</u>

7. **How can we conclude this point?** <u>We might ask them: Do you believe in Jesus?</u>

8. **What is the sixth point of our practical Gospel Message? Provide a Scripture.** <u>We share the importance of putting our Faith in Jesus by confessing Him as Lord and confession that we believe that He is the Son of God. We also confess our sins and ask for His forgiveness. Romans 10:9-10, Romans 10:13, Acts 2:38.</u>

9. **We conclude this with the seventh point.** <u>We ask concluding questions: Do you want to open your heart and ask Jesus into your life today? May I lead you in a Prayer to accept Jesus as your Lord and Savior?</u>

10. **Write out the Prayer for Salvation.** <u>"Father God in Heaven, I confess that I am a Sinner. I repent of my sins and ask for Your Forgiveness. I ask You to be my Lord and Savior. Please forgive me, save me from my sin,</u>

and make me Your Child today. Wash me with Your Blood, Cleanse me by the Power of Your Holy Spirit. In Jesus Name. Amen"

11. How do we close our conversation? *We conclude the practical Gospel message by congratulating them on their decision, as well as, affirm that Jesus accepted their confession of sins, according to 1 John 1 verse 9, and that He forgave them their sins; and that He washed them with His Blood. We also affirm that they are now children of God.*

PART IV

OVERCOMING WEEKEND ENCOUNTER

WEEKEND FOUR

ENCOUNTER SCHEDULE

- Session 1 – INTRODUCTION
- Session 2 – CARES OF THE WORLD
- Session 3 – FEAR AND UNBELIEF
- Session 4 – UNFORGIVENESS
- Session 5 – LUST OF THE FLESH
- Session 6 – FAITH AND OBEDIENCE

INTRODUCTION
SESSION ONE

Christ paid a deer price that we could be free from slavery to sin. To ensure that we grow, develop and bring into fruit the gracious work of the Holy Spirit in us, we need to weed out those encumbrances that will keep us from seeing our full harvest. Christ set us free from sin and slavery. He broke the yoke of slavery to sin; however, we learn from John that young believers overcome the evil one by applying the Blood of the Lamb and standing on the Truth of God's Word.

This weekend is about overcoming the evil one. This weekend is about taking the yoke off and walking away with the Freedom Christ brought to us.

> *Galatians 5:1 (NIV) Freedom in Christ "1 It is for freedom that Christ has set us free. Stand firm, then, and do not let yourselves be burdened again by a yoke of slavery."*

> *1 John 2:13-14 (NIV) "13 I am writing to you, fathers, because you know him who is from the beginning. I am writing to you, young men, **because you have overcome the evil one**. 14 I write to you, dear children, because you know the Father. I write to*

> *you, fathers, because you know him who is from the beginning. I write to you, **young men**, because you are strong, and **the word of God lives in you, and you have overcome the evil one.**"*

> *Revelation 12:11 "11 **They triumphed over him by the blood of the Lamb and by the word of their testimony;** they did not love their lives so much as to shrink from death."*

Every time we read the Word, every time we pray, every time we sow seeds of the Gospel by sharing our testimony, every time we sow financial seed, we plant towards a spiritual harvest. Jesus promised that we could expect a 30, 60 or 100-fold harvest if we have been planted in the right soil, grown roots and weeded out of our lives those things that might choke the fruit from coming into harvest.

> ***Matthew 13:22 (NKJV)**, "Now he who received seed among the thorns is he who hears the word, and the cares of this world and the deceitfulness of riches choke the word, and he becomes unfruitful."*

This course is designed to remove those obvious, and sometimes not so obvious, encroaching and encumbering habits, aptitudes, pursuits, and practices that will inhibit our growth and enjoyment of the harvest, of our service unto the Lord.

The "<u>cares</u> of the world, deceitfulness of <u>riches</u>, and <u>pride</u>" often consume much needed nourishment away that would have seen our harvest and expected outcome realised. Lingering aptitudes, such as undealt hurt, fear, unforgiveness, rejection, and resentment, often keep us from reaching our Promised Land.

Where we observe these things remaining in our disciples' lives, we take time during this weekend encounter to deal with those decisively. This course is also designed to set our affections on the right things. Setting your affections on the wrong things will most certainly distract you from the purposes of God.

The Bible outlines how these things affect us in the Parable of the

Sower, in Matthew 13. Interestingly, thorns only required removal at this stage of the seed's growth, as it posed a threat when it is about to reproduce. Therefore, it makes sense that once you've developed spiritual values and disciplines, you must get rid of these "thorns" that might keep you from being fruitful.

The Bible also outlines those things that kept Israel from reaching their Promised land; they were **unbelief and disobedience.** These two thorns still keep good people out of their promised land today. Through the years we have seen the terrible impact *fear, doubt and unbelief* has on people, but also the devastation for those who continued with **unforgiveness and bitterness.**

Finally, we will look at *faith and obedience* as sure tenets to ensure our successful possession of the Full Harvest and Good Land God promised us.

CARES OF THE WORLD, DECEITFULNESS OF RICHES, AND PRIDE
SESSION TWO

Let us look at each of these areas individually during this session.

CARES OF THE WORLD

Right from the outset of Jesus' teachings he addressed the *"cares of the world"* as a weed which we need to guard ourselves against, and which we should root out by placing our complete trust and faith in God. At its core the *"cares of the world"* challenges the Source of our **Provision**, and His ability to **Protect** us.

> *Matthew 13:22 (NKJV),* "Now he who received seed among the thorns is he who hears the word, and **the cares of this world** and the deceitfulness of riches choke the word, and he becomes unfruitful."

Cares are concerns that we worry about. Some people are even known are **"worry-ers."** They worry about everything. What Jesus was saying in this Parable was that the "cares of the world" robs us from seeing our expected **harvest**, and even can cause us to become

unfruitful. It challenges us greatly when we worked for something and then don't get to see the end result of it, or see the project through to completion, or enjoy the fruit of our hard labour or investment.

What do the world care about? They care about what we eat, drink and wear. They care about position, possessions, and their pride drives them to have more, keep more, and self-sustain more.

> *Matthew 6:25-34 Do Not Worry "Therefore, I tell you, do not worry about your life, what you will eat or drink; or about your body, what you will wear. Is not life more important than food, and the body more important than clothes? Look at the birds of the air; they do not sow or reap or store away in barns, and yet your heavenly Father feeds them. Are you not much more valuable than they? Who of you by worrying can add a single hour to his life? And why do you worry about clothes? See how the lilies of the field grow. They do not labor or spin. Yet I tell you that not even Solomon in all his splendor was dressed like one of these. If that is how God clothes the grass of the field, which is here today and tomorrow is thrown into the fire, will he not much more clothe you, O you of little faith? So do not worry, saying, 'What shall we eat?' or 'What shall we drink?' or 'What shall we wear?' For the pagans run after all these things, and your heavenly Father knows that you need them. But seek first his kingdom and his righteousness, and all these things will be given to you as well. Therefore, do not worry about tomorrow, for tomorrow will worry about itself. Each day has enough trouble of its own."*

More often, than not, the things people worry about are shared in this message of Jesus. God is our source. He is the One who feeds us, clothes us and protects us.

Israel, at one point, thought that it was their strength that brought them the victories, the provisions and the security they treasured, but the Lord sternly reminded them that it was His Power that accomplished all that for them. These encapsulate the essentials of the cares and concerns people carry with them on a daily basis, the very thing the Lord teaches us not to do.

> *Deuteronomy 8:10-18 "When you have eaten and are satisfied, praise the Lord your God for the good land he has given you. 11* ***Be careful that you do not forget the Lord your God, failing to observe his commands, his laws and his decrees that I am giving you this day.*** *12 Otherwise, when you eat and are satisfied, when you build fine houses and settle down, 13 and when your herds and flocks grow large and your silver and gold increase and all you have is multiplied, 14* ***then your heart will become proud and you will forget the Lord your God,*** *who brought you out of Egypt, out of the land of slavery. 15 He led you through the vast and dreadful desert, that thirsty and waterless land, with its venomous snakes and scorpions. He brought you water out of hard rock. 16 He gave you manna to eat in the desert, something your fathers had never known, to humble and to test you so that in the end it might go well with you. 17 You may say to yourself,* ***"My power and the strength of my hands have produced this wealth for me." 18 But remember the Lord your God, for it is he who gives you the ability to produce wealth, and so confirms his covenant,*** *which he swore to your forefathers, as it is today."*

We are encouraged to not be anxious about anything since God is our Provider, Protector and the One who blesses us.

> *1 Peter 5:7 Cast all your anxiety on him because he cares for you.*

> *Psalms 55:22 Cast your cares on the Lord and he will sustain you; he will never let the righteous fall.*

Today we declare that God is our strength, it is He who gives us the ability to produce wealth! We also declare that it is He who saved us and brought us into a good land, flowing with Milk and Honey. It is He who gives us victories. It is He who enables us to build houses and to study and to succeed in business. It is He who enables us to have the privileges we currently enjoy. We declare our gratitude to Him for the clothes we are able to wear, the food we are able to eat, and the drinks we are able to drink.

Take a moment and declare your complete gratitude and trust in Him as the source of your life!

Deceitfulness of riches

Now, this portion also addresses the second part of the weeds that robs us from our intended and expected harvest, and that is the "***deceitfulness of riches***." The Israelites was forewarned that when their gold and silver increases, that they needed to remind themselves that it was indeed the Lord who gave them these riches and that it was not their own goodness or ability that gave it to them.

People often have a false sense of security built around their wealth and ***treasures.***

People think that their ***wealth*** secures them from pandemics, misfortune or even poverty, however, we are warned against such false thinking.

> *Deuteronomy 8:17 You may say to yourself, "My power and the strength of my hands have produced this wealth for me." 18 But remember the Lord your God, for it is he who gives you the ability to produce wealth, and so confirms his covenant, which he swore to your forefathers, as it is today.*

These words stand as an eternal warning and guidance for all those who will place their trust in their wealth.

The Lord is the One who gives us *wealth* and He is the One who allows us to *prosper*.

We should eternally be grateful when He grants us such blessings to be enjoyed.

> *1 Samuel 2:7 The Lord sends poverty and wealth; he humbles, and he exalts.*

> *Proverbs 8:18 With me are riches and honor, enduring wealth and prosperity.*

God is the source of all riches, wealth and prosperity. We will be wise to always remember from whom we have received such blessings. The defining principle is to remain grateful and not to become proud and arrogant, and to forget the Lord. We have what we have because of His great Grace. The Bible teaches us that it is through His blessing that we increase our wealth.

> *Proverbs 10:22 (NIV) The blessing of the Lord brings wealth, and he adds no trouble to it.*

The Apostle Paul taught Timothy to **"teach those who are rich"** to not put their hope in their wealth, but to put their hope in God. If we remain dependent on God, even though He has given us great wealth, then we will most certainly see the Good seed sown into our lives come into producing a multiplied harvest. It is this self-reliance, self-sufficiency and independence that deceives us, and eventually chokes the fruit from producing and multiplying.

> *1 Timothy 6:17-19 (NIV) Command those who are rich in this present world not to be arrogant nor to put their hope in wealth, which is so uncertain, but to put their hope in God, who richly provides us with everything for our enjoyment. 18 Command them to do good, to be rich in good deeds, and to be generous and willing to share. 19 In this way they will lay up treasure for themselves as a firm foundation for the coming age, so that they may take hold of the life that is truly life.*

The Apostle Paul also taught that people who become rich often find themselves enticed by foolish and harmful desires which plunge them into ruin and destruction. Many people wander away from their faith and pierce themselves with many griefs, as a result of pursuing these evil desires and pleasures. Our attention is drawn to the *"deceitfulness of riches,"* in as far as it can make us forget who granted us the blessings, and lead us to a false sense of security.

> *1 Timothy 6:9-10 (NIV) People who want to get rich fall into temptation and a trap and into many foolish and harmful desires that plunge men into ruin and destruction. For the love of money is a root of all kinds of evil. Some people, eager for money, have wandered from the faith and pierced themselves with many griefs.*

The desire and dream God have for us is known: He desires to give us an expected end. The very things we work towards in our faith, that's the fruit God desires for us to bear. The Lord desires for us to be fruitful and to multiply greatly and to see the expected end of our faith pursuits.

Riches bring with it a sense of false security that we will be <u>ok</u> even if bad things happen to us.

This false security chokes us from fruitfulness, whereas gratefulness, reliance and dependency on God keeps the expectations alive, to see fruit on our labour. This is the very thing God constantly exhorts and encourages us towards.

> *Jeremiah 29:11 (KJV) For I know the thoughts that I think toward you, saith the Lord, thoughts of peace, and not of evil, **to give you an expected end.***

> *Galatians 6:9 (NIV) 9 Let us not become weary in doing good, for at the proper time we will reap a harvest if we do not give up.*

Pride

Another area which often chokes our fruitfulness is pride.

- ***Pride is that self-esteemed attitude of vein egotism.***
- Pride can be described as that conceited and over-perceived value of one's importance or stature.
- Pride is that pre-occupation with self-care, caring only about yourself and your own interest.

Since the time Satan was cast out of the presence of God because of his pride, people have fallen prey to pride, and it too kept them from seeing their fruitful multiplication.

Ezekiel 28:2 (NIV) *"Son of man, say to the ruler of Tyre, This is what the Sovereign Lord says: 'In **the pride of your heart you say**, I am a god; I sit on the throne of a god in the heart of the seas. But you are a man and not a god, though you think you are as wise as a god.'"*

Ezekiel 28:4 (NIV) *By your wisdom and understanding you have gained wealth for yourself and amassed gold and silver in your treasuries. 5 By your great skill in trading you have increased your wealth, and **because of your wealth your heart has grown proud.***

Ezekiel 28:17
Your heart became proud *on account of your beauty, and you corrupted your wisdom because of your splendor.* **So, I threw you to the earth;** *I made a spectacle of you before kings.*

Satan's pride cost him his privileged position in Heaven. The Bible teaches us to guard against pride.

> *Proverbs 16:18 (NIV)* ***Pride goes before destruction,*** *And a haughty spirit before a fall.*

Pride will most certainly keep us away from fruitfulness. If pride is not of the Father, then pride should not live in us if we desire fruitfulness. The Apostle John, in his first pastoral letter, outline the very things that is of the world, but more importantly, those things that are not of the Father. As people who are grafted in the **"Vine,"** we draw our sap from the Nature of our Heavenly Father.

> *1 John 2:16 (KJV) For all that is in the world—the lust of the flesh, the lust of the eyes,* **and the pride of life**—*is not of the Father but is of the world.*

The New International Version defines this **"pride"** as **"the boasting of what he has and does."** You can spend a few minutes with someone and quickly know how much pride exist.

> *1 John 2:16-17 (NIV) For everything in the world–the cravings of sinful man, the lust of his eyes and* **the boasting of what he has and does**–*comes not from the Father but from the world. 17 The world and its desires pass away, but the man who does the will of God lives forever.*

In Jesus' message in John 15 on the Vine, the branches and the fruit, we learn that there is a direct correlation between our connectedness to Christ, as the Vine, and the fruit we bear. If pride does not come from the Father, then drawing our sap from pride will not produce the fruit we desire to bear in our lives.

If pride got Satan kicked out of Heaven, how much more will it keep us from God's Presence?

In Conclusion

Search your heart and dispose of any and all pride in your life. Our pursuit through this course is to help you to bring the good seed of the Word, sown into your life, come into a fruitful harvest. What we learnt in this session is how that the cares of this world, the deceitfulness of riches, and pride are those aptitudes that choke the seed from becoming and producing a multiplied harvest.

Assimilation Sheet for
Cares of the World, deceitfulness of riches, and pride.

1. Complete the sentence. *At its core the "cares of the world" challenges the Source of our Provision, and His ability to Protect us.*

2. How will the cares of the world leave us with our expectations? *They will leave us with a feeling of being robbed and unfruitful.*

3. What are the cares of the world? *The cares of the world are typically related to what we eat, drink or wear. It also concerns us about our position, possessions and our pride.*

4. Which Scriptures best defines, and addresses the Cares of the world to you? *Matthew 6:25-34; Deuteronomy 8:10-18; 1 Peter 5:7; and Psalms 55:22.*

5. Complete this sentence. *People think that their wealth secures them from pandemics, misfortune or even poverty, however, we are warned against such false thinking.*

6. Complete the sentence. *People often have a false sense of security built around their wealth and treasures.*

7. Complete this sentence. *The Lord is the One who gives us wealth and He is the One who allows us to prosper.*

8. Which Scriptures best guides us to think soundly about treasures, riches and wealth? *Deuteronomy 8:17; 1 Samuel 2:7; Proverbs 8:18; Proverbs 10:22; 1 Timothy 6:17-19.*

9. Complete the sentence. *Pride is that self-esteemed attitude of vein egotism.*

10. What impact did pride have on Satan? *Support your answer from Scripture. Satan was cast out of the Presence of God. He lost his place and position in Heaven. Ezekiel 28:2, 4, 17.*

11. Which Scriptures warns us against the impact of Pride? *Proverbs 16:18, 1 John 2:16-17.*

12. Complete the sentence. *Pride will most certainly keep us away from fruitfulness.*

17

FEAR AND UNBELIEF
SESSION THREE

Fear and <u>unbelief</u> are two enemies that can keep us from seeing the fruit of our labour. These two wars against the good seed sown in us. This session is about identifying *fear and unbelief* in our hearts, and to displace them with *faith and obedience* so that we will reap our harvest.

FEAR

Fear is a thistle and thorn that keep many believers from reaping their expected harvest. Fear can keep us out of our Promised land. We are constantly confronted with circumstances which call on us to fear or to face by faith. The New Testament teaches us a powerful principle to remember, and that is that God did not give us a Spirit of fear.

> *2 Timothy 1:7 (KJV) [7] For God hath not given us **the spirit of <u>fear</u>**; but of power, and of love, and of a sound mind.*

The Spirit of the Lord is a Spirit of Love, Power and a Sound mind, yet many, even believers, struggle with a Spirit of fear tormenting them. ***Living with Fear is not from God.*** I pray that you will know the truth and allow the truth of God's Word to flood your soul today that you can be free from fear and filled with faith and hope.

> *John 8:32 (KJV) "Then you will know the truth, and the truth will set you free."*

The King James Bible record **63** instances where the Lord commands His followers to *"fear not."* The NIV records **107** instances where the Lord says: **"Do not be afraid."**

The Bible challenges us to not give way to fear, but to live by faith.

Whenever we are faced with a challenge, **we have a choice** to make, either give in to the spirit of fear or face it by faith.

Unbelief

<u>Unbelief</u> is that act of embracing one's fears and doubt over against the promises of God. Doubt and unbelief kept the Israelites, whom God delivered out of the hands of the mighty Egyptian Rulers' might, out of their Promised land.

> *Hebrews 3:19 (KJV) So we see that they were not able to enter, because of their unbelief.*

Unbelief is rife in so many people, no wonder that so few people reach their promised land. You can quickly detect unbelief when you listen to people. It is not uncommon to hear people say:"*I don't believe that.*" Though they might be speaking about everyday things, they have become accustomed to constantly stating what they don't believe as opposed to stating what they belief. This becomes systemic of How they act and respond to life in general. As Believers we are called to live by faith, in other words, by what we believe.

The Old Testament present to us a number of wonderful examples to which many of us can relate in our present circumstances.

Hagar

The first is that of Hagar, a servant girl, without rights or means for justice in her precarious situation. She had a child with her master, and now the wife of the master threw her out to fend for herself and her son. Even though Sarai was a willing part to this original arrangement with Hagar having a child with Abram, it spiralled out of control and sanity once Ismael was born.

> *Genesis 16:2, 4 (NIV) "so, she said to Abram, 'The Lord has kept me from having children. Go, sleep with my maidservant; perhaps I can build a family through her.' Abram agreed to what Sarai said. 4 He slept with Hagar, and she conceived. When she knew she was pregnant, she began to despise her mistress."*

This pregnancy and despising by Hagar infuriated Sarai that she got rid of her with Abram's consent.

> *Genesis 16:6 (NIV) "Your servant is in your hands," Abram said. "Do with her whatever you think best." Then Sarai mistreated Hagar; so she fled from her.*

After the Angel of the Lord met her, she returned into that hostile situation, but 14 years later when Isaac was born, she was finally ousted from the household.

> *Genesis 21:8 (NIV) The child grew and was weaned, and on the day Isaac was weaned Abraham held a great feast. 9 But Sarah saw that the son whom Hagar the Egyptian had borne to Abraham was mocking, 10 and she said to Abraham, "Get rid of that slave woman and her son, for that slave woman's son will never share in the inheritance with my son Isaac." 11 The*

> *matter distressed Abraham greatly because it concerned his son.*

This matter greatly, and rightly, distressed Abraham. He had to send his son, Ismael, and the mother of his son away. I am sure he too was anxious about their welfare. What blessed me from this portion is that God saw his distress and comforted him prior to him sending them off. God has a good plan for each one of us, even though in our distress we might not see it, He has a plan for each of our lives.

> *Genesis 21:12 (NIV) But God said to him, "Do not be so distressed about the boy and your maidservant. Listen to whatever Sarah tells you, because it is through Isaac that your offspring will be reckoned. 13 I will make the son of the maidservant into a nation also, because he is your offspring."*

Hagar went away with her son and wandered around until their provisions was up. In her desperation she put her son down in a place where she could not hear his cries and sat down and wept out of pure distress and destitution.

> *Genesis 21:17 (NIV) God heard the boy crying, and the angel of God called to Hagar from heaven and said to her, "What is the matter, Hagar? Do not be afraid; God has heard the boy crying as he lies there.*

Every time Hagar found herself in this desperation the Word of God tells us that God saw and heard her.

> *"Fear grips our hearts because we think that God does not <u>see</u> or <u>hear</u> the desperation of our circumstances."*

Before the Lord gave her an outcome to her desperation, He first required of her to take a step in obedience and faith. She had to lift her son up and take him by the hand. Once she did, the Word of God tell us that God opened her eyes and she saw the well of water. God also gave her a wonderful promise of her son's future well-being.

> *Genesis 21:18* (NIV) *"Lift the boy up and take him by the hand, for I will make him into a great nation." 19 Then God opened her eyes and she saw a well of water. So she went and filled the skin with water and gave the boy a drink. 20 God was with the boy as he grew up. He lived in the desert and became an archer.*

This situation plays itself out in modern society daily: girls become pregnant with the children of their employers, bosses, or simply people more powerful and of greater standing than them, and then when their pregnancy becomes known, are thrown out to fend for themselves. Even mentioning it sends up shivers up my spine. Just the thought of the desperation, the injustice, and the cruelty is enough to propel even the kindest into becoming an activist for human rights.

The truth is that those to whom such injustices happen are often filled with fear and anxiety, and rightly so, wouldn't you? I can almost feel their fear and anxiety. The desperation of the predicament you find yourself in. *What is going to happen to me? What is going to happen with my child? How am I going to live? What shall we eat? Where can we go? Where will we live? What will people say?* These are just some of the many questions that I think people in such desperations find themselves asking.

What is important to know from this desperate situation is that; **God hears, God sees, and God will make a way** where there seems to be no way or outcome.

> *Genesis 21:17* (NIV) *God heard the boy crying, and the angel of God called to Hagar from heaven and said to her, "What is the matter, Hagar?* ***Do not be afraid****; God has heard the boy crying as he lies there.*

The Lord answered her with those tremendously comforting

words: "***Do not be afraid!***" Fear grips even the most toughest of us. May we take courage from how the Lord intervened in the desperation of Hagar.

Isaac

During Isaac's journeys there was a great famine in the land.

> *Genesis 26:1 (NIV) Now there was a famine in the land–besides the earlier famine of Abraham's time–and Isaac went to Abimelech king of the Philistines in Gerar.*

Isaac was a herdsman with lots of livestock, so the onset of a famine would bring within him anxiety and fear for what the future holds for him and his livestock. The amazing thing is that, no sooner was the consideration uttered in Isaac's heart, when God gave him, not just guidance and instruction as to what to do, but also a wonderful confirmation of the Promise He first gave to his Father Abraham. This Promise of God not just secured guidance for the present challenge they faced but also secured hope for the future. The key response of Isaac in his distress is seen in verse 6 when the Word says: "***So Isaac stayed.***" He overcame a terrible fearful situation by obeying the directive of the Lord.

> *Genesis 26:2 (NIV) "The Lord appeared to Isaac and said, 'Do not go down to Egypt; live in the land where I tell you to live. 3 Stay in this land for a while, and I will be with you and will bless you. For to you and your descendants I will give all these lands and will confirm the oath I swore to your father Abraham. 4 I will make your descendants as numerous as the stars in the sky and will give them all these lands, and through your offspring all nations on earth will be blessed, 5 because Abraham obeyed me and kept my requirements, my commands, my decrees and my laws.' 6 So Isaac stayed in Gerar."*

Isaac then faced a challenge with Abimelech, since he feared for his life since he anticipated that the men of the city might kill him for his beautiful wife, Rebekah. In his fear he told everyone that she was his sister, when in fact she was his wife. When he was found out by the king, he even feared more for his life, but in his fear, God came and consoled him again.

> *Genesis 26:9 (NIV) "So Abimelech summoned Isaac and said, 'She is really your wife! Why did you say, 'She is my sister'? Isaac answered him, 'Because I thought I might lose my life on account of her.'"*

Staying in obedience, even though the circumstances seemed to stack up against him, kept Isaac in a position where God could bring great blessings upon him. ***The place where he feared for his life is the very place where God brought great increase upon Isaac.*** Genesis 26 verses 12 and onwards tell us how God prospered him.

> *Genesis 26:12 (NIV) Isaac planted crops in that land and the same year reaped a hundredfold, because the Lord blessed him. 13 The man became rich, and his wealth continued to grow until he became very wealthy.*

His obedience to stay where God wanted him, even though the natural circumstances called him to move and to be confronted with fearing for his life, he stayed, and God rewarded his faith and obedience by prospering him greatly.

He became so prosperous that King Abimelech requested him to leave. As far as what he travelled, he opened up old wells, however, the local herdsman kept closing the wells up, or dispossessing him from the wells. This might have been such a fearful and challenging experience.

> *Genesis 26:16 (NIV)* Then Abimelech said to Isaac, "Move away from us; you have become too powerful for us."

After a number of dispossessions no one quarrelled over one of the wells which he named Rehoboth. Perseverance and persistence always pay off when we remain obedient to God and trust him in all things. When Isaac eventually moved on to Beersheba, God appeared to him at night and comforted him with a Promise again, but not before first assuring him of His Presence: "**Do not be afraid, for I am with you.**"

> *Genesis 26:22 (NIV) He moved on from there and dug another well, and no one quarrelled over it. He named it Rehoboth, saying, "Now the Lord has given us room and we will flourish in the land."*

> *Genesis 26:23-25 (NIV) [23] From there he went up to Beersheba. [24] That night the LORD appeared to him and said, "I am the God of your father Abraham. **Do not be afraid, for I am with you;** I will bless you and will increase the number of your descendants for the sake of my servant Abraham." [25] Isaac built an altar there and called on the name of the LORD. There he pitched his tent, and **there his servants dug a well.***

Isaac faced famine, fearing for his life as he lived among people who could kill him for his wife, but in the midst of facing all these fearful situations, He followed the directives of the Lord. Many people find themselves in sudden famines. Some live in circumstances where they fear for their own lives. Some fear that they might lose their spouses.

Finding comfort in the directives of God, in the midst of fear, always carry with it a rich reward from the Lord. Isaac overcame his fear by "staying" when God said stay. Him remaining in the land not just kept him but also brought him to a place of abundance.

Moses

When I think of Moses, I think of the many times He faced impossible, fearful situations. **Firstly,** when God called him to go to Pharaoh to let his people go, and then, with all the plagues. **Secondly,** we have the time when they left Egypt and was caught between the Red Sea and the approaching furore of Pharaoh with his descending army. What looked like a certain death situation turned out to be one of the most victorious moments for Israel, but not before Moses faced the mumbling anger of his own people on the one hand, the approaching Egyptian Army, and a Red Sea at the same time. The Bible tells us that it was Moses' faith that brought him through the many fearful circumstances.

> *Hebrews 11:24-29 (NIV) [24]* ***By faith Moses, when he had grown** up, refused to be known as the son of Pharaoh's daughter.*
> *[25]* ***He chose*** *to be mistreated along with the people of God rather than to enjoy the pleasures of sin for a short time.*
> *[26]* ***He regarded disgrace for the sake of Christ as of greater value than the treasures of Egypt,*** *because he was looking ahead to his reward. [27]* ***By faith he left Egypt, not fearing the king's anger;*** *he persevered because he saw him who is invisible.*
> *[28]* ***By faith he kept the Passover*** *and the sprinkling of blood, so that the destroyer of the firstborn would not touch the firstborn of Israel. [29]* ***By faith the people passed through the Red Sea*** *as on dry land; but when the Egyptians tried to do so, they were drowned.*

Moses spoke to the Israelites when they were caught between the desert and the Red Sea. His message was clear: **"Do not be afraid. Stand firm!"** He even spoke words of hope and trust into them: **"You will see the deliverance the Lord will bring today."** These were such encouraging words to the hearts of those Israelites, and they continue to encourage many of us today as we face encumbering situations in our lives.

> *Exodus 14:13-14 (NIV) [13]* Moses answered the people, **"Do not be afraid. Stand firm and you will see the deliverance the LORD will bring you today.** *The Egyptians you see today you will never see again. [14]* **The LORD will fight for you; you need only to be still."**

When Israel faced their enemies, Moses reminded them, and comforted them with the Words God spoke to him when they faced insurmountable situations.

> *Deuteronomy 20:1-4 (NIV) [20:1]* **When you go to war against your enemies** *and see horses and chariots and* **an army greater than yours, do not be afraid of them,** *because the LORD your God, who brought you up out of Egypt,* **will be with you.** *[2] When you are about to go into battle,* **the priest shall come forward and address the army.** *[3] He shall say: "Hear, O Israel, today you are going into battle against your enemies.* **Do not be fainthearted or afraid; do not be terrified or give way to panic before them.** *[4] For the LORD your God is the one who goes with you to fight for you against your enemies to give you victory."*

Joshua

The Lord instructed Joshua and the Israelites to not fear as they prepared themselves to go to possess the promised land.

> *Joshua 1:9 (NIV) "Have I not commanded you? Be strong and courageous.* **Do not be terrified; do not be discouraged,** *for the Lord your God will be with you wherever you go."*

Just after Israel got a mighty hiding in a battle with the people of Ai, the Lord encouraged them again to not fear.

> *Joshua 8:1 (NIV) [8:1] Then the LORD said to Joshua,* **"Do not be**

afraid; do not be discouraged. Take the whole army with you and go up and attack Ai. *For I have delivered into your hands the king of Ai, his people, his city and his land.*

It is easy for us to read these encouragements today, but the same encouragement is given to us as we face our Red seas, our enemies, our dire and challenging circumstances.

David

David once faced a giant, Goliath. One-man instilled fear in an entire army. They feared for their lives. This situation continued for 40 days. The Bible tells us of the extent of the threat and How it impacted them.

> *1 Samuel 17:10-11 (NIV) [10] Then the Philistine said,* **"This day I defy the ranks of Israel!** *Give me a man and let us fight each other." [11]* **On hearing the Philistine's words, Saul and all the Israelites were dismayed and terrified.**

> *1 Samuel 17:16 (NIV) [16] For* **forty days** *the Philistine came forward every morning and evening and took his stand.*

David came to bring refreshments to his brothers, but while he was still speaking to them, he heard the thundering voice of Goliath, and saw all the army run from Goliath with great fear.

> *1 Samuel 17:23-24 (NIV) [23] As he was talking with them, Goliath, the Philistine champion from Gath, stepped out from his lines and shouted his usual defiance, and* **David heard it.** *[24]* **When the Israelites saw the man, they all ran from him in great fear.**

David was filled with faith, even though he saw and faced the same enemy. He chose to act in faith and not in fear. He spoke his faith and not his fear.

> *1 Samuel 17:32-36 (NIV) [32] David said to Saul, "Let no one loose heart on account of this Philistine; your servant will go and fight him." [33] Saul replied, "You are not able to go out against this Philistine and fight him; you are only a boy, and he has been a fighting man from his youth." [34] But David said to Saul, "Your servant has been keeping his father's sheep. When a lion or a bear came and carried off a sheep from the flock, [35] I went after it, struck it and rescued the sheep from its mouth. When it turned on me, I seized it by its hair, struck it and killed it. [36] Your servant has killed both the lion and the bear; this uncircumcised Philistine will be like one of them, because he has defied the armies of the living God.*

When fear grips your heart, it brings you down into earthly, faithless speech, however, for David, he rose to the occasion with faith to go and fight this enemy of Israel. His superiors did not think that he had what it took to take on such an experienced warrior, but **David was confident, not in his own strength, but in the God whom he served.** This is such a wonderful example for us who face giants too strong and powerful for us.

> *1 Samuel 17:37 (NIV) [37]* **The LORD who delivered me from the paw of the lion and the paw of the bear will deliver me from the hand of this Philistine."** *Saul said to David, "Go, and the LORD be with you."*

David spoke by faith, not in his own strength or ability, but in faith in the living God.

> *1 Samuel 17:45-46 (NIV) [45] David said to the Philistine, "***You come against me with sword and spear and javelin, but I come against you in the name of the LORD Almighty, the God of the armies of Israel, whom you have defied. [46] This day the LORD will hand you over to me, and I'll strike you down and cut off your head.*** Today I will give the carcasses of the*

Philistine army to the birds of the air and the beasts of the earth, and **the whole world will know that there is a God in Israel**.

The widow of Zarephath

The widow of Zarephath faced debtors who threatened to take her sons as slaves. When Elijah heard of her plight, he spoke hope into her.

> *1 Kings 17:13 (NIV) [13] Elijah said to her, "**Don't be afraid**. Go home and do as you have said. **But first make a small cake of bread for me from what you have and bring it to me**, and then make something for yourself and your son.*

Once again, we see that the Lord's instruction was to first take an action of faith before she would see God bring tremendous provision. **Obedience and Faith in God is always richly rewarded.** The Bible tells us of How her faith and actions in obedience to the Word of the Lord, was rewarded.

> *1 Kings 17:14-16 (NIV) [14] For this is what the LORD, the God of Israel, says: 'The jar of flour will not be used up and the jug of oil will not run dry until the day the LORD gives rain on the land.'" [15] She went away and did as Elijah had told her. So there was food every day for Elijah and for the woman and her family. [16] For the jar of flour was not used up and the jug of oil did not run dry, in keeping with the word of the LORD spoken by Elijah.*

Isaiah

A prophetic Word came through the prophet Isaiah to encourage us on how to deal with fearful situations.

Isaiah 41:10-14 (NIV) [10] **So do not fear, for I am with you; do not be dismayed, for I am your God. I will strengthen you and help you; I will uphold you with my righteous right hand.** [11] *"All who rage against you will surely be ashamed and disgraced; those who oppose you will be as nothing and perish.* [12] **Though you search for your enemies, you will not find them.** *Those who wage war against you will be as nothing at all.* [13] *For I am the LORD, your God, who takes hold of your right hand and says to you,* **Do not fear; I will help you.** [14] **Do not be afraid, O worm Jacob, O little Israel, for I myself will help you,"** *declares the LORD, your Redeemer, the Holy One of Israel.*

You can live by faith or you can live by fear. Our senses open the doorway to fear or faith. We can look at the same situation through the eyes of fear, or we could look at it with the eyes of faith.

Elisha

The King of Aram was at war with Israel and decided to set up camp against them, however, Elisha sent word to the King of Israel to warn him of the impending ambush and attack. When the King of Aram found out that the man of God foiled his plans by declaring it to the King of Israel, he set out to kill Elisha. During the night the Aramean army surrounded the town where Elisha and his companion was overnighting. Early in the morning when Gehasi woke up, he saw that the whole town was surrounded by this army, and he was afraid. He was fearful, however, when he told the man of God about them being surrounded, the man of God came out and he said: "why are you fearful? Those who are for us, are more than those who are against us." Elisha prayed for his eyes to be opened. When the Lord opened his eyes, he saw the Angels of God, on Chariots of fire, all around them. Gehasi saw that those who were for them were more than those who were against them. They saw the same thing in the natural, however, Elisha also saw in the supernatural, and that made all the difference. May God open our eyes to see, in every situation, that those who are for us are more than those who are against us.

> *2 Kings 6:15-17 (NIV) [15] When the servant of the man of God got up and went out early the next morning, an army with horses and chariots had surrounded the city. "**Oh, my lord, what shall we do?**" the servant asked. [16] "**Don't be afraid,**" the prophet answered. "**Those who are with us are more than those who are with them.**" [17] And Elisha prayed, "O LORD, open his eyes so he may see." Then the LORD opened the servant's eyes, and he looked and saw the hills full of horses and chariots of fire all around Elisha.*

How do we overcome fear?

We overcome fear by faith.

<u>Faith</u> opens the doorway to God's protection, provision and guidance. The Word of God teaches us that we can live by sight or we can live by <u>faith</u>. Fear is often, and mostly, driven by our senses. The more we allow ourselves to be directed through what we see, hear and feel, the more we will fuel the fear in us. However, the more we fuel our decisions by our faith in what God said in His Word, and act accordingly, by faith, we fuel hope and positivity.

> *2 Corinthians 5:7 (KJV) [7] **For we walk by faith, not by sight:***

> *2 Corinthians 4:18 (NIV) [18] **So we fix our eyes not on what is seen, but on what is unseen.** For what is seen is temporary, but what is unseen is eternal.*

> *2 Corinthians 4:13 (NIV) [13] It is written: "**I believed; therefore I have spoken.**" With that same spirit of faith we also believe and therefore speak,*

We overcome fear through our words

We activate the spirit of faith through our words and by focusing our attention on what we see in the spirit rather than what we see in the natural.

Fear is a <u>spirit</u>, and we need to take charge of it since we know that **it is <u>not</u> from God,** and that God did not give us a spirit of fear.

> *2 Timothy 1:7 (KJV) [7] For God hath not given us the **spirit of fear;** but of power, and of love, and of a sound mind.*

Life and death are in the power of our tongues. We need to learn to speak by faith. Speak to your mountain. Speak to your fear. Speak to your circumstances. Speak and declare your faith.

> *Proverbs 18:21 (NIV) [21] **The tongue has the power of life and death,** and those who love it will eat its fruit.*

> *Romans 10:17 (KJV) [17] So then **faith cometh by hearing,** and **hearing by the word of God.***

> *Mark 11:22-23 (NIV) [22] "**Have faith in God,**" Jesus answered. [23] "I tell you the truth, if anyone says to this mountain, 'Go, throw yourself into the sea,' and does not doubt in his heart but believes that what he says will happen, it will be done for him.*

> *2 Corinthians 4:13 (NIV) [13] It is written: "I believed; therefore I have spoken." With that same spirit of faith we also believe and therefore speak,*

Speak what you <u>believe</u>, not what you fear. Faith is speaking what you believe, not what you fear. Activate the spirit of faith by your words, and then act on your faith, not on your fear.

We overcome fear by thinking right.

Our thoughts set a pathway for our faith to follow. **Faith follows your thoughts.**

> *Proverbs 23:7 (KJV) [7]* ***For as he thinketh in his heart, so is he:*** *Eat and drink, saith he to thee; but his heart is not with thee.*

Activate the spirit of faith by your thoughts. Set your mind on things that is above. Setting our thoughts on things that are above us, is to think on the promises of God. It is to think on the goodness and greatness of God.

If we think on the things we fear, they are the things that will come upon us, but if we think on the God who is greater and stronger, and more powerful, then His power will be unlocked over our situation.

> *Job 3:25 (KJV) [25]* ***For the thing which I greatly feared is come upon me, and that which I was afraid of is come unto me.***

Fear is activated when we give precedence to it in our thoughts, however, the same is true for faith. We need to activate our faith in God in every possible way we can. Activate your faith, over your fears, in your thought dimension, through your words and your actions.

We overcome fear by our faith.

Act by faith and not by what you fear. **We overcome our fears by the profession of our faith.** We overcome fear by acting out our faith in God, His Word and His promises.

> *Hebrews 11:1 (NIV) [11:1]* ***Now faith is being sure of what we hope for and certain of what we do not see.***

> *Hebrews 11:6 (NIV) [6] And **without faith it is impossible to please God, because anyone who comes to him must believe that he exists and that he rewards those who earnestly seek him.***

The men and woman we read about in Chapter 11 were all commended for their faith. In the face of fear, they walked, talked, acted, continued by faith, and that walk by faith was richly rewarded.

There are men and woman going through this session today, and you are facing difficulties, battles, Giants, sickness, debt, storms, and enemies. You might be facing famine and desperate circumstances. The Lord wants me to tell you: "Don't <u>fear</u>. Have <u>faith</u> in God."

There are people today who are **in the midst of the storm**, you find that the **enemy already set up camp around you**. The Lord wants me to tell you: "**Don't fear. Have faith in God.**"

I believe we need to pray against that spirit of fear. I believe we need to speak and make faith declarations. I believe we need to set our minds on things above and not below. I believe we need to live by faith and not by sight. Warfare against that spirit of fear according to the Word of God.

Closing declaration

> *2 Timothy 1:7 For God hath not given us the spirit of fear; but of power, and of love, and of a sound mind.*

God has not given me a spirit of fear, but a spirit of <u>love</u>, power and a sound <u>mind</u>.

Assimilation Sheet for
Fear and Unbelief.

1. Complete the sentence. *Fear and <u>Unbelief</u> are two enemies that can keep us from seeing the fruit of our labour.*

2. What Spirit has God given us according to 2 Timothy 1 verse 7? <u>*A Spirit of Love, Power and a Sound Mind.*</u>

3. Complete the sentence. *<u>Unbelief</u> is that act of embracing one's fears and doubt over against the promises of God.*

4. Complete the sentence. *Fear grips our hearts because we think that God does not <u>see</u> or <u>hear</u> the desperation of our circumstances.*

5. What is one of the main messages we learn from this account of Hagar? <u>*We learn that God sees and hears our cries, and that He answers us in all of our desperations.*</u>

6. Isaac experienced famine, defrauding, many battles with family and enemies who obstructed his work. Give at least two portions of Scriptures of How God helped and encouraged him in dealing with his despondency, fear and unbelief? <u>*God said to him to not fear. Genesis 26 verses 1-25.*</u>

7. Moses faced many challenges. Name at least two occasions where Moses faced situations that would generally make people succumb to fear and unbelief. <u>*He approached Pharaoh to ask for the Israelites to go. He was caught between the furious Egyptian Army and the Red Sea. They needed to feed an entire Nation in the Wilderness. They needed water in the Wilderness.*</u>

8. Moses had two messages for the Israelites. Complete the two sentences. Provide the Scriptural reference as well. "**Do not be <u>afraid</u>. Stand firm!**" He even spoke words of hope and trust into them: "**You will see the deliverance the <u>Lord</u> will bring today.**" <u>*Exodus 14 verses 13-14.*</u>

9. Name any other biblical character we discussed in this session, and what fearful situation they overcame. Provide Scriptural support for your answer. <u>*David overcame Goliath. 1 Samuel 17. The Widow of Zarephath was debtors. 1 Kings 17. Isaiah encouraged those Israelites in Captivity and Slavery. Isaiah 41. Elisha was pursued by the Aramean Army. They surrounded the city. 2 Kings 6.*</u>

10. Complete the sentence. *We overcome fear by **faith**.*

11. Complete the sentence. *We overcome fear through our **words**.*

12. Provide at least one Scripture to support this strategy of overcoming fear. *Proverbs 18 verse 21, Romans 10 verse 17, Mark 11 verses 22 to 23, 2 Corinthians 4 verse 13.*

13. Complete the sentence. ***Fear is a spirit**, and we need to take charge of it since we know that **it is not from God**, and that God did not give us a spirit of fear.*

14. Complete the sentence. *We overcome fear by thinking right. Faith follows your **thoughts**.*

15. Complete the sentence. *God has not given me a spirit of fear, but a spirit of **love**, power and a sound **mind**.*

18

UNFORGIVENESS
SESSION FOUR

Unforgiveness is one of the most devastating things, both for the offended and offender, one can embrace and hold onto. Bad things happen to people of all ages, positions and statuses.

The bad things that happen to us could be **the result of the intentional causing of hurt** or insult, **or of misguided, unintentional causing of hurt and pain.** For most, as victims, we often feel that we were hurt by intention. This felt feeling, experience or encounter of hurt, pain, injustice or rejection triggers within us self-communication which could either be channeled to forgive or to not forgive and excuse the offence. The effects on those who choose to not forgive, especially if it is held onto for an extended period of time, are devastating. We've all been hurt, been offended, been mis-understood, rejected and affected by injustice, however, the way we forgive ultimately determine how we cope with these kinds of challenges today.

This session is not going to be a session to open up every wound or dissect every injustice, however, we will rather attempt to learn ways in which we can more astutely deal with it in a righteous and God-honouring way, by forgiving.

One of the most prominent Teachings of Jesus is on forgiveness. He repeated it on a number of occasions, through a variety of messages, to bring home the power of forgiving others, as well as connecting it to our constant need for forgiveness ourselves. We all desire to be forgiven when we have faulted, but much fewer people are willing to reciprocate such forgiveness where they are wronged. The extent to which we desire to be forgiven is the extent to which we need to understand and apply forgiveness in our lives.

Definition of Forgiveness:

Forgiveness is the renunciation or cessation of <u>resentment</u>, indignation or anger as a result of a perceived offence, disagreement, or mistake, or ceasing to demand <u>punishment</u> or restitution.

Forgiveness Balance

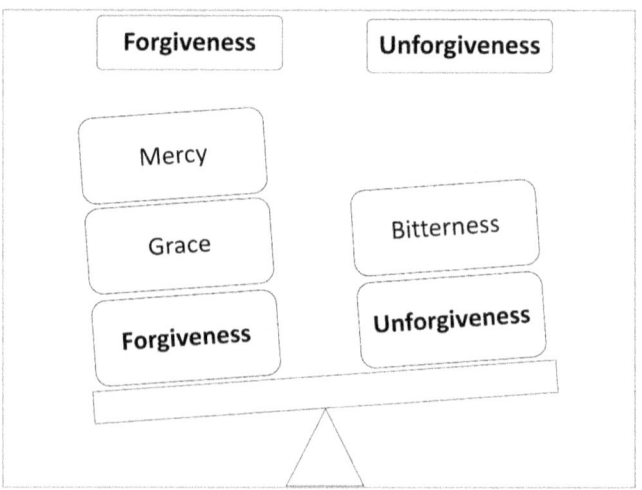

The purpose of this session is to help us outweigh unforgiveness with the weightier effects of forgiveness, grace and mercy.

Jesus is our Example

Jesus is our ultimate example of someone who practiced forgiveness. He set the example when He experienced the ultimate betrayal, hurt, pain, insult, and intentional injustice and still chose to forgive. So, to address unforgiveness, let us explore forgiveness from the WORD OF GOD.

> *Luke 23:34 (NIV) [34] Jesus said, "Father, forgive them, for they do not know what they are doing." And they divided up his clothes by casting lots.*

One of the pillars of our Faith is the value we place on <u>FORGIVENESS</u>. FORGIVENESS, alongside LOVE, FAITH, HOLINESS, HUMILITY, FAITHFULNESS, HONESTY, SUBMISSION, OBEDIENCE, COURAGE, COMPASSION, SERVANTHOOD, GENTLENESS, and many more, form the basis of the way we live and ultimately die.

> *<u>FORGIVENESS</u> is the ability to pardon an offence without holding resentment."* Hendrik J. Vorster

Harold S. Kushner wrote in his book: ***When Bad Things Happen to Good People;***

> *"Forgiveness always seems so easy, when we need it, and so hard when we need to give it."*
>
> *"The ability to <u>forgive</u> and the ability to <u>love</u> are the <u>weapons</u> God has given us to live fully, bravely, and meaningfully in this less-than-perfect world."*

One of the greatest needs in our day, is the need to be forgiven and be given another chance!

Pandemic Proportions

This need for Forgiveness is so great that it has reached **PANDEMIC** proportions, as it is one of the main reasons for depression, health causes, relationship break-ups, child behavioural disfunction and many more of societies challenges.

God, in His Graciousness and Compassion made eternal provision to meet our need for forgiveness.

Defining Forgiveness

There are primarily two GREEK words for forgiveness and describing its meaning:

- **Aphiemi** - means to: send away, leave alone, or "*To abandon.*"

- **Charizomai** - means to: show favor, give freely, graciously forgave, forgive.

The Basis for giving and receiving Forgiveness is found in God. Today we will explore the Biblical requirements for Forgiveness. We will also look at the provision for forgiveness by Christ, and His message to each one of us today.

THE BASIS OF FORGIVENESS IS FOUND IN GOD.

God is a God of Forgiveness. Throughout the Bible we read that God is a "Forgiving God."

> *Numbers 14:18 (NIV) [18] 'The LORD is slow to anger, abounding in love and **forgiving sin** and rebellion. Yet he does not leave the guilty unpunished; he punishes the children for the sin of the fathers to the third and fourth generation.'*

Daniel 9:9 (NIV) [9] **The Lord our God is merciful and forgiving,** *even though we have rebelled against him;*

Nehemiah 9:17 (NIV) [17] They refused to listen and failed to remember the miracles you performed among them. They became stiff-necked and, in their rebellion, appointed a leader in order to return to their slavery. ***But you are a forgiving God, gracious and compassionate, slow to anger and abounding in love.*** *Therefore, you did not desert them,*

The Nature of God is that He is a Forgiving God, Gracious and Compassionate. The Psalmists remind us of this truth.

Psalms 86:5 (NIV) [5] ***You are forgiving and good, O Lord,*** *abounding in love to all who call to you.*

Psalms 130:4 (NIV) ***[4] But with you there is forgiveness; therefore, you are feared.***

There is Forgiveness with God.

The God we serve is a forgiving God. Any pursuit of Him will find Him to be the most forgiving, understanding and compassionate God we hope to have dealing with our shortcomings, faults, mistakes, intentional and unintentional sins.

THE BIBLICAL REQUIREMENTS FOR FORGIVENESS.

When God gave the law to Moses, He also gave instructions for sacrifices to be made for the redemption and forgiveness of sins. The sacrifice had to be consistent with the offence for which pardon was sought. The "bigger the sin," the larger the sacrifice that was required.

Leviticus 4:19-20 (NIV) ***[19] He shall remove all the fat from it and burn it on the altar, [20] and do with this bull just as*** *he did with the bull for the sin offering. In this way the priest will make atonement for them, and they will be forgiven.*

A. The offering of sacrifices is the first part of seeking Forgiveness.

According to the transgression, the sinner brought sin offerings under the Old Testament law. So, when you sinned, and wanted to be pardoned for your sin, you will bring to the priest a sacrifice to be offered, to be killed, to give its life, as a sin offering for your sin. The Priest will slaughter the dove, lamb or bull, after hearing your confession, and then pardon you. The sacrifice will pay for your sins and you will be free from the guilt and punishment. It was the blood that was shed that satisfied the requirements of God to forgive and pardon sinners. The Bible teaches that **"without the shedding of blood there is no forgiveness."**

> *Hebrews 9:22 In fact, the law requires that nearly everything be cleansed with blood, and **without the shedding of blood there is no forgiveness.***

For us as New Testament Believers, we are blessed since Christ became our Sacrificial Lamb who took away the sins of the world and paid for our sins by shedding **His Blood** and being our Atoning Sacrifice.

> *Ephesians 1:7 In him **we have redemption through his blood, the forgiveness of sins**, in accordance with the riches of God's grace*

> *Hebrews 9:13-14 The blood of goats and bulls and the ashes of a heifer sprinkled on those who are ceremonially unclean **sanctify them so that they are outwardly clean. 14 How much more, then, will the blood of Christ**, who through the eternal Spirit offered himself unblemished to God, **cleanse our consciences***

from acts that lead to death, so that we may serve the living God!

B. The second part of this redemptive process was that, the sacrifice, or offering, had to be acceptable to God, before forgiveness was given.

Right from when the very first offerings were brought to God by Cain and Abel, we see that one was accepted, and the other not. When Adam and Eve sinned in the Garden, the covering God made to cover the sin and shame, was made of skin. An animal lost its life to cover the sin of Adam and Eve.

Only the death of a sacrificial animal could appease the Father for the sins committed. This action of the Father set in motion a principle for what was acceptable to pardon sin; it was the shedding of blood that would bring a covering and pardon for sin. The sacrifice needed to be <u>**unblemished to be acceptable**</u>. No deformed, cripple or blemished sacrifice would suffice.

> *Genesis 3:21 The **Lord God made garments of skin** for Adam and his wife and clothed them.*
>
> *Genesis 4:4 But Abel brought fat portions from some of the firstborn of his flock. **The Lord looked with favor on Abel and his offering**, 5 but on Cain and his offering he did not look with favor. So, Cain was very angry, and his face was downcast.*
>
> *Leviticus 1:3-4 "'If the offering is a burnt offering from the herd, he is to offer a male without defect. He must present it at the entrance to the Tent of Meeting so that **it will be acceptable to the Lord**. 4 He is to lay his hand on the head of the burnt offering, and it will be accepted on his behalf to make atonement for him."*

It was essential to bring sacrifices that would be acceptable to

God, in order to receive forgiveness of sins. When Christ became our Sacrificial Lamb, His sacrifice was accepted. We see in Romans that: *"God presented Jesus as a sacrifice of atonement."* In the Words of John: *"God so loved the world that He gave His One and Only Son."* This level and kind of giving, of a Redeemer, is beyond our reason or understanding. God truly loves us.

> *Romans 3:25* **God presented him as a sacrifice of atonement,** *through faith in his blood. He did this to demonstrate his justice, because in his forbearance he had left the sins committed beforehand unpunished–*

> *1 John 2:2* **He is the atoning sacrifice for our sins,** *and not only for ours but also for the sins of the whole world.*

> *John 1:29* *The next day John saw Jesus coming toward him and said, "Look,* **the Lamb of God, who takes away the sin of the world!**

<u>**Christ**</u> became our Sacrificial Lamb, who took away our sins. It is through Christ meeting the requirements to pay the price for our sins, that forgiveness is offered to all who believe in Him and trust in Him for their Forgiveness. If the blood of animals brought pardon to the offenders, how much more did the Blood of Christ accomplish forgiveness to those who confess, repent and believe in His Gracious Pardon.

It is so true what the Word tells us in Hebrews: **"How much more, then, will the blood of Christ cleanse our consciences from acts that lead to death."** Christ sacrifice, and offering His Blood, cleanses us from all sin and unrighteousness.

> *Hebrews 9:13-14* *The blood of goats and bulls and the ashes of a heifer sprinkled on those who are ceremonially unclean* **sanctify them so that they are outwardly clean.** *14* **How much more, then, will the blood of Christ,** *who through the eternal Spirit*

> offered himself unblemished to God, **cleanse our consciences from acts that lead to death,** so that we may serve the living God!
>
> *1 Peter 1:18-19* For you know that it was not with perishable things such as silver or gold that **you were redeemed** from the empty way of life handed down to you from your forefathers, 19 but **with the precious blood of Christ,** a lamb without blemish or defect.

We have been redeemed by the Blood that Jesus Christ shed. He paid the price for our sins. Through His sacrifice and the shedding of His Blood we have forgiveness of our sins.

This forgiveness is extended to all who believe. This forgiveness covers all sin. This forgiveness is for everyone.

C. The Third part is for us to accept His Forgiveness.

We need to accept His forgiveness. The New Testament proclaimed the same message that: *"without the shedding of blood there is no forgiveness."* Conversely, with the Blood of Christ there is Forgiveness. Christ shed His blood for your and my sins. We are forgiven because of His great sacrifice.

If God accepted Christ's sacrifice and His blood offered for the remission of our sins, then **we ought to accept His sacrifice and forgiveness of our sins** as well. There is a direct connection between the shedding of Christ's Blood and our forgiveness.

> *Hebrews 9:22 (NIV)* [22] In fact, the law requires that nearly everything be cleansed with blood, and **without the shedding of blood there is no forgiveness.**
>
> *Hebrews 9:12 (NIV)* [12] He did not enter by means of the blood of goats and calves; but he entered the Most Holy Place once for all **by his own blood,** having **obtained eternal redemption.**

> *Colossians 2:13 (NIV) [13] When you were dead in your sins and in the uncircumcision of your sinful nature, God made you alive with Christ.* **He forgave us all our sins,**

> Acts 10:43 (NIV)
> *[43] All the prophets testify about him that* **everyone who believes in him receives forgiveness of sins through his name."**

Every time we partake of the Lord's Table we celebrate and accept His forgiveness of our sins.

> *Matthew 26:28 (NIV) [28]* **This is my blood** *of the covenant, which is poured out for many* **for the forgiveness of sins.**

We all thank God for His Grace and Mercy to forgive us of our sins, however, there is an extremely important aspect to receiving this forgiveness that, if missed or not applied, might leave you in the same misery as if you never confessed your sin and sought forgiveness, and that is that God requires us to extend forgiveness to those who "sinned" against us.

God's Forgiveness is conditional.

Christ offers us unreserved forgiveness, but **there is a condition** attached to it: **we need to also forgive.** Jesus taught us in the "Our Father" prayer, to *"forgive us our sins as we forgive those who have sinned against us."*

> *Matthew 6:12-15 (NIV) "[12]* **Forgive us our debts, as we also have forgiven our debtors.** *[13] And lead us not into temptation but deliver us from the evil one.' [14]* **For if you forgive men when they sin against you, your heavenly Father will also forgive you. [15] But if you do not forgive men their sins, your Father will not forgive your sins."**

Forgiving others is as important to God as receiving forgiveness from Him for our sins. Jesus told a number of Parables to emphasise the importance of forgiveness. Jesus reminds us of the practice of forgiveness through parables. In two parables Jesus points us to forgive like God and not like man.

The unmerciful servant.

Jesus precedes this Parable by teaching the principle of forgiveness.

> *Matthew 18:21-22 The Parable of the Unmerciful Servant "Then Peter came to Jesus and asked, **'Lord, how many times shall I forgive my brother when he sins against me? Up to seven times?'** 22 Jesus answered, **'I tell you, not seven times, but seventy-seven times.'"***

In this Parable Jesus taught that the Kingdom of Heaven is like a Master who wanted to settle accounts, or the debts, that his servants had with Him. When one of the servants was brought to Him because of his Large debt, into the millions in today's terms, he begged for mercy when his Master wanted to have him and his whole family, including all he owned, sold to cover the debts. His Master took pity on him and forgave him his debt and let him go debt-free. However, as that pardoned servant went out, he saw another servant who owed him only a few dollars, but instead of pardoning him, he put him in prison until his debt was paid. When the Master heard of this ungrateful and inconsistent behaviour of someone whom he pardoned of so much, he called him to account because of his unmerciful behaviour.

> *Matthew 18:32-35 "Then the master called the servant in. 'You wicked servant,' he said, 'I cancelled all that debt of yours because you begged me to. 33 Shouldn't you have had mercy on your fellow servant just as I had on you?' 34 In anger his master turned him over to the jailers to be tortured, until he*

should pay back all he owed. 35 'This is how my heavenly Father will treat each of you unless you forgive your brother from your heart.'"

This parable epitomises our response in many respects; we plead our case for forgiveness daily for the things in which we transgressed, yet at the same time, almost without consideration, refuses to engage the thought of leniency, grace, pardon or forgiveness towards those who offended, hurt or transgressed towards us.

Although we could see it clearly explained and understood in this parable, we often fail to connect this parable to the realities of our actions and how we practice forgiveness. The concluding words of the Lord Jesus should serve as a stern warning and reminder that our "**Heavenly Father will treat each one of us**" with the same measure, unless we "*forgive our brother from our heart.*"

This conversation would not be complete if we did not revisit the "yardstick" or "**Rule of Thumb**" for practicing forgiveness: "**I tell you, not seven times, but seventy-seven times.**"

The Millstone

The teaching of Jesus on Sin and the Millstone serves as another reminder to watch ourselves, that we do not cause others to sin, but also to live with a certain preparedness to forgive those who "sin" against us without reservation. Here again we learn the same principle on forgiveness: "*If your brother sins, rebuke him, and if he repents, forgive him. If he sins against you seven times in a day, and seven times comes back to you and says, 'I repent,' forgive him.*"

> Luke 17:1-4 Jesus said to his disciples: "Things that cause people to sin are bound to come, but woe to that person through whom they come. It would be better for him to be thrown into the sea with a millstone tied around his neck than for him to cause one of these little ones to sin. So, watch yourselves. If your brother sins, rebuke him, and **if he repents, forgive him.** If he sins

against you seven times in a day, and seven times comes back to you and says, 'I repent,' forgive him."

Someone has said, "**We are never more like God than when we can forgive others.**"

Let us take a few moments to explore this connection between receiving forgiveness for our sins and the forgiveness we are willing to offer to others. Throughout the Scriptures we are taught four basic principles of forgiveness.

Principle 1: God Forgives sins.

> *Matthew 6:12-13 (NIV) [12]* **Forgive us our debts,** *as we also have forgiven our debtors. [13] And lead us not into temptation but deliver us from the evil one.'*

The first principle is that **God is the Author of Forgiveness.** He desires to be Merciful to all who seek forgiveness from Him for their sins. The reason for us praying: "*Forgive us our sins*" is rooted in the deepest desire of man to live without guilt, rejection or guilt, and an acknowledgment that true forgiveness is only found in Him.

> *Mark 2:7* "*Why does this fellow talk like that? He's blaspheming!* **Who can forgive sins but God alone?**"

Many times, people struggle with unforgiveness since they fail to accept the forgiveness of the Father, even after repeated offerings of repentance. Settle this today: **His Forgiveness stands secure for all who confess and repent of their sins.**

Principle 2: Forgive Those Who Sin Against you.

> *Matthew 6:12(NLT)* "*And forgive us our sins, just as we have forgiven those who have sinned against us.*"

> Matthew 18:21 – Then Peter came to Him and said, "Lord, how often shall my brother sin against me, and I forgive him? Up to seven times?"

To forgive completely requires one of the most difficult of all adjustments, but Jesus describes it so simply: **"Just as we need forgiveness, so we must forgive others."**

Principle 3: Forgive and be forgiven

If we forgive, God will **forgive** us.

> Matthew 6:14 "For if you forgive men their trespasses, **your heavenly Father will also forgive you.**"

> Luke 6:37 "Judge not, and you shall not be judged. Condemn not, and you shall not be condemned. Forgive, **and you will be forgiven.**"

It all depends on us. As we forgive, we will be forgiven. As we show mercy, mercy shall be shown to us.

> *"We need not climb up into heaven to see whether our sins are forgiven. Let us look into our hearts and see if we can forgive others."*
>   - *Thomas Watson*

Principle 4: If we do not Forgive, we will not be forgiven.

Jesus gave this warning about forgiveness: If we refuse to forgive others, God will also refuse to forgive us.

> Matthew 6:15 (NIV) "[15] **But if you do not forgive men their sins, your Father will not forgive your sins.**"

> Mark 11:25 And when you stand praying, if you hold anything

against anyone, forgive him, so that your Father in heaven may forgive you your sins.'"

This is the reality check on holding on to unforgiveness. If we hold back, or refuse to forgive men their trespasses against us, then our Heavenly Father will also refuse to forgive us our sins. We are warned against the sin of an unforgiving heart, which often results in a bitter spirit that robs us of the blessings God reserved for us.

Hebrews 12:15 (NIV) [15] See to it that no one misses the grace of God and that no bitter root grows up to cause trouble and defile many.

In one sense refusing to forgive others reveals a lack of appreciation for the mercy received from God.

AFTERWORD

As Followers of Jesus Christ **we clothe ourselves with the forbearance** to be merciful and to forgive whatever grievances we may have with others.

Ephesians 4:32 Be kind and compassionate to one another, forgiving each other, just as in Christ God forgave you.

Colossians 3:12-13 Therefore, as God's chosen people, holy and dearly loved, clothe yourselves with compassion, kindness, humility, gentleness and patience. 13 Bear with each other and forgive whatever grievances you may have against one another. Forgive as the Lord forgave you.

Almost nothing shows the love we have for one another, as does the way we are merciful, forgiving and forbearing with others.

Biblical Examples

Every believer should seek to practice the forgiving spirit of these examples:

Joseph

Joseph endured unjust treatment and the ultimate betrayal from his family, by being sold as a slave into a foreign nation. His brothers essentially ensured that he was as good as dead when they sold him. Joseph endured false accusation from Potiphar's wife, which landed him in prison. His companions in prison also let him down by not keeping their word. He almost endured a lifetime of betrayal, false accusation and rejection, yet he forgave his perpetrators.

> *Genesis 50:19-21 (NIV) [19] But Joseph said to them, "Don't be afraid. Am I in the place of God? [20] You intended to harm me, but God intended it for good to accomplish what is now being done, the saving of many lives. [21] So then, don't be afraid. I will provide for you and your children." And he reassured them and spoke kindly to them.*

His kindness not only extended to forgiving and pardoning them, he also provided for them and their families. Many people live the proverbial *"Joseph's Life,"* they have been betrayed, been rejected and experienced false accusations levelled against them. Like Joseph found it in his heart to forgive those who subjected him a life-time of abuse and living a degenerated life, we too should forgive those who intentionally and purposefully hurt and abused us.

Stephen

Stephen was this powerful witness for Jesus Christ who, in the midst of preaching and defending the faith, was stoned to death. He did not defend himself against his assaulters, or retaliated with threats and accusations, but chose to continue to testify and to pray for his oppressors that God would forgive them and not hold their sin against them. What an example of the ultimate test to practice forgiveness. Stephen did it: He forgave those who stoned him to death for preaching and testifying for Jesus Christ.

> *Acts 7:60 (NIV) [60] Then he fell on his knees and cried out, "Lord, do not hold this sin against them." When he had said this, he fell asleep.*

As principle-centered people, we are called upon again and again to forgive. The principles of forgiveness are given priority throughout the scriptures to be placed into practice.

Jesus

Jesus modelled forgiveness to us, even when He faced the most challenging of circumstances. Sometimes we think that: *"if I was just in a better headspace,"* or *"if I wasn't in so much pain and discomfort, then I would possibly more easily forgive,"* however, Christ set us an example to follow.

> *Luke 23:34 (NIV) [34] Jesus said, "Father, forgive them, for they do not know what they are doing." And they divided up his clothes by casting lots.*

Jesus remains our ultimate example of someone who endured the harshest of unjust treatments any human ever endured, yet chose to forgive.

Communion

It is through our participation of communion that we affirm the forgiveness of our sins. Every time we take the cup, we partake of the Blood of Jesus Christ. His Blood washes and cleanses us from all sin and shame. One of the sure-fast ways we deal with unforgiveness is by consciously partaking of the blood of Jesus. When we take the cup, after examining ourselves, we both pardon others of their offences against us, and we receive and accept our forgiveness and pardon from the Lord.

> *Matthew 26:28 (NIV) [28] This is my blood of the covenant, which is poured out for many for the forgiveness of sins.*

How do we deal with unforgiveness?

- Affirm Almighty God as the Forgiver of sin.
- Affirm that He made significant and complete provision for the remission of all the sins of the world, including yours.
- Take time to consider all the people who committed offences against you and forgive them. Once you truly forgiven them, and asked God to forgive them and to pardon them, then address your own needs for forgiveness.
- Confess your sins and ask God to forgive you.
- Affirm that you seek and accept His Forgiveness for all your sins.

Assimilation Sheet for Unforgiveness.

1. Complete the sentence. *One of the most prominent Teachings of Jesus is on forgiveness.*

2. Complete the definition of Forgiveness. *Forgiveness is the renunciation or cessation of resentment, indignation or anger as a result of a perceived offence, disagreement, or mistake, or ceasing to demand punishment or restitution.*

3. Complete the sentence. *The ability to forgive and the ability to love are the weapons God has given us to live fully, bravely, and meaningfully in this less-than-perfect world.*

4. Which Scriptures teach that God is a forgiving God? *Numbers 14 verse 18, Daniel 9 verse 9, Nehemiah 9 verse 17, Psalms 86 verse 5 and Psalms 130 verse 4.*

5. Provide Scriptural proof that: **"without the shedding of blood there is no forgiveness."** *Hebrews 9 verse 22, Ephesians 1 verse 7, and Hebrews 9 verses 13-14.*

6. Provide Scriptural proof that: "Jesus is the Lamb of God." *John 1 verse 29, 1 John 2 verse 2, Romans 3 verse 25, Hebrews 9 verses 13-14, 1 Peter 1 verses 18-19.*

7. Jesus taught about a condition upon which God will forgive us of our sins. What is that condition for us to receive our forgiveness? Provide Scriptures. *Jesus taught that He will forgive us our sins as we forgive those who sin against us. Matthew 6 verses 12-15, Matthew 18 verses 32-35, and Luke 6 verse 37.*

8. We looked at Four Principles of Forgiveness. Name the Four and provide at least one Scripture for each.

- *Principle 1: God forgives sins. Matthew 6 verse 12, Mark 2 verse 7.*
- *Principle 2: Forgive those who sin against you. Matthew 6 verse 12, Matthew 18 verse 21.*
- *Principle 3: Forgive and be forgiven. Matthew 6 verse 14, Luke 6 verse 37.*

- *Principle 4: If we do not forgive, we will not be forgiven. Matthew 6 verse 15, Mark 11 verse 25, Colossians 3 verses 12-13.*

9. Complete the sentence. *As Followers of Jesus Christ* **we clothe ourselves with the forbearance** *to be merciful and to forgive whatever grievances we may have with others.*

19

LUST OF THE FLESH AND THE LUST OF THE EYES
SESSION FIVE

*1 John 2:15-17 Do not love the world or anything in the world. If anyone loves the world, the love of the Father is not in him. 16 For everything in the world—**the cravings of sinful man, the lust of his eyes** and **the boasting of what he has and does**—comes not from the Father but from the world. 17 The world and its desires pass away, but the man who does the will of God lives forever.*

Lust is a terrible **evil root** in many people's lives. It manifests itself in numerous ways. Most will deny its existence in them until the Holy Spirit's conviction unlayer the masks behind which they hide to attempt to disguise it.

When Jesus taught us through the Parable of the Sower, He emphasised how the thistles and thorns would choke the seed and make it unfruitful.

To choke something means that you block its breathing capacity and enforcing a cruel destructive death.

This is exactly what lust does in one's life; it deprives the good seed in you to remain alive. It essentially kills it and makes all the good potential to be eliminated and to be made unfruitful.

> *Mark 4:18-19 "Still others, like seed sown among thorns, hear the word; 19 but the worries of this life, the deceitfulness of wealth and **the desires for other things come in and choke the word, making it unfruitful**."*

> *Luke 8:13-14 "Those on the rock are the ones who receive the word with joy when they hear it, but they have no root. They believe for a while, but in the time of testing they fall away. 14 The seed that fell among thorns stands for those who hear, but as they go on their way **they are choked by** life's worries, riches and **pleasures**, and they do not **mature**."*

It is this **"desire"** for other things and for **"pleasures"** that choke the good seed of the Word in our lives and ultimately make us unfruitful and keep us from maturing in our faith. Nowadays you can't watch regular television without being bombarded with "pleasures." It is the encompassing extent and result of these "pleasures" that is not openly disclosed.

The Bible teaches us, both what these acts are, which responds to the sinful nature, as well as the outcome for those who persist in such acts. May the Lord grant us a soberness to assess ourselves in the light of Scripture.

Galatians chapter 5 unpacks those acts of the sinful nature that ultimately "choke" us and lead us to a place where we will miss out on inheriting the Kingdom of God.

> *Galatians 5:19-21 "The acts of the sinful nature are obvious: sexual immorality, impurity and debauchery; idolatry and witchcraft; hatred, discord, jealousy, fits of rage, selfish ambition, dissensions, factions and envy; drunkenness, orgies, and the like. **I warn you, as I did before, that those who live like this will not inherit the kingdom of God**."*

When we allow ourselves to be lured by *"**the lust of our eyes**,"* or *"**the lust of the flesh**"* then we find these very things present: *"sexual immorality, impurity and debauchery; idolatry and witchcraft; hatred, discord, jealousy, fits of rage, selfish ambition, dissensions, factions and envy; drunkenness, orgies, and the like."*

These Scriptures do not address those who still live under the blindfold of their old nature, no, these Scriptures address those in the Church. These Scriptures exhorts us to address these carnal aptitudes in a deep yieldedness to the sanctification work of the Holy Spirit. It is not to spoil our fun or to deprive us from living with a sense of gratification, but to bring us to a place of true, and lasting fulfilment.

> *Romans 13:14 Rather, **clothe yourselves** with the Lord Jesus Christ, and **do not think about how to gratify the desires of the sinful nature**.*

It seems from this Scripture that it is essential that we make a concerted effort to rather please the Holy Spirit's desires inside of us, rather than the unsatisfiable promptings of the flesh. The outcome of continuing to live for the gratifications of the flesh will leave you empty, unsatisfied and unfulfilled. They will also deprive you of seeing the seed of your efforts bearing lasting fruit.

> *Galatians 5:16-17 So, I say, live by the Spirit, and you will not gratify the desires of the sinful nature. For the sinful nature desires what is contrary to the Spirit, and the Spirit what is contrary to the sinful nature. They are in conflict with each other, so that you do not do what you want.*

> *Galatians 5:24 Those who belong to Christ Jesus have crucified the sinful nature with its passions and desires.*

> *Ephesians 2:3 All of us also lived among them at one time, **gratifying the cravings of our sinful nature and following its***

> *desires and thoughts. Like the rest, we were by nature objects of wrath.*

It is this, succumbing to the gratifications of the flesh that will keep you from seeing fruit on your labour in the Lord. When we sow to please the Holy Spirit, we will reap eternal benefits, however, if we continue to sow to satisfy the gratifications of the flesh, it will only bring forth a harvest of sin.

How do we crucify the lust of the flesh?

Fast and Pray.

Nothing breaks the back of fleshly desires as does fasting and prayer. Jesus ones said that: *"this kind does not come out expect by fasting and prayer."* This remains true for every Believer. When we submit ourselves to a time of Fasting and prayer, we actively crucify the lust and desires of the flesh.

> Mark 9:29 (NIV) 29 He replied, "This kind can come out only by prayer and fasting."

In the well-known chapter on Fasting, Isaiah outlines the very things we need to crucify in our lives through fasting.

> Isaiah 58:6-9 (NIV) 6 "Is not this the kind of fasting I have chosen: to loose the chains of injustice and untie the cords of the yoke, to set the oppressed free and break every yoke? 7 Is it not to share your food with the hungry and to provide the poor wanderer with shelter — when you see the naked, to clothe them, and not to turn away from your own flesh and blood? 8 Then your light will break forth like the dawn, and your healing will quickly appear; then your righteousness will go before you, and the glory of the LORD will be your rear guard. 9 Then you will call, and

the LORD will answer; you will cry for help, and he will say: Here am I.

Take a 21-day Spiritual food challenge.

Take a 21-day Spiritual Food challenge. The purpose of this is simply to fill yourself with more of God as we believe that God will set you free from the spirit of lust this weekend. Jesus' warning in Luke chapter eleven compels us to take this action to ensure that we replace every area lust occupied and fill it with the Word and the Holy Spirit.

> Luke 11:24-26 (AMP) 24 When the unclean spirit has gone out of a person, it roams through waterless places in search [of a place] of rest (release, refreshment, ease); and finding none it says, I will go back to my house from which I came.
> 25 And when it arrives, it finds [the place] swept and put in order and furnished and decorated.
> 26 And it goes and brings other spirits, seven [of them], more evil than itself, and they enter in, settle down, and dwell there; and the last state of that person is worse than the first.

Take 21 days to only feed yourself with the Word of God, before taking any physical food. Read and pray through 21 New Testament Books, starting with Revelation. Some days will take you 90 minutes, but others just a few short minutes, however, take the time to ask the Holy Spirit to help you and lead you out of lust. How we feed and fill our mind with the Word of God, will help us overcome whatever is tormenting and enslaving us.

Confess your deliverance.

Make confessions of what you are trusting God to accomplish in your life. We overcome the evil one by applying the **Blood** of Jesus and by the **confession** of our mouths.

> *Revelation 12:11* **They overcame him by the blood of the Lamb and by the word of their testimony;** *they did not love their lives so much as to shrink from death.*

Get an accountability partner.

The Bible teaches that we should confess our sins **one to another** so that we may be healed. Being free from lust will bring healing to your life. Many times, when people confess their sins, especially to those counted as elders, they help us by holding us **accountable**. Their prayers have tremendous power and are effective in seeing us free and delivered.

> *James 5:16 Therefore,* **confess your sins to each other** *and pray for each other so that you may be healed. The prayer of a righteous man is powerful and effective.*

Be filled, and remain filled, with the Spirit.

Nothing is as sure a guard against the enemy's assaults as remaining filled with the Holy Spirit. The more we remain filled with the Holy Spirit, the more we will find ourselves suppressing the evil desires of the flesh. Remember, the flesh and the spirit are in competition and opposition to each other. The one you feed and give pre-eminence to, is the one who will reign and bear fruit in your life.

> *Galatians 5:16-17 Life by the Spirit "So, I say, live by the **Spirit**, and you will not gratify the **desires** of the sinful nature. 17 For the sinful nature desires what is contrary to the Spirit, and the*

Spirit what is contrary to the sinful nature. They are in conflict with each other, so that you do not do what you want."

Galatians 5:24-25 "Those who belong to Christ Jesus have crucified the sinful nature with its passions and desires. 25 Since we live by the Spirit, let us keep in step with the Spirit."

I pray that you will find true freedom in Christ Jesus. The next part is dedicated to maintaining the freedom Christ brought into our lives.

Assimilation Sheet for
The Lust of the flesh and the Lust of the Eyes.

1. Complete the sentence. *Lust is a terrible* **evil root** *in many people's lives.*

2. Which things are not from the Father according to 1 John 2 verses 15 to 17? *The things that are not of the Father are Love for the world and the cravings of sinful man, the lust of the eyes and the boasting of what he has and does.*

3. What two things does the thorns do in our lives, according to Mark chapter 4 verses 18 to 19. *The thorns will choke the seed of the Word and make it unfruitful.*

4. Write down those things that are described in Galatians chapter 5 as "acts of the sinful nature." *They are sexual immorality, impurity and debauchery; idolatry and witchcraft; hatred, discord, jealousy, fits of rage, selfish ambition, dissensions, factions and envy; drunkenness, orgies, and the like.*

5. Write down the five things we can do to deal with Lust in our lives. *1. We can Fast and pray; 2. We can take a 21 day Spiritual Food challenge; 3. We can over come lust by applying the blood of Jesus and by the confession of our mouths; 4. We can make confession to an Accountability Partner; and 5. We can ensure that we remain filled with the Holy Spirit.*

6. Give one Scriptures to substantiate the first two approached of dealing with Lust. *Mark 9 verse 29; Isaiah 58 verses 6 to 9; Luke 11 verses 24 to 26.*

7. Complete the sentence. *We overcome the evil one by applying the* **Blood** *of Jesus and by the* **confession** *of our mouths.*

8. Why is it important to confess your sins, one to another? What Scripture do you base this belief on? *We confess our sins so that we might be healed. James chapter 5 verse 16.*

9. Complete the sentence. *"Live by the* **Spirit**, *and you will not gratify the* **desires** *of the sinful nature."*

20

FAITH AND OBEDIENCE
SESSION SIX

Luke 11:24-26 "When an evil spirit comes out of a man, it goes through arid places seeking rest and does not find it. Then it says, 'I will return to the house I left.' 25 When it arrives, it finds the house swept clean and put in order. 26 Then it goes and takes seven other spirits more wicked than itself, and they go in and live there. And the final condition of that man is worse than the first."

The last thing any of us want is to see all the good work God accomplished in your life, this weekend, become undone in weeks to come.

- *How do we remain free and delivered?*
- *How do we retain the good measure God poured out into our lives this weekend?*

Our **first defence** is to stay in a place of being full of the **Holy Spirit**. Our **second defence** is to **stay in contact** with those who will encourage and spur us on in this journey with Christ. Our **third**

defence is to stay in the _Word_ and _pray_ together with fellow Believers as often as what we are able.

I believe that we will do well to head to the advice and action steps we've taken throughout this weekend to decisively deal with the affected areas of our lives, however, there is another aspect that requires our attention, and that is the _faith to obey_. Hebrews chapter 4 recounts the reasons why a generation of Israelites did not enter into the land promised to them, as well as why only 2 people, out of an entire generation, entered into the Promised land.

Many people experience deliverance from the power of slavery, but only a few take possession of the promised land God set before them. I pray that you will set your heart on the Promises God set before you, and consciously turn your back on the Egypt – place of slavery — and by faith take possession of the land occupied by giants.

Faith to Obey.

> *Hebrews 4:1-2 NIV "Therefore, since the promise of entering his rest still stands, let us be careful that none of you be found to have fallen short of it. For we also have had the good news proclaimed to us, just as they did; but **the message they heard was of no value to them, because they did not share the faith of those who obeyed."***

In this session I want to speak about **Faith to Obey**. One morning, whilst reading the Word of God, the Lord spoke to me through His Word. Allow me to share this thought with you.

> *Hebrews 4:2 (NIV) "For we also have had the good news proclaimed to us, just as they did; but the message they heard was of no value to them, **because they did not share the faith of those who obeyed."***

The latter part of this verse spoke to me: "**the faith of those who obeyed.**" The Word of God is powerful and is full of benefits, however these benefits are reserved for those who **combine their _faith_ with obedience.**

An entire nation received a promise of a Promised Land; however, it was only Joshua and Caleb who entered that Promised Land. **Their Promised land was connected to their faith to obey.** The Amplified Bible states it beautifully:

> *Hebrews 4:2 (AMP) [2] For indeed we have had the glad tidings [Gospel of God] proclaimed to us just as truly as they [the Israelites of old did when the good news of deliverance from bondage came to them]; but the message they heard did not benefit them, because it was not mixed with faith (with *the leaning of the entire personality on God in absolute trust and confidence in His power, wisdom, and goodness) by those who heard it; *neither were they united in faith with the ones [Joshua and Caleb] who heard (did believe).*

I was thinking about the Faith of a Joshua and Caleb. They were remarkable men. They were part of the 12 spies, whom Moses selected to go and spy out the Promised land. Only Joshua and Caleb came back believing that they could conquer and possess the Promised land. _**Two out of twelve**_ became two out of an entire nation. 12 Spies went out, 10 came back with a negative report, a report of unbelief, a report of impossibility, a report of fear and of rebellion, and two came back with a report of Hope, Faith, Obedience, and possibility. The Bible says that the twelve reported and confirmed that it was a "land flowing with milk and honey," but the main emphasis of ten of them was on the impossibilities of conquering the powerful possessors of the land.

> *Numbers 13:27-28 (NIV) [27] They gave Moses this account: "We went into the land to which you sent us, and it does flow with milk and honey! Here is its fruit. [28]* **But the people who live**

> there are powerful, and **the cities are fortified and very large. We even saw descendants of Anak there.**"

Among the same 12 spies was Joshua and Caleb, who silenced the revolting people, and said that they "**should go up and take possession of the land.**"

> Numbers 13:30 (NIV) Then Caleb silenced the people before Moses and said, "**We should go up and take possession of the land, for we can certainly do it.**"

Caleb and Joshua found themselves among unbelievers who did not believe that the God who miraculously delivered them from the hands of the mighty Pharaoh could give them a land that He promised to them. 10 of the 12 spies kept on discouraging the Israelites to the extent that the Israelites were filled with fear and unbelief.

> Numbers 13:31-33 (NIV) [31] But the men who had gone up with him said, "We can't attack those people; they are stronger than we are." [32] And **they spread among the Israelites a bad report about the land** they had explored. They said, "**The land we explored devours those living in it. All the people we saw there are of great size.** [33] We saw the Nephilim there (the descendants of Anak come from the Nephilim). **We seemed like grasshoppers in our own eyes, and we looked the same to them.**"

This back and forth struggle went on. It will be the same in your and my Christian walk, many will continue to echo the impossibilities. Many might say to you that the Promises of God has impossible conditions attached to them. Many might say that you will not be able to accomplish what was impossible for past generations. Many might say that you should simply settle for "your lot." There are not many Joshua's and Caleb's, who resolve to heed to the voice of faith inside of them and trust in the God who is able to make the impossible possible.

> *Numbers 14:6-9 (NIV) [6]* **Joshua** *son of Nun and* **Caleb** *son of Jephunneh, who were among those who had explored the land,* **tore their clothes** *[7] and said to the entire Israelite assembly,* "*The land we passed through and explored is exceedingly good. [8] If the LORD is pleased with us,* **he will lead us into that land***, a land flowing with milk and honey, and* **will give it to us***. [9]* **Only do not rebel against the LORD***. And do not be* **afraid** *of the people of the land, because we will swallow them up. Their protection is gone, but the LORD is with us. Do not be afraid of them.*"

Finally, the Lord expressed His dismay with the people's response of rebellion and fear. Was it not for **Moses** who **interceded** before the Lord for the people, the whole nation would have been wiped out. May Father find in us a "Moses" who would stand in the gap on behalf of our Nation, City, Family and even church, to pray for their unbelief to be replaced with faith and obedience.

> *Numbers 14:20-24 (NIV)* "*[20] The LORD replied,* "*I have forgiven them, as you asked. [21] Nevertheless, as surely as I live and as surely as the glory of the LORD fills the whole earth, [22] not one of the men who saw my glory and the miraculous signs I performed in Egypt and in the desert but* **who disobeyed me** *and* **tested me ten times**— *[23] not one of them will ever see the land I promised on oath to their forefathers. No one who has treated me with contempt will ever see it. [24] But because my servant Caleb has a different spirit and follows me wholeheartedly, I will bring him into the land he went to, and his descendants will inherit it.*"

> *Numbers 14:30-31 (AMP)* "*[30] Surely none shall come into the land in which I swore to make you dwell,* **except Caleb** *son of*

> *Jephunneh and Joshua son of Nun. [31]* **But your little ones whom you said would be a prey, them will I bring in and they shall know the land** *which you have despised and rejected.* **God** *said: 'Go and possess the Land.'"*

Two men <u>believed</u> that, regardless of the Giants in the land, regardless of their fortified cities, **the Lord was able to do what He said He would do.** They had faith to obey God. They added obedience to their faith in God. 40 years later we see them entering in the land promised them.

> *Numbers 26:64-65 (NIV)* "*[64]* **Not one of them was among those counted** *by Moses and Aaron the priest when they counted the Israelites in the Desert of Sinai. [65] For the LORD had told* **those Israelites they would surely die in the desert, and not one of them was left except Caleb** *son of Jephunneh and* **Joshua son of Nun.**"

I pray that God will fill our hearts with Faith to obey Him, to do everything He wants us to do for Him, so that in we might see the fulfilment of all that He Promised us.

How will we see the Good Promises fulfilled in our lives?

Persevere in Prayer and Trusting God

We need to learn from the Persistent woman who never gave up on making her requests known, until she was met with justice for her case.

> *Luke 18:1-8 (NIV) The Parable of the Persistent Widow [18:1] Then Jesus told his disciples a parable to show them that they should always pray and not give up. [2] He said: "In a certain town there was a judge who neither feared God nor cared about men. [3] And there was a widow in that town who kept coming to*

*him with the plea, 'Grant me justice against my adversary?' [4]
"For some time he refused. But finally, he said to himself, 'Even
though I don't fear God or care about men, [5] yet because this
widow keeps bothering me, I will see that she gets justice, so
that she won't eventually wear me out with her coming!'" [6]
And the Lord said, "Listen to what the unjust judge says. [7]*
**And will not God bring about justice for his chosen ones, who
cry out to him day and night? Will he keep putting them off?
[8] I tell you; he will see that they get justice, and quickly.**
However, when the Son of Man comes, **will he find faith on the
earth?"**

What kind of faith is required?

Faith to trust God for the impossible.

Every one of us know that God called us for a purpose. We will never be fulfilled until we fulfill His purpose on our lives.

How many actually take that Call serious to Obey?

Romans 8:28 NIV "And we know that in all things God works for the good of those who love him, who have been called according to his purpose."

There is an ever-increasing amount of road rules, yet no one gets in behind the steering wheel of a car and complains about having to get on the road and having to obey every road rule and every sign on the road, even though there might be many. You don't complain every time you see a traffic light or stop sign and say: "*look, another one! Do I* ***have to stop at every single traffic light, yield at every single stop sign, obey every single road sign, even when no one might be looking?***" No, we know that it is in our best interest to obey the rules.

In our faith, in our walk with God, it is the same. **We need to add to our profession, <u>obedience</u>, and faith to obey!** Whether that is in trusting God for **His provision**, when we stepped out by faith to tithe. Whether that is in trusting God **for salvation** in someone's life when we stepped out to share with them about God's Love for them and that He died for them. Whether it is trusting God for **justice**, or **Favour**, or **deliverance**, or **breakthrough**, or **reconciliation** or **restoration**, we apply faith to our obedience.

Whatever He asks you to do, be <u>obedient</u> and do it.

- **Gideon** did what God asked him to do. *Judges chapters 6 to 9.*
- **The widow of Zarephath** acted on the Word when the prophet spoke to her. She received her miracle and never experienced famine again. All her debts was paid. *1 Kings 17 verses 9 to 16.*
- **Naaman** did what the prophet told him to do. He applied obedience to his faith and received his <u>*miracle*</u>. He was cured of leprosy. 2 Kings chapter 5.

Conclusion

In closing, let us make a decision today to <u>***trust* God**</u> and to <u>***obey* Him**</u>. This will ensure that the good work God started in our lives will be accomplished.

> *Hebrews 3:7-14 (NIV) Warning Against Unbelief "[7] So, as the Holy Spirit says: "Today, if you hear his voice, [8] do not harden your hearts as you did in the rebellion, during the time of testing in the desert, [9] where your fathers tested and tried me and for forty years saw what I did. [10] That is why I was angry with that generation, and I said, 'Their hearts are always going astray, and they have not known my ways.' [11] So I declared on oath in my anger, 'They shall never enter my rest.' [12] See to it, brothers, that none of you has a sinful, unbelieving heart that turns away from the living God. [13] But*

encourage one another daily, as long as it is called Today, so that none of you may be hardened by sin's deceitfulness. [14] We have come to share in Christ if we hold firmly till the end the confidence, we had at first."

Let's have Faith to Obey God's Word!

Let us be that generation who benefit from the Word spoken into our lives. May our obedience match the faith we profess.

Assimilation Sheet for
Faith and Obedience.

1. Complete the sentence. *Our first defence is to stay in a place of being full of the <u>Holy Spirit</u>.*

2. What is the main message we derived from Hebrews chapter 4 verses 1 and 2. *<u>We derived from these two verses that if we want to reach our Promised land, then we need to apply obedience to our faith.</u>*

3. Complete the sentence. *The <u>Word</u> of God is powerful and is full of <u>benefits</u>, however these benefits are reserved for those who combine their faith with <u>obedience</u>.*

4. What was Joshua and Caleb's report when they returned from spying out the Promised Land? Give Scriptural Proof. *<u>They reported that it was " a land flowing with milk and honey," and that they "should go up and take possession of the land." Numbers 13 verses 27 to 28, and 30.</u>*

5. Joshua and Caleb pleaded with the people to go and take possession of the Land and not to rebel against the Lord. Where do we find this Pleading of Joshua and Caleb? *<u>Number 14 verses 6 to 9.</u>*

6. How many of the Twelve Spies, and How many of the people eventually entered the Promised Land? Provide Scriptural Reference. *<u>Only Joshua and Caleb went into the Promised Land. Numbers 26 verses 64 to 65.</u>*

7. Name three other people who received their miracle because they combined obedience with their faith. Give Scriptures. *<u>Gideon in Judges chapters 6 to 9; The Widow of Zarephath in 1 Kings chapter 17 verses 9 to 16; Naaman in 2 Kings chapter 6.</u>*

8. Complete the sentence. *Let us make a decision today to <u>trust</u> God and to <u>obey</u> Him.*

PART V

SHEPHERD LEADER WEEKEND ENCOUNTER

WEEKEND FIVE

ENCOUNTER SCHEDULE

- Introduction
- Session 1 – THE BIBLICAL SHEPHERD
- Session 2 – THE HEART OF A SHEPHERD
- Session 3 – THE PURPOSE OF A SHEPHERD
- Session 4 – DEVELOPING DEEP AND MEANINGFUL RELATIONSHIPS
- Session 5 – PRACTICAL KEYS
- Session 6 – PRACTICAL APPLICATION
- Session 7 - CONSECRATION

INTRODUCTION

Once you've led two or more people to Christ, you need to gather them for **teaching**, like Jesus did with His Disciples. By teaching our disciples the teachings of Jesus, we in effect **disciple** them. The most time-efficient way to disciple new Believers is in a **group**.

> *Acts 20:28 (NIV) "Keep watch over yourselves and all the flock of which the **Holy Spirit has made you overseers**. Be shepherds of the church of God, which he bought with his own blood."*

As this Scripture highlights, being **a shepherd,** or overseer of the flock of God, is an honourable appointment of the **Holy Spirit**. It is both a huge responsibility and an honour to be entrusted with the welfare of the lives of the children of God.

This weekend encounter will teach us the *how-to* care for our disciples and equip us with skills that will help us to do so with excellence.

Together, we will explore the following areas:

Session One: The Biblical Shepherd

What does the Biblical Shepherd look like? What is the Lord's desire for Shepherds?

Session Two: The heart of a Shepherd

We will look at How we can have a Shepherd's heart. We will look at the Biblical characteristics of a good Shepherd.

Session Three: The purpose of a Shepherd

In this session we will explore what God wants us to do with and for His Sheep.

Session Four: Developing deep and meaningful relationships

This session marks the beginning of a few practical sessions on the "How-to" of building life-long and purposeful relationships.

Session Five: Practical Keys

This session outlines practical and helpful steps to take to lead well, and to provide an atmosphere where people's lives can be transformed by the Power of God.

Session Six: Practical application

This session concludes extremely helpful guidelines on the processes at play in bringing people from various backgrounds together, to ultimately serve together to reach the lost for God.

Session Seven: Consecration Session

During this final session, we conclude, not just this weekend's equipping, but also the entire equipping series of Step Three - Developing Gifts and skills. It would seem appropriate that we take time to present ourselves before God as equipped workers to be sent out to go and to preach the gospel, to make disciples by teaching them and to care for them like Jesus would.

I pray that this Weekend will bring conclusion in your heart as to How you will serve the Father and the expansion of His Kingdom. I pray that it will serve as a huge blessing to you.

SESSION ONE: THE BIBLICAL SHEPHERD

This weekend is all about learning to be a **Good Shepherd**. I am most certain that most of you have at this point of your journey started sharing your faith, with positive outcomes.

This weekend we will answer the question that many of you might have:

"Now that I have led someone to the Lord, what do I do with them?"

During this weekend we will explore how to Shepherd those entrusted to our care. We will learn how to take care of the sheep entrusted to our care. Shepherds usually take care of their sheep in a **flock**. We will learn how to bring the flock together and how to help them become a fully functioning part of the Body of Christ.

In the Acts of the Apostles, we read a clear instruction to Shepherds, which we will attempt to address in a responsible manner throughout this weekend course.

> *Acts 20:28 (NIV) "Keep watch over **yourselves** and all the flock of which the Holy Spirit has made you overseers. Be shepherds of the church of God, which he bought with his own blood."*

We are offered such an amazing privilege to be entrusted with the care of those whom we have the privilege to lead to Christ. Over the following hours together, we will learn all about being a good Shepherd.

Let us start by looking at Shepherds in the Bible.

<u>Abel</u> was the first shepherd we read about in the Bible. The Bible says that: "**Abel kept flocks.**" He was taking care of his flocks.

> *Genesis 4:2 Later she gave birth to his brother Abel. Now **Abel kept flocks**, and Cain worked the soil.*

<u>Rachel</u> is the second Shepherd we read about in the Bible as she was tending the sheep of her father.

> *Genesis 29:9 While he was still talking with them, **Rachel came with her father's sheep, for she was a shepherd.***

Through Jacob's marriage to Rachel, He also became a shepherd who tended the sheep of his Father-in-law, at first, but later overseeing a huge livestock of several thousand.

> *Genesis 30:29-30 Jacob said to him, "You know how **I have worked for you and how your livestock has fared under my care**. The little you had before I came has increased greatly, and the Lord has blessed you wherever I have been. But now, when may I do something for my own household?"*

When Jacob was old, before giving up his spirit, he blessed Joseph, and here we see him referencing our Heavenly Father as His <u>Shepherd</u>. He learnt about God as being his Shepherd.

> *Genesis 48:15-16 Then he blessed Joseph and said, "May the God before whom my fathers Abraham and Isaac walked faithfully,*

the God who has been my <u>shepherd</u> all my life to this day, the Angel who has delivered me from all harm —may he bless these boys. May they be called by my name and the names of my fathers Abraham and Isaac, and may they increase greatly on the earth."

<u>Moses</u> was tending his Father-in-law's sheep when God called him to be His Servant to deliver Israel.

*Exodus 3:1 Now **Moses was tending the flock of Jethro his father-in-law**, the priest of Midian, and he led the flock to the far side of the wilderness and came to Horeb, the mountain of God.*

<u>David</u> was tending his Father's sheep when God called and anointed him to be the next King of Israel.

*1 Samuel 16:11 So he asked Jesse, "Are these all the sons you have?" "There is still the youngest," Jesse answered. **"He is tending the sheep**." Samuel said, "Send for him; we will not sit down until he arrives."*

David learnt to care for the sheep of his Father before the Lord used him to become the <u>shepherd</u> of His people, Israel. The Bible teaches that he cared for them with integrity of heart, and with great skill.

*Psalms 78:70-72 **He chose David his servant and took him from the sheep pens; from tending the sheep he brought him to be the shepherd of his people Jacob**, of Israel his inheritance. **And David shepherded them with integrity of heart; with skillful hands he led them.***

<u>Amos</u> was a shepherd before God called and anointed him to be a prophet to His people.

> *Amos 7:15 But **the Lord took me from tending the flock** and said to me, 'Go, prophesy to my people Israel.'*

In his great Psalm, David present us with the true heart of a **Shepherd**.

> *Psalm 23:1-6 The Lord is my shepherd, **I lack nothing**. He makes me lie down in green pastures, **he leads me** beside quiet waters, **he refreshes** my soul. **He guides me** along the right paths for his name's sake. Even though I walk through the darkest valley, I will fear no evil, for **you are with me**; your rod and your staff, they **comfort me**. **You prepare a table before me** in the presence of my enemies. **You anoint my head with oil**; my cup overflows. Surely your goodness and love will follow me all the days of my life, and I will dwell in the house of the Lord forever.*

David presents the Good Shepherd as a <u>**Provider**</u>, a Guide, a Protector, an Anointer, and an ever-present Presence through every circumstance of life.

<u>**Jesus**</u> presents Himself to us as the Good Shepherd.

> *John 10:11 "**I am the good shepherd**. The good shepherd lays down his life for the sheep."*

Many times, and through many of the Prophets, God spoke about raising up "<u>*a Shepherd*</u>" to save His people, to rescue them, and to take proper care of them. One of the most outstanding portions of Scripture, addressing the Biblical role and expectation of a Shepherd, is found in the Book of Ezekiel. God was looking for a Shepherd who will tend His Sheep with His Heart.

> *Ezekiel 34:15-16 "**I myself will tend my sheep** and have them lie down, declares the Sovereign Lord. I will search for the lost and bring back the strays. I will bind up the injured and strengthen*

> *the weak, but the sleek and the strong I will destroy. I will shepherd the flock with justice."*

Ezekiel 34:31
"You are my <u>sheep</u>, the sheep of my pasture, and I am your God, declares the Sovereign Lord."'

The Shepherd is that personification of someone who cares, even if it requires to lay down your own life for the sake of the safekeeping of the sheep. The Biblical Shepherd is that person who cares for God's people as if they belonged to them. Very few Shepherds actually care for their own sheep, they normally tend the sheep of others. For the purpose of our time together, God is calling each one of us to walk in the footsteps of Jesus, and to be a Good Shepherd like He is, and wants us to be.

In conclusion on our session on the Biblical Shepherd, let us take a moment to identify the key hallmarks of a biblical shepherd.

Assimilation Application

Group breakout session:

What are the key Hallmarks of a Biblical Shepherd?

Identify Five Good characteristics of a shepherd from Ezekiel 34:1-16.

- 1.
- 2.
- 3.
- 4.
- 5.

Identify Five good characteristics of a good shepherd from John 10:1-18.

- 1.
- 2.
- 3.
- 4.
- 5.

Identify five bad characteristics of bad shepherds from Ezekiel 34:1-16.

- 1.
- 2.
- 3.
- 4.
- 5.

Identify five bad characteristics of bad shepherds from John 10:1-18.

- 1.
- 2.
- 3.
- 4.
- 5.

Which other Scriptures really spoke to you of being a good Shepherd, and what specifically do you aspire to take home with you from that Scripture?

SESSION TWO: THE HEART OF A SHEPHERD

In this session we will look at what the <u>heart</u> attitude of a Biblical Shepherd looks like. The Word of God teaches us about this heart attitude in a number of Scriptures. Let us look at these for a few moments.

In this session we will look at the heart of a Shepherd, and then also what it is not. Shepherds are those people who take care of the welfare of other believers, by leading them, guiding them, caring and protecting them.

Shepherds have a Self-sacrificing heart

Almost every Shepherd works in the care of someone else. They care for someone else's sheep. The first heart attitude for us to adopt is that of a self-sacrificing <u>servant</u>. We are entrusted with taking care of God's sheep. Christ purchased the sheep that we care for with his own blood.

> Ezekiel 34:31 *<u>You</u> are my sheep, the sheep of my <u>pasture</u>, and I am your God, declares the Sovereign Lord.'"*

Psalms 100:3 Know that the Lord is God. It is he who made us, and we are his; we are his people, the sheep of his pasture.

Revelation chapter 5 present us with "**the Lamb**" who purchased men from '**every tongue, tribe and nation**' for our God. He became the Lamb of God to purchase the precious lives of those who would become sheep of His pasture, under the care of the Great Shepherd. Jesus became our example of the perfect Shepherd who <u>lay</u> down His life for the life of the sheep.

John 10:11 "I am the good shepherd. The good shepherd lays down his life for the sheep."

The Shepherd lives for the welfare of the sheep of God. One of the hallmarks of a Follower of Jesus Christ is that he lays down his life for the sake of Christ. This is one of the requirements Jesus laid down for His Followers.

Luke 9:23 Then he said to them all: "If anyone would come after me, he must <u>deny</u> himself and take up his cross daily and follow me."

*1 Corinthians 4:15 Even though you have ten thousand guardians in Christ, **you do not have many fathers**, for **in Christ Jesus I became your father** through the gospel.*

Every Shepherd lays down his life for the sheep entrusted to his care. One way of looking at it is like having and caring for your own children. Who of us, as parents, won't do anything we can for the welfare of our children? We do whatever it takes to care for our children. Being a Shepherd is like being a spiritual father or mother who have been entrusted with the care of spiritual children.

To assume responsibility for those whom Jesus paid a high price for their salvation, requires of us to lay down our lives for the welfare of the sheep. Being a Shepherd is a selfless, self-sacrificing vocation.

Shepherds have a Willing heart

God is calling on us to be His Shepherds, not because we must, "**But because we are willing**." Our eagerness to serve is no better expressed than by our willingness to serve the Will of the Father by caring for His Sheep whom He purchased with His blood and sacrifice. One aspect of this is to commit oneself to be an example for others to follow.

> 1 Peter 5:2-4 Be shepherds of God's flock that is under your care, watching over them—not because you must, but **because you are willing**, as God wants you to be; not pursuing dishonest gain, but **eager to serve**; 3 not lording it over those entrusted to you, but **being examples to the flock**. 4 And when the Chief Shepherd appears, you will receive the crown of glory that will never fade away.

We also see from this Scripture in 1 Peter, the extension of this idea of it being the Will of God to take care of the sheep and to watch over their welfare and well-being. It is God's Will that we take care of His Sheep. God wants and desires us to take care of His Sheep. Our "willingness" to serve the Father, in caring for His Sheep, shows the true heart with which we serve Him. May God find in each one of us a "willingness" to care for His Sheep like He would if He was doing it Himself.

Shepherds have a Caring heart

God is calling us to take **care** of ourselves and over all the flock He placed under our care. To take care requires both to protect and to provide for the sheep what they need most.

There is this saying:

> "*People don't care how much you know until they know how much you care.*"

Once people know that you love them, warts and all, they feel loved and cared for. One other hallmark of Believers is their love for one another.

> John 13:34-35 *"A new command I give you: Love one another. As I have loved you, so you must love one another. 35 By this all men will know that you are my disciples, if you love one another."*

For us as under-shepherds it is to provide **protection** from all evil and worldliness, as well as **leading** them to green pastures where they will find rest and restoration of their souls. The greatest care we could provide is constantly leading those entrusted to our care, to the Word of God and reliant submissions of prayer. By constantly praying with them and submitting everything through prayer unto God, and exploring and sharing the Word of God together, we actively care for their spiritual wellbeing.

This exhortation is carefully explained in the first letter of Peter, as well as the well-known Psalms 23.

> *1 Peter 5:2-4* **Be shepherds of God's flock that is under your care, watching over them**—*not because you must, but because you are willing, as God wants you to be; not pursuing dishonest gain, but eager to serve; 3 not lording it over those entrusted to you, but being examples to the flock. 4 And when the Chief Shepherd appears, you will receive the crown of glory that will never fade away.*

> *Psalms 23:2-3 He makes me lie down in green pastures, he leads me beside quiet waters, he refreshes my soul. He guides me along the right paths for his name's sake.*

In the words of the Prophet Ezekiel it is extended in greater detail. The Lord spoke through Ezekiel and expressed His dismay that the Shepherds of Israel only took care of themselves and not of the flock over which He assigned them. Shepherds should take care of the flock, and not only for what they may benefit from them.

> Ezekiel 34:2 *"Son of man, prophesy against the shepherds of Israel; prophesy and say to them: 'This is what the Sovereign Lord says:* **Woe to you shepherds of Israel who only take care of yourselves! Should not shepherds take care of the flock?**

The Lord continues throughout this entire chapter to outline what that care looks like.

Caring requires us to:

- *strengthen the <u>weak</u>,*
- *<u>heal</u> the sick,*
- *<u>bind</u> up the injured,*
- *search for the <u>lost</u>, and to*
- *Bring back those who have <u>strayed</u> away from God.*

To this end, each one of us, as followers of Jesus Christ, have been called to strengthen the weak, heal the sick, bind up the injured, search for the lost, and to bring back to Him those who have strayed away from their faith in Him.

> Ezekiel 34:4 *You have not strengthened the weak or healed the sick or bound up the injured. You have not brought back the strays or searched for the lost. You have ruled them harshly and brutally.*

Every shepherd is like a parent over their own children. One of the ways we care and protect them is by never exposing the weaknesses of our children to others. When we get close to people, we get close to their weaknesses and failures. Sheep smell. When we get close to our sheep we deal with where they are at with compassion.

Frequently we read about God's concern and care for his people when he refers to them being *"sheep without a shepherd."* May we care in such a way that the Lord knows that there exists a compassionately caring shepherd in their lives.

Shepherds knows the heart of their sheep

One of the key essentials of being a good shepherd is that you **know** your sheep. It is essential that we know our sheep by **name** and that they know our **voice**. Know the condition of their lives and that of their family situation.

> *John 10:3 The watchman opens the gate for him, and the sheep listen to his voice.* **He calls his own sheep by name** *and leads them out.*

> *John 10:14 "I am the good shepherd;* **I know my sheep** *and my sheep know me–*

The heart of a shepherd is seen in how he relates with the sheep. How we talk about those entrusted to our care, tells of our intimate knowledge of their wellbeing and condition.

We are Good Shepherds when *we protect them, watch over them* and constantly *watch over their growth, condition and development*. Whenever we observe areas of need or diversions, we address those in a private and caring manner.

Sheep quickly know that you've got their best interest at heart and that you know them better than they know themselves. This intimate knowledge is not for lording it over them or for being busy bodies into their private affairs, but we observe enough, *through prayer and travailing*, that we can help and guide them, and *ultimate care for them effectively*.

We will often find that *the Holy Spirit will* **enlighten** *us to areas of growth and activation* in our disciples' lives, but He will also *forewarn us* of encroaching and encumbering situations that might hinder the growth and development in their lives. As Good Shepherds we keep a careful watch over our disciples, as to How we may best care, protect and guide them in their walk with the Lord.

Shepherds are Committed to lead

Shepherds **lead** the sheep. Shepherds do not drive the sheep. In Psalm 23 we read about how the Good Shepherd *"leads"* his sheep to green pastures and still waters.

- We lead by our **example**.
- We lead by modelling Christ through our behavior, **actions** and words.
- We lead by seeing and **knowing** where they need to go.

True shepherds are those who **constantly look ahead** and know where they are leading towards, and carefully take every precaution to ensure that they lead all the sheep towards that place.

> *Psalms 23:2 2 He makes me lie down in green pastures,* **he leads me** *beside quiet waters, 3 he restores my soul.* **He guides me** *in paths of righteousness for his name's sake.*

> *John 10:3-4 3 The watchman opens the gate for him, and the sheep listen to his voice. He calls his own sheep by name and* **leads them out.** *4 When he has brought out all his own,* **he goes on ahead of them,** *and his sheep follow him because they know his voice.*

Shepherds leads people by going **ahead** of them. The hireling tells people where they need to go whereas the Shepherd shows the people where he is leading them towards.

The heart with which we lead is observed in the commitment we make to being an example that they can follow.

Assimilation Application

David was known for being a man *"after God's own heart."* I pray that God will find in each one of us, a man or a woman, after His own heart.

> Jeremiah 3:15 (NIV) 15 Then *I will give you shepherds after my own heart*, who will lead you with knowledge and understanding.

> Acts 13:22 (NIV) 22 After removing Saul, he made David their king. God testified concerning him: 'I have found David son of Jesse, *a man after my own heart*; he will do everything I want him to do.'

Let us take a moment and commit ourselves to being good Shepherds. May God find in us people who have a heart after Him, and a heart for His work and for His people. May our actions show the heart we have for Him and for His Sheep. I almost want us to pray the words of David, when He asked God to create in him "a new heart."

> Psalms 51:10 (NIV) 10 Create in me a pure heart, O God, and renew a steadfast spirit within me.

I pray that God will create in us *"a pure heart"* so that we will serve His Sheep with integrity of heart, with sincerity to see the best God has for them accomplished. I pray that God will remove the heart of stone and give us a heart of flesh so that we can serve with love, care, forbearance, understanding, and compassion.

> Ezekiel 11:19 (NIV) 19 *I will give them an undivided heart* and put a new spirit in them; I will remove from them their *heart of stone* and *give them a heart of flesh*.

> Ezekiel 36:26 (NIV) 26 I will give you a new heart and put a

new spirit in you; I will remove from you your heart of stone and give you a heart of flesh.

As an expression of this desire to have a heart after God, let us articulate our commitment to Him in prayer. Take a few moments in quiet prayer and meditation and make these commitments to God (*Give about 10 minutes for this prayerful conclusion of this session*):

- *Lord, I lay down my life for the sheep You entrusted to me, and*
- *I commit to be a willing servant eager to do all that is required of me as an under-shepherd, and*
- *I commit to care for the sheep as if it is You Yourself caring for Your sheep, and*
- *I commit to know the sheep intimately, and*
- *To lead them, by example, to wherever You desire them to go and grow.*
- *Today I declare my eagerness, willingness and desire to strengthen the weak, heal the sick, bind up the wounded, seek the lost and search with eagerness those who have strayed from their faith in You Lord Jesus. Amen!*

May our heart tell of the love we have for God, His work, and His people.

Have a heart for God, His work and His Sheep!

SESSION THREE: THE PURPOSE OF A SHEPHERD

The purpose of a Shepherd is to **care** for the sheep by **protecting** and **providing** for them.

"We all have a need and a desire to be loved and to be cared for."

As we've discussed and seen so far, it is both God's desire to care for His sheep, as well as to Shepherd His sheep through His Servants. We are His Servants when we avail ourselves to love and care for others, on His behalf.

Many times, we see young people showing great interest in children. This is wonderful, however, the depth of this love and care for children is only truly observed when they have their own children, when the reality of commitment, care and devotion truly come into play. It is fairly easy to love God's children from afar, especially if you don't assume responsibility for their well-being, development and growth. For us, as Shepherds of God's Sheep, **it requires a whole other level of commitment** and **devotion**.

In this session we will explore **the best ways** in which we can take up our responsibility to care and provide for those entrusted to our care.

The best way to Disciple someone is to step up into the role of being a **Shepherd** for them. The greatest expression of making a Disciple is seen in those who shepherd people on Christ's behalf. Our eagerness to serve the Lord is seen by the way in which we seek to save the lost and those who have gone astray, and to then follow through by taking care of them.

Jesus called us to "*go and make disciples of all nations*" and that includes "*baptizing and teaching*" them. The '*teaching*' part is the most comprehensive and engaging part and requires the greatest level of **commitment** and endurance.

> Matthew 28:19 "Therefore, **go and make disciples** of all nations, **baptizing them** in the name of the Father and of the Son and of the Holy Spirit, 20 and **teaching them** to obey everything I have commanded you. And surely, I am with you always, to the very end of the age."

To be a Shepherd requires skills

To serve as a Shepherd to those God entrusted to our care is a noble call and task and requires **skills** beyond our willingness to answering such a call. The skills required are varied, however if we keep at the forefront of our minds who we do this for, and the joy of knowing the eternal impact in the lives of those entrusted to our care, it will move us to apply ourselves with diligence and to continually give our best.

Shepherds provide a caring environment within which they will practice protection and provision.

To develop a **caring** environment, we need to develop an "one another," edifying and encouraging, kind of deep relationship between the group members.

> 1 Thessalonians 5:11 Therefore **encourage** one another and **build each other up**, just as in fact you are doing.

How do we encourage and build each other up?

- We **affirm** one another continually, especially in those areas where we observe growth and development in our faith.
- We speak the **truth** in love, even when it requires confrontation.
- We **spur** each other on towards love and good deeds.
- We pray for each other and **share** words of encouragement to one another.
- We **carry** each other's burdens.
- We love one another by actively **practicing** felt ways to give expression of our love.

Encouragement takes place when we unconditionally love one another. Edification takes place when people have a deep sense of feeling that they are being heard, understood and then, as a result of this feeling of *"being heard,"* they open up to accept and receive, through words of **affirmation**, forgiveness, grace, mercy and clear encouragement for the pathway ahead.

In a later session we will look specifically on how to effectively lead our disciples into edifying and encouraging each other. Suffice to say that we ought to love each other as we love God. Loving in ways that is both intentional and felt is the goal. This is how we are known to be His Disciples – by the way we love one another.

Shepherd not only provide an environment where disciples can edify one another, they also provide a **place** where they can help their disciples to grow.

Shepherds protect and provide for the sheep.

We protect by keeping the sheep together, and by keeping them from wondering away, straying and endangering themselves. We protect them against **false** doctrines, **worldly** mindsets and destructive relationships and environments.

Shepherds protect their sheep by prayerfully watching over them.

> *1 Peter 5:2* ***Be shepherds of God's flock that is under your care, watching over them****—not because you must, but because you are willing, as God wants you to be; not pursuing dishonest gain, but eager to serve;*

The awareness of **watching** starts with us keeping watch over our own walk and stand in the Lord continually. One of the men of God who helped the Church understand "watching" is Watchman Nee, a Chinese evangelist. He said;

> *"We must not only be watchful in keeping the time of prayer but also be watchful during the prayer time so that we may really be effective in prayer."*

Definition of Watching

> "Watching is anticipative spiritual awareness or **alertness** concerning things that are happening around us."

"Alertness" is defined as ***"the ability to anticipate right responses to that which is taking place around us."***

This alertness is especially observed through prayer. It is while we pray for, and over, our disciples, that we respond to those things that come to our mind by the Holy Spirit, which then may prompt us to pray more intentionally and thoroughly for things. We respond to the impulse or promptings of the Holy Spirit in prayer.

Jesus modelled watching

On one occasion Jesus modelled this *"**watching**"* and *"**Alertness**"* when He told Peter that; *"**Satan wanted to sift him, but He prayed for him.**"*

> Luke 22:31-32 (NIV) 31 "Simon, Simon, **Satan has asked to sift all of you** as wheat. 32 **But I have <u>prayed</u> for you, Simon, that your faith may not fail.** And when you have turned back, strengthen your brothers."

Peter's life was spared as a direct result of Jesus' awareness and alertness in prayer as He watched over those entrusted to His care.

The Holy Spirit is amazing. He always helps us and guides us when we keep our disciples in our prayers. He always teaches us and directs us. The more we live in step with the Holy Spirit, the more we will find ourselves alert and aware of things around us, and in the lives of those entrusted to our care. The Holy Spirit will reveal to us things that might happen, good or bad. The Holy Spirit might make us aware of things He is busy working out in our disciple's lives. The more we spend time being aware and spiritually alert, the more we will find ourselves at the crest of the wave in what the Lord is busy doing in and around our lives. This alertness helps us work more efficiently for God.

"Watching" might be more fully defined as,

- Keeping spiritually awake in order to <u>**guard**</u>.
- To observe closely.
- To be on the <u>**alert**</u>.

Spiritual alertness is vital to effective shepherding of those entrusted to our care. Such alertness includes our ability to anticipate or comprehend what is taking place around us.

To *"anticipate"* means *"to act in advance as to prevent."* Watching is <u>**prayerful**</u> shepherding.

How do we watch over our sheep?

- We keep watch when we constantly <u>**pray**</u> over those entrusted to our care.
- We keep watch over them when we <u>**ask**</u> God to show us

His greater purpose for each one of them. As we speak the purpose of God into their lives, we keep watch over them to ensure that they walk and develop in accordance with the purpose God has for each one of them.
- We keep watch when we **observe** their lives and prayerfully consider what guidance, teaching, instruction, or help they might need that will help them become more like Christ.

Shepherds protect their sheep by keeping them together.

As Biblical Shepherds we bring and keep our sheep together so that we can better protect them. Jesus spoke about the shepherd going in through the gate to tend his sheep. That speaks of having them together. Jesus modelled this kind of shepherding by discipling his disciples in a **group**. The Shepherd has two pieces of equipment with which to shepherd his sheep: *a Rod and a Staff.* **The Rod** was used for **protecting** them from dangerous animals, as well as for **discipline**, and **the Staff** was used to **keep the straying** sheep together as a flock, as well as **guiding them**.

> *Psalms 23:4 (Amplified) Yes, though I walk through the [deep, sunless] valley of the shadow of death, I will fear or dread no evil, for You are with me;* ***Your rod [to protect]*** *and* ***Your staff [to guide], they comfort me.***

In His rebuke of the Shepherds of Israel, one of the chief concerns was that the Shepherds allowed the sheep to scatter without **keeping them gathered**. As Shepherds we need to remain with our sheep to look after them.

> *Ezekiel 34:11-13 "For this is what the Sovereign Lord says: 'I myself will search for my sheep and look after them. 12 As* ***a shepherd looks*** *after his scattered flock when he is with them, so will I look after my sheep. I will rescue them from all the places*

*where they were scattered on a day of clouds and darkness. 13 **I will bring them out from the nations and gather them** from the countries, and I will bring them into their own land. I will pasture them on the mountains of Israel, in the ravines and in all the settlements in the land.'"*

We look after our disciples by keeping them in fellowship together. Jesus discipled His Disciples by gathering them and teaching them in a group. In one sense he kept His sheep together to such an extent that at the end of His earthly ministry He declared that He "*protected them and kept them safe*," and that He "*lost none*" of those given Him.

*John 17:12 While I was with them, **I protected them and kept them safe** by that name you gave me. **None has been lost** except the one doomed to destruction so that Scripture would be fulfilled.*

How do we keep our Disciples together?

- We bring them **together** regularly for times of ministering to them as a group.
- We stay in contact with our disciples on **daily** basis by phoning them, sharing meals together, visiting them, or by meeting for coffee at some cafe.
- We keep our disciples in the forefront of our hearts and minds by **praying** for our disciples on a daily basis.
- We meet together as a group so that we can **teach** them together.
- When we bring them together, we allow for equally fair times of **sharing**.
- We take time to **worship** together.
- We practice the **WWM's** during our time together.

Shepherds protect their sheep by harnessing them with the Truths of God's Word.

We protect them by teaching them the **truths** of God's Word in a systematic and structured way. We protect them by ensuring that they feed and live by the Word of God, and not by the sensory impulses of the world. The antidote for false teachings is to form a hedge of protection around our disciples by bringing them **sound** doctrine and teaching. Sound doctrine and teaching harnesses our sheep from wolves.

> *2 Timothy 3:14 But as for you, continue in what you have learned and have become convinced of, because you know those from whom you learned it, 15 and how from infancy you have known* **the Holy Scriptures, which are able to make you wise for salvation through faith in Christ Jesus. 16 All Scripture is God-breathed and is useful for teaching, rebuking, correcting and training in righteousness, 17 so that the servant of God may be thoroughly equipped** *for every good work.*

A large portion of Titus chapter 2 is devoted on what he needed to teach the flock. He instructs Titus to teach sound doctrine to the old and young men, the woman, the slaves and the children.

> *Titus 2:1 You, however, must teach what is appropriate to* **sound** *doctrine.*

> *Titus 2:11-14 "For the grace of God has appeared that offers salvation to all people.* **It teaches us to say "No" to ungodliness and worldly passions, and to live self-controlled, upright and godly lives** *in this present age, while we wait for the blessed hope—the appearing of the glory of our great God and Savior, Jesus Christ, who gave himself for us, to* **redeem us from all wickedness and to purify for himself a people that are his very own, eager to do what is good"**

> *Titus 2:15 **These, then, are the things you should teach**. Encourage and rebuke with all authority. Do not let anyone despise you.*

We protect our sheep by teaching the truths of God's Word in a systematic and sound way.

How do we teach them?

- We teach them by ensuring that they live on the Word of God on a **daily** basis.
- **We teach** them that the Word of God is the **Foundation** and **Handbook** that relates to **every part of our lives.**
- **We teach** them How to **apply** the Word of God.
- **We equip** them by **practicing** the Equipping Model.
- We teach them by helping and providing a **shared learning experience** by being more facilitating than telling, especially as they mature in their walk with God.

Shepherds provide an example for their disciples to follow.

We provide for our Disciples by providing them with **an example to follow.** We provide them a safe learning atmosphere where they can learn the Word of God, appreciate the Voice of the Holy Spirit, and grow in their faith. Nothing prepares us for life like the Word of God.

The greatest legacy anyone can leave is **their example.** Maybe in your life it might be your Mom or your Dad, or your Pastor who is that model or example that you follow. For each Believer we have this instruction to be good examples.

> *Titus 2:7-8 In everything **set them an example** by doing what is good. In your teaching show integrity, seriousness and soundness of speech that cannot be condemned, so that those who oppose you may be ashamed because they have nothing bad to say about us.*

> *1 Timothy 4:12 Don't let anyone look down on you because you are young, but **set an <u>example</u> for the believers** in speech, in conduct, in love, in faith and in purity.*

> *1 Peter 5:2-4 **Be shepherds of God's flock that is under your care, watching over them**—not because you must, but because you are willing, as God wants you to be; not pursuing dishonest gain, but eager to serve; 3 not lording it over those entrusted to you, but **being <u>examples</u> to the flock**. 4 And when the Chief Shepherd appears, you will receive the crown of glory that will never fade away.*

We provide for our Disciples by giving them **a living example** to follow. Jesus called us to follow in His Footsteps. The Apostle Paul became an example to the Believers and urged them to follow his example. We ought to provide our disciples with an example to follow, otherwise we subscribe to the rule of the pharisees who instructed people to comply to rules and regulations which they themselves did not practiced in their own lives. This instruction came right from the top. **Jesus** told His Disciples that **He gave them an example to follow**, and insisted that they follow His example. By all accounts of what we read in the New Testament, they followed the example Jesus set for them.

> *John 13:15 **I have set you an <u>example</u>** that you should do as I have done for you.*

The Apostle Paul followed this same approach in his ministry by appealing to his disciples to follow his example in the same way as what he was following the example set by Jesus.

> *1 Corinthians 11:1 **Follow my example**, as I follow **the example of Christ**.*
> *Ephesians 5:1 **Follow God's example**, therefore, as dearly loved children*

The Apostle Peter echoed this approach, both in exhorting Believers to follow Christ' example by following in His footsteps, and by exhorting us, as His under-Shepherds, to *"be examples."*

> *1 Peter 2:21 To this you were **called**, because **Christ suffered for you, leaving you an example, that you should follow in his steps.***

Make a commitment in your life to be an example that others can follow.

Shepherds lead and guide their sheep.

Another way in which we provide for the flock entrusted to our care and watch is that **we <u>lead</u> them** to *"green pastures and still waters"* and a place where their souls can be refreshed.

> *Psalms 23:2-3 He makes me lie down in green pastures, **he leads me** beside quiet waters, he refreshes my soul. **He guides me** along the right paths for his name's sake.*

Every opportunity we have to open the Word of God, read it together, hear what the Holy Spirit is saying to us, and how we may apply it to our lives, provide us with an opportunity to effectively care, protect and provide for our sheep. The Word restores us, refreshes us, guides us, leads us, and ultimately directs us.

> *Psalms 1:2-3 but whose delight is in the law of the Lord, and who meditates on his law, day and night. **That person is like a tree planted by streams of water**, which yields its fruit in season and whose leaf does not wither—whatever they do prospers.*

As Shepherds we lead our disciples to the green pastures of the Word, the green pastures of encounters in the Holy Spirit, and green pastures of building each other up through the gifts and power of the

Holy Spirit. Nothing refreshes us like time spent in the Presence of God.

Conclusion

This session would not be concluded without us making a conscious decision to commit being such a purposeful Shepherd.

We explored together:

The Shepherd provides a caring environment within which they can practice protection and provision. We learned How best we may encourage and build each other up within the walls of this protected environment.

We also looked at How **Shepherds prayerfully protect their sheep by watching over them.** We protect and keep them by being spiritually alert and watchful in prayer. We also protect them by keeping them together as well as teaching them sound doctrine.

We looked at **providing our Disciples with an example to follow**, and finally at **committing to lead and guide** them along right paths and to places where their soul's would be refreshed.

> *"I pray that you will make a commitment to be that shepherd to provide such an example that others can follow. I pray that God will help us to keep and protect those entrusted to our care, "That none should perish." I also pray that we will have open hearts and minds to be spiritually alert and aware as to know what the Lord might be doing in our disciple's lives, to enable us to lead, guide, and protect them more efficiently. May God bless you in your pursuit of being the Best Shepherd you could ever be with the help of the precious Holy Spirit. Amen"*

Session Three: The purpose of a Shepherd | 283

Assimilation Sheet for
The Purpose of a Shepherd

1. Complete the sentence. *The purpose of a Shepherd is to **care** for the sheep by **protecting** and **providing** for them.*

2. Complete the sentence. *The best way to Disciple someone is to step up into the role of being a **Shepherd** for them.*

3. Complete the sentence. *The **'teaching'** part is the most comprehensive and engaging part and requires the greatest level of **commitment** and endurance.*

4. Which Scripture particularly encourages us to provide a caring environment. *1 Thessalonians 5 verse 11.*

5. Name two ways in which we can encourage and build one another up. *We **affirm** one another continually, especially in those areas where we observe growth and development in our faith. We speak the **truth** in love, even when it requires confrontation. We **spur** each other on towards love and good deeds. We pray for each other and **share** words of encouragement to one another. We **carry** each other's burdens. We love one another by actively **practicing** felt ways to give expression of our love.*

6. Complete the sentence. *We protect them against **false** doctrines, **worldly** mindsets and destructive relationships and environments.*

7. What is the most efficient way to keeping watch over our disciples? Give a Scriptural reference from the life of Christ. *By praying for them like Jesus prayed for Simon Peter in Luke 22 verses 31-32.*

8. Complete the sentence. Watching is ***prayerful*** shepherding.

9. Shepherds protect their sheep. Which two pieces of equipment do they use and what is the purpose of each one of them? *The Shepherd has two pieces of equipment with which to shepherd his sheep: **a Rod and a Staff**. The Rod was used for **protecting** them from dangerous animals, as well as for **discipline**, and the Staff was used to **keep the straying** sheep together as a flock, as well as **guiding them**.*

10. Jesus made three claims in His prayer in John 17 verse 12 What was His three claims? *He claimed that He "**protected them and kept them safe**," and that He "**lost none**" of those given Him.*

11. Give three Scriptures that exhorts us to protect our disciples by

teaching them sound doctrine. *Titus 2 verse 15, Titus 2 verses 11 to 14, Titus 2 verse 1, 2 Timothy 3:14.*

12. The greatest legacy anyone can leave is their example. Provide some Scriptural support for this statement. *Titus 2 verses 7-8, 1 Timothy 4 verse 12, 1 Peter 5 verses 2-4, John 13 verse 15, 1 Corinthians 11 verse 1, Ephesians 5 verse 1 and 1 Peter 2 verse 21.*

13. What purpose does the Good Shepherd have in Psalms 23 verse 2-3? *He leads and he guides.*

SESSION FOUR: DEVELOPING DEEP AND MEANINGFUL RELATIONSHIPS

The most effective part of Shepherding is *providing a place where people's lives could be <u>transformed</u>, renewed, encouraged, and built up.*

This session is about **How to develop deep and meaningful <u>relationships</u>** that will last the test of time. To enable us **to effectively disciple our disciples**, we, in the **first place**, need to be **fully <u>committed</u> to shepherd and care** for those entrusted to our care, and secondly, purpose-fully <u>develop</u> deep and meaningful relationships within which, **thirdly**, **true transformation** can take place, as well as where, **fourthly**, our disciples can ultimately **serve the purpose God** has for their lives.

Developing deep and meaningful relationships

We develop deep and meaningful relationships along a known pathway. **Understanding how to** responsibly pace oneself in **developing deep and meaningful relationships** will **help you to impact others** more **effectively.**

The ebb and flow of how we develop purposeful relationship requires "**know how**" as well as <u>**prayerful**</u> **diligence.**

If you go deep too quickly you might find yourself at a **vulnerability beyond the depth of the relationship**, and that will unnecessarily expose you to getting hurt.

May your ministry in the Spirit and accompanied systematic equipping, form the solid base timeline along which you will pursue the development of lifelong relationships. To help us, let us look at a few key principles to helps us in our understanding.

JOHARI WINDOW

The Johari window is an **imaginary tool** we use to think about relationships. The **JOHARI** Window consist of **four quadrants**; each representing a different aspect and **dimension of how we are perceived** and **what people know about us**, and **what we know about ourselves**, and **how we relate to others.**

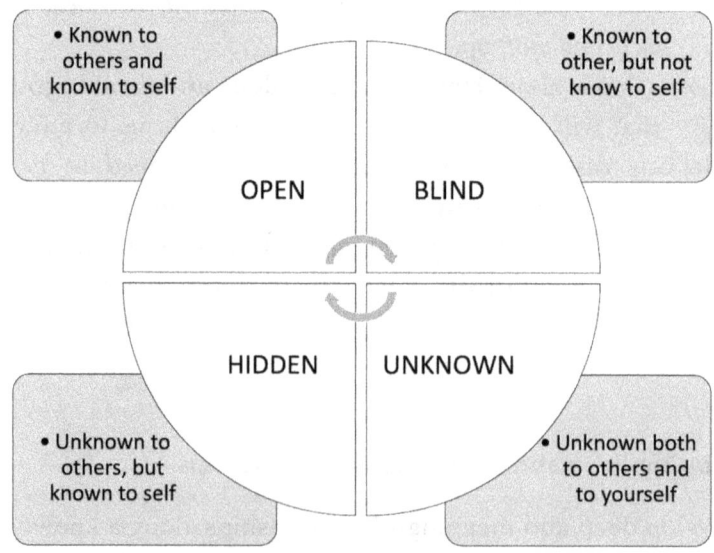

Johari Window Graphic

The JOHARI WINDOW brings to us an awareness that not everything we know about ourselves is known to others, but also, that others see and know things about us that we are not necessarily aware of.

There are four aspects to consider when developing self-awareness, both for ourselves and within those we are leading: the first is the **OPEN** area, then there is an area that is **HIDDEN** (undisclosed) by ourselves yet unknown to others, the third area represents what might be seen and known to others yet unknown to us, to which we are totally **BLIND** to, and finally there is an undiscovered and **UNKNOWN** area, within each one of us, not known to either ourselves, or others.

Let us explore them individually.

The OPEN dimension

The **OPEN dimension** to our lives represents that aspect of our lives that is <u>known</u> to both ourselves and by others. This could be **our Name**, the **colour of our eyes**, the **place we live in**, the **language** we speak, the **relationships** we have, our **education**, and our **beliefs**. Generally these are the things we choose to share with others, to varying degrees, as we will see later. This represents things that we are comfortable to share, or that might be known about us that is also known to others.

The HIDDEN dimension

The **HIDDEN dimension** represents that side of us where **we know things about ourselves** that is <u>hidden</u> **from the knowledge of others**. People might know you as an English-speaking person and assume that you are English, not knowing that you are actually a German-born Swede. Others might know you as a Brunette when in fact you are a blond. Other hidden things might represent your **belief-system, practices, habits, hobbies, education, heritage** or **preferences**. These might be **known to you** but **hidden from the sight or knowledge of others.**

The BLIND dimension

The BLIND dimension represents that side of our lives that **others see and know about us** that we are completely blind to. Others see and observe things in us, or about us which is <u>unknown</u> **to us**. They see behavioural patterns, attitudes and ways that might be apprehensible, yet we might be blind to the fact that we are behaving in unbecoming ways.

Before we were "*Born Again*" we spoke like the world, behaved and acted like the world, blinded to the fact that our sins blinded us from seeing how far away from God we've been and how apprehensible our conduct has been. Once we open ourselves to Jesus Christ, the blindfolds are removed, and we become aware of our sins and shortcomings.

There are areas or aspects of our lives, that we need to be open to, that others observe in and about us, to which we are currently blind to. Our journey with others should always bring within us *an awareness that the world does not only exist as we see or understand it*, and to *be open to learn and understand things better*, both about ourselves and about others. This aptitude will help us, and others, to grow together and develop deeper and more meaningful relationships.

UNKNOWN dimension

The UNKNOWN dimension represents *that part of our lives* to which *we have never woken up to* or *become aware of*, or discovered, *but the same is true for others* who come into a relationship with us. *The UNKNOWN dimension is unchartered and <u>undiscovered</u> territory for others as well as for us.*

The OBJECTIVE of understanding the Johari Window

The objective of understanding the **JOHARI** window is to *help us understand* the dynamics that is involved when we *lead people to self-discovery, openness, vulnerability and ultimate transformation*. This helps us understand that people might be *open in some areas* but *intentionally close in other areas.* Our journey into developing deep and meaningful, God-honouring relationships, will pursue ways in which we will **work on making the OPEN dimension larger** and the other areas smaller and smaller.

No deep relationship is possible if we do not open ourselves up to others, and at the same time allow others to help us become aware of possibilities to which we have been closed to before.

As Shepherds, we desire to help our disciples to become more like Jesus. We desire for them to open themselves up to the dream God has for them. We want to see people transformed by the power of the Holy Spirit. We desire to see them grow and develop and operate in ways that they never dreamt of. **We desire to see the Purposeful, Destined for Greatness Person discovered** and **unlocked**, and this require prayer, skill and intentional focus on the end goal.

Five levels of deepening relationships.

Another help in developing deep relationships is to have an understanding of the *Five levels of deepening relationships.* Let us explore the different levels of communicating. *The purpose is to help us learn* to understand *the pathway along which sound depths of relationships are developed*. This will both help us in understanding how to develop deeper relationships with our disciples along a responsible pathway, as well as to guide our disciples, through the various stages of developing the group, and their inter-relationships with each other, to do so in a responsible way.

If people disclose of themselves too quickly, they **make themselves vulnerable** beyond the level of relationship they've developed. This is dangerous and might lead to people exiting the group unnecessarily since they become uncomfortable with their premature disclosure. Disclosure is good, but only at a time when it is warranted and where the atmosphere for transformation is right. Let us look at the five levels:

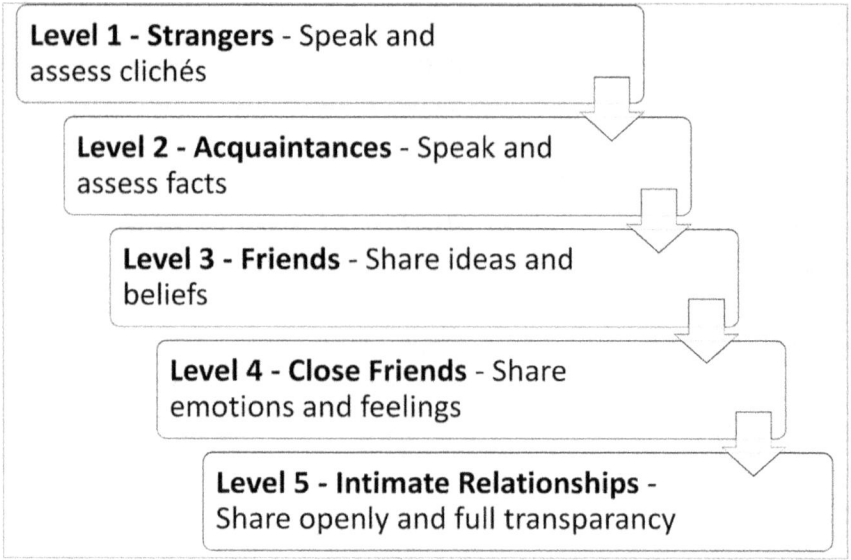

Diagram: Five levels of deepening relationships

Strangers – Speak clichés.

In the beginning of every relationship our conversations are based on *clichés*. We hardly say anything meaningful except what is common knowledge. For example, *"It's hot,"* or *"the bus is full."*

Acquaintances – Speak facts.

Once *we become acquainted* with people, the more *we speak verifiable facts*, in order that the relationship will develop. If facts do not stack up, the relationship will remain courteous but will never go deeper. Since **trust is one of the key essential ingredients** to good long-lasting relationship, it is imperative that you **ensure that what you communicate is true and factual.** Before people like or even love you for who you are, without knowing it, they assess you based on your words: *what you say, how you say it and the confidence with which you speak.* **If people trust the facts you share, they most certainly will seek to keep and develop the relationship.**

Friends – Ideas and beliefs.

Once people go *from acquaintances to become known on a first name basis* and *mutual engagement is pursued,* **the sharing of <u>ideas</u> and <u>beliefs</u> will be entertained.** If people **trust the facts you share**, they are **more likely to embrace the thought patterns of your ideas and beliefs.** This progressive sharing and entertaining of ideas and beliefs almost always predicates transformational and deeper relationships.

The potential to impact people's lives become greater at this point. The opportunity to lead people to transformation becomes greater at this point. *It requires*, beyond the sharing of your ideas and beliefs, *an intentional pursuit* of *"knowing the friend"* to ultimately equip them into their God purpose. Building purposeful relationships is of paramount importance if we desire to see lives <u>*changed*</u> and <u>*transformed*</u>. No casual relationship has any real meaning or serve any purpose for life.

Close Friends - Share emotions and feelings.

Over time, as people entrench themselves into each other's lives, and for us towards seeing people grow in the Lord, maturing, and ultimately become Fathers and Mothers of Nations, the premium is to *stay focused on prayerfully developing the relationships deeper* so that we can ultimately together impact others for the advancement of the Gospel of Jesus Christ.

During this phase of developing deep and meaningful relationships we can move to a place where we should be able *share how we <u>feel</u>* and *express our emotions* without guilt or a feeling of being guarded. If you trust someone whose ideas and beliefs you embrace, then the natural next step is to let them into how you truly feel. This might be the expression of disappointment, gladness, fulfillment, love and even fear. As we share our emotions and feelings more freely, and receive appropriate and reciprocal response we will find the relationship deepen even more. If there is no reciprocation or appropriate response, as what you would expect from your sharing, then the likelihood of the relationship going deeper stalemates here.

Our goal is to help our disciples to develop deep and more meaningful relationship to enable them to bring transformation in their lives. When we become open and honest about our ***hopes and dreams***, our ***fears and failures***, we develop relationships for life. This phase draws people into becoming ***more vulnerable and exposed***, however, if we've taken the cautious path of developing the relationship carefully, then true transformation will take place and people will be more likely changed and transformed into the likeness of Christ.

My caution is this: ***never move or develop relationships beyond reciprocal open sharing and transparency.***

Intimate Relationships – open and complete transparent relationships.

The deepest level of relationship is really reserved for covenantal relationships, or marriage to be more specific.

In developing these relationships, it is importance to know that the deeper the relationship level, the more transparency and therefor vulnerability will exist. ***Transformation only exists along the pathway of becoming transparent** and **vulnerable**.* As we help and guide our disciples along this pathway of disclosure, vulnerability and transformation their lives will be enriched, and the result will be a unified Body of Believers fulfilling the purpose of God for each of their lives.

Simultaneously, and alongside this pathway of developing deep and transformational relationships, there exist another dynamic that we need to be aware of and it is the ***relationship cycle***.

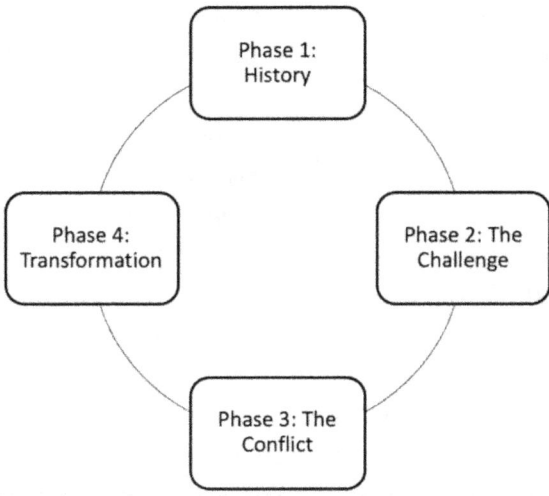

Relationships develop through cycles.

Phase 1: History

The first phase of building purposeful relationships is defined by the status quo; each one being his or her own person, seeing life and things from their *one-dimensional perspective*. This marks the starting point for each relationship.

In this phase, since we evangelise, we might start with *Level One and Level Two communication*. This phase is also identified by our pursuits to open up conversation with strangers. *We open conversations with sincere <u>compliments</u> and then by asking <u>open</u> questions to know them better.*

People open up quicker if we show *sincere interest in non-threatening situations*. Non-threatening situations are those where you will potentially part ways within minutes. If you are more likely to "bump" into these strangers more frequently then you *keep it consistent* and at a *low level of asking intruding questions*. They should, on the surface, seem casual, as if you are just showing interest. Remember, *we are engaging with strangers to find "men of peace'* with whom we can share Christ. We are looking for open hearts where it seems that we could see ourselves build deep and meaningful relationships that would potentially advance the Kingdom of God greatly.

When we bring our *"worthy men"* together for the first time, they will start their joint relationship at this point as well. **Help them bridge the unknown by communicating the things they have in common and share.** It helps them connect in a positive atmosphere.

When **Philip brought Nicodemus to Jesus**, He made it easy by telling him about Jesus. When Andrew left John the Baptist to follow Jesus, he took his brother along. On both of these occasions the disciples **prepared the way** for their "friends and family" to meet the Lord. In one sense we need to do the same when building our discipleship groups.

> *John 1:41-42 The first thing Andrew did was to find his brother Simon and tell him,* **"We have found the Messiah"** *(that is, the Christ). 42 And* **he brought him to Jesus.** *Jesus looked at him and said, "You are Simon son of John. You will be called Cephas" (which, when translated, is Peter).*

> *John 1:43, 45 The next day Jesus decided to leave for Galilee. Finding Philip, he said to him, "Follow me."* **45 Philip found Nathanael and told him, "We have found the one Moses wrote about in the Law, and about whom the prophets also wrote—Jesus of Nazareth, the son of Joseph."**

The beginning of establishing a relationship is for the most part easy, unless you just don't connect with the people you are pursuing. On both of these occasions we see that the common denominator was one's knowledge of Jesus, and then sharing it with the other.

Sharing something <u>positive</u> about those whom you're introducing to each other, always sets a good positive departure point to starting new relationships. Jesus immediately connected with those who were introduced to Him, by ministering to them by the Holy Spirit. We need to be constantly tuned into the Holy Spirit to connect with people more effectively. *Divine connections has the capacity to catapult relationships deep within one or two encounters.*

Phase 2: The Challenge

The second phase of building purposeful relationships is where things become a little trickier as *we become aware of what we like and don't like about the other person*. If we could keep in the forefront of our minds the reason why we felt to start and pursue the specific relationship, it will help us to develop "that" person. *During this phase people are <u>confronted</u> and often have a sense of being challenged.*

- We are challenged <u>culturally</u> by observing the *different values* people uphold.
- We are challenged by *what people endorse* and see as *normal behaviour*.
- We are challenged by people's *educational status*.
- We are challenged by *our own emotional adaptabilities*.
- We are challenged by *other's habits, practices and sayings*.
- We are challenged by *the way people respond to <u>changing</u> circumstances*.
- We are challenged *<u>spiritually</u>* as we face our own short comings and need of God.
- We are challenged as *we come to know the purpose God has for our lives*.
- We are challenged as *we become aware of the changes that is required* to obey God.
- We are also challenged when we consider *how much time we wasted in not following God*.

During this phase we open ourselves up, by becoming more transparent and vulnerable. It is this openness that challenges us as we come to terms with how vulnerable it's making us. One of the areas we are challenged in, on the pathway of openness and vulnerability, is towards *being transformed into the likeness of Christ*. *We*, of necessity, *have to confront the challenge* to our upbringing, our values, cultural habits and practices, and this leads to *the next phase of conflict.*

Whenever *we are challenged in our beliefs, behavior and thought patterns*, we become aware that much of *our adamic nature is in opposition to sound biblical wisdom*, and that brings us to *a Gospel Conflict which needs resolving with the help of the Holy Spirit* and *a Good Shepherd.* We are often confronted with our sins and how it has impacted our lives. We are confronted with how we lived our lives, and thought it was right and normal, just to discover that it was wrong.

These things bring us to a confrontation of who we are and how change is required to become the people we want to become, and what God want us to be. The constant agent working primarily in us is *the Holy Spirit* who brings on this confrontation, or conviction. *A conviction calls for change.* When the Holy Spirit convicts us of sin in our lives, it calls us to change our ways.

> *John 16:8 When he comes,* ***he will convict the world of guilt in regard to sin*** *and righteousness and judgment:*

When the Apostle Paul wrote to the *Thessalonians*, he addressed them on a number of issues which ***brought deep conviction within them.***

> *1 Thessalonians 1:5 because our gospel came to you not simply with words, but also with power, with* ***the Holy Spirit*** *and* ***with deep conviction.*** *You know how we lived among you for your sake.*

Phase 3: Conflict

Any challenge of our values, habits, behavior, beliefs and knowledge always is followed by a period of conflict. *The outcome of conflict determines the values, practices and behaviours we will uphold or adapt to in our lives.* This conflict is often more on *a spiritual level* than on a physical level. Depending on the depth of our *upheld mindsets*, the *conflict might be a more painful experience* in one area than in other parts of our lives where we can more easily *observe the wisdom towards change and transformations.*

We always need to remind ourselves of what Scripture teaches us.

> *Ephesians 6:12 For **our struggle is not against flesh and blood**, but against the rulers, against the authorities, against the powers of this dark world and against the spiritual forces of evil in the heavenly realms.*

> *2 Corinthians 10:3-6 For though we live in the world, **we do not wage war as the world does**. The weapons we fight with are not the weapons of the world. On the contrary, they have divine power to demolish strongholds. We demolish arguments and every pretension that sets itself up against the knowledge of God, and we take captive every thought to make it obedient to Christ. And we will be ready to punish every act of disobedience, once your obedience is complete.*

This spiritual conflict, fought with spiritual weapons and armament, aligns us with the Will and Purpose of God. The hope is that *conviction brings us to a place of obedience to God* and the favor of God. For some, conviction could come in a moment of prayer and contemplation in the Word, for others it might be more of a process.

Transformation takes place through conflict.

Our purpose as Shepherds is to help our disciples through this phase of conflict. *Never make their conflict your conflict, neither trivialise the conflict* and trauma they might experience in "*letting go*" or "*leaving*" things of the past behind. *Never take it personal* as they might vent themselves in the process of trying to come to terms with the change that is required to grow in their faith and stature in Christ. *Without being challenged*, through the Word, the Holy Spirit, or through us, as we share the Truths of God's Word to our disciples, *no change or transformation is possible.*

The Apostle Paul wrote to the church in Corinth and emphasised the way in which they were challenged by his letter, but more importantly the conviction it brought and ultimate transformation in their character and ministry, was clearly observed. This is what we are trusting God for in our disciples.

> 2 *Corinthians 7:8-12 Even **if I caused you sorrow by my letter, I do not regret it.** Though I did regret it—I see that my letter hurt you, but only for a little while – 9 yet now I am happy, not because you were made sorry, but because **your sorrow led you to repentance.** For you became sorrowful as God intended and so were not harmed in any way by us. 10 **Godly sorrow brings repentance that leads to salvation** and leaves no regret, but worldly sorrow brings death. 11 **See what this godly sorrow has produced in you:** what earnestness, **what eagerness to clear yourselves,** what indignation, what alarm, what longing, what concern, **what readiness to see justice done.** At every point you have proved yourselves to be innocent in this matter.*

This conviction is nothing more than a major conflict which results in godly sorrow and repentance, and ultimately a transformed life.

Phase 4. Transformation

Phase four is defined by being transformed in your life. I learned about transformers at school. Transformers take one kind of electricity from one source and transform it to another form and consistency out on the other end. *Transformation takes place when we input our old selves as clay into the hands of the Almighty God*, submits to him, allowing Him to form us and creating something beautiful of our lives.

> "Transformation is the process by which our old nature, encompassing our will, intellect, emotions, values, habits, ambitions and practices is transformed by a combined process of submitting our own selves, with willingness to permanently change, together with desiring the Holy Spirit to bring the sanctification and renewed creation forth on the other end."

Once we come to a place of conviction, as those led by the Holy Spirit, and constantly under Him working consecration in us, we repent, we change, and we turn for good. This change is called *transformation*.

> *1 Corinthians 7:11 NIV 11* **See what this godly sorrow has produced in you:** *what earnestness, what eagerness to clear yourselves, what indignation, what alarm, what longing, what concern, what readiness to see justice done. At every point you have proved yourselves to be innocent in this matter.*

God has our best interest at heart, and so should we for those who we lead and care for during their transformation process. **Constantly remind yourself**, and those you lead, of the goal before us. *Let us keep our eyes focused on the goal of becoming and being like Jesus.*

> *Philippians 2:5* **Your attitude should be the same** *as that of Christ Jesus:*

> *Philippians 3:10* **I want to know Christ** *and the power of his resurrection and the fellowship of sharing in his sufferings,* **becoming like him** *in his death,*

Change for good

This kind of change is good, *it makes us better people*, and *better people to be around with*. This kind of change presents Jesus to others in a real and transferable way. This change brings about **change in our speech, actions, behavior and reactions.**

Transformation

Our goal is to see people transformed in their person, character and nature. *We desire to equip them with every good thing that will lead them to be fully transformed until Christ is formed in them.*

> *Romans 12:2 Do not conform to the pattern of this world but **be transformed by the renewing of your mind.** Then you will be able to test and approve what God's will is —his good, pleasing and perfect will.*

> *2 Corinthians 3:18 And we all, who with unveiled faces contemplate the Lord's glory, are **being transformed into his image** with ever-increasing glory, which comes from the Lord, who is the Spirit.*

The purpose of transformation is that Christ is formed in us. Our work as Shepherds is to help our disciples to be transformed until Christ is formed in them.

> *Galatians 4:19 My dear children, for whom I am again in the pains of childbirth **until Christ is formed in you,***

The Apostle Paul speaks of God's goal and means of seeing His people equipped and mobilised for service. *We are so much more effective in building the Church up when we are mature and Christ formed in us.*

> *Ephesians 4:12 **His intention was the perfecting and the full equipping of the saints** (His consecrated people), [that they should do] the work of ministering toward building up Christ's body (the church),*

*Romans 8:29 For those God foreknew he also predestined to **be conformed to the image of his Son**, that he might be the firstborn among many brothers and sisters.*

*1 Corinthians 15:49 And just as we have borne the image of the earthly man, **so shall we bear the image of the heavenly man.***

God desires that we bear the image of His Son just as we borne the image of our adamic nature. This is possible with the Power of the Holy Spirit.

"Transformation takes place when we combine being vulnerable, transparent and humble, with a <u>willingness</u> and openness to <u>change</u> and be renewed into the person God dreamed us to be."

Vulnerability and transparency

One of **the greatest expressions of vulnerability and transparency is when we confess our sins to God.** When we are in a caring Shepherding relationship and confess our sins, it provides opportunity for change and transformation to takes place.

*James 5:16 Therefore, **confess your sins to each other** and pray for each other so that you may be healed. The prayer of a righteous person is powerful and effective.*

*Acts 19:18 Many of those who believed now came and **openly confessed what they had done.***

It takes great humility to say to your "shepherd" that you have sinned, and that you need help and forgiveness. It requires a loving and accepting environment where you can be held accountable to turn from wicked ways and practices. As Shepherds of God, we desire to see our disciples turn from worldly ways to walk in godly, exemplary ways.

So, step one is to keep the focus clear in our hearts and minds, that we serve as His Servants to equip our disciples to be transformed into the likeness of Christ Jesus. To do this efficiently, **we need to create an environment where people can be vulnerable and transparent,** but also where they can be held **accountable, to ensure they truly change and transform into the people God desires them to be.**

Built up

Our goal is defined: that *the Body be built up in Him*!

> *Ephesians 4:12-13 "to prepare God's people for works of service, **so that the body of Christ may be built up until we all reach unity in the faith** and in the knowledge of the Son of God and become mature, attaining to the whole measure of the fullness of Christ."*

Our prayer is that you will grow in understanding these simple, yet powerful skills to assist you to help your disciples develop deep and kingdom advancing relationships.

Session Four: Developing deep and meaningful relationships | 303

Assimilation Sheet for
Developing deep and meaningful Relationships

1. Complete the statement. *The most effective part of Shepherding is providing a place where people's lives could be <u>transformed</u>, renewed, encouraged, and built up.*

2. Complete the sentence. *The ebb and flow of how we develop purposeful relationship requires "<u>know how</u>" as well as <u>prayerful</u> diligence.*

3. Name the four quadrants of the Johari Window, and briefly explain the importance of each aspect for us to consider in developing deep and meaningful relationships.

- *<u>The Open Dimensions - It relates to what is known to both yourself and others.</u>*
- *<u>The Hidden Dimension - It relates to that side of us where we know things about ourselves that is hidden from the knowledge of others.</u>*
- *<u>The Blind Dimension - It represents that side of our lives that others see and know about us that we are completely blind to.</u>*
- *<u>The Unknown Dimension - It represents that part of our lives to which neither us or others have become aware of, or discovered.</u>*

4. What is the objective to understanding the Johari Window? *<u>The objective of understanding the JOHARI window is to help us understand the dynamics that is involved when we lead people to self-discovery, openness, vulnerability and ultimate transformation.</u>*

5. Name the Five levels of deepening relationships, and provide a brief description for each level.

- *<u>Level 1 - Strangers - Speak and assess clichés.</u> <u>The purpose is primarily to simply connect to strangers in a non-threatening friendly way.</u>*
- *<u>Level 2 - Acquaintances - Speak and assess facts.</u> <u>To take the relationship deeper you convey facts, and assess the facts</u>*

sharing from the person being pursued to determine whether it is a "worthy person" with whom you can develop a "Man of Peace" relationship.
- **Level 3 - Friends - Share ideas and Beliefs.** *Once you've determined that you want to take the relationship deeper you start sharing ideas and beliefs. The affirmative response to you sharing your beliefs will be an indicator whether this could develop into a discipling relationship.*
- **Level 4 - Close Friends - Share emotions and feelings.** *In a discipling relationship we endeavour to have people respond to the sanctification work of the Holy Spirit. It is at this level of ministry into the vulnerabilities of people's lives that change and transformation take place. We also see deep and meaningful, kingdom advancing relationships develop during this level.*
- **Level 5 - Intimate Relationships - Share openly and full Transparancy.** *Jesus shared with His Disciples that He "now call you friends," since He lived a fully transparant life with them. Our goal is to live such transparent lives with our disciples.*

6. Complete the sentence. **We open conversations with sincere compliments and then by asking open questions to know them better.**

7. Complete the sentence. **Sharing something positive about those whom you're introducing to each other, always sets a good positive departure point to starting new relationships.**

8. Name a few areas in which we often find ourselves challenged when we develop new relationships.

- We are challenged **culturally** by observing the **different values** people uphold.
- We are challenged by **what people endorse** and see as **normal behaviour.**
- We are challenged by people's **educational status.**
- We are challenged by **our own emotional adaptabilities.**
- We are challenged by **other's habits, practices and sayings.**

• *We are challenged by **the way people respond to changing circumstances**.*

• *We are challenged **spiritually** as we face our own short comings and need of God.*

• *We are challenged as **we come to know the purpose God has for our lives**.*

• *We are challenged as **we become aware of the changes that is required** to obey God.*

• *We are also challenged when we consider **how much time we wasted in not following God**.*

9. Which are the four phases of relationship building? *The History phase, the Challenge phase, the Conflict phase, and the Transformation phase.*

10. Complete the sentence. *Any challenge of our values, habits, behavior, beliefs and knowledge always is followed by a period of conflict.*

11. Define the process of Transformation. *"Transformation is the process by which our old nature, encompassing our will, intellect, emotions, values, habits, ambitions and practices is transformed by a combined process of submitting our own selves, with willingness to permanently change, together with desiring the Holy Spirit to bring the sanctification and renewed creation forth on the other end."*

12. What is the purpose of transformation? Give Scriptural support for your answer. *The purpose of transformation is that Christ be formed in us. Romans 12 verse 2, 2 Corinthians 3 verse 18, and Galatians 4 verse 19, and Ephesians 4 verse 12.*

13. Complete the sentence. *"Transformation takes place when we combine being vulnerable, transparent and humble, with a willingness and openness to change and be renewed into the person God dreamed us to be."*

SESSION FIVE: PRACTICAL KEYS

This session will provide us with practical ways to lead a group effectively and efficiently.

Meeting Place setup.

Set out the meeting place in a <u>circle</u> as opposed to a classroom setting. Make sure that you have a comfortable amount of seating available for everyone. Preferably, no one should sit at a lower level than others. If your culture is comfortable to be seated on the floor, then make room that everyone sits on the floor. If your culture sits on chairs, make sure that everyone sits within a reasonable height to each other, and that *everyone can see everyone else in the room.* We *encourage open and transparent communication* and this arrangement will assist in helping people to be open and *free to minister to each other*, as well as to observe and share together.

WWM's

Once we bring our disciples together in a group, there are a number of practical keys that will assist us to coordinate these gatherings in an orderly and functional way. There is something that is now commonly known as the WWM's for effective group functioning. The **WWM's stand for: Welcome, Worship, Ministry,** and **Word, Witness, Mission.** These four W's and 2 M's form the broad outline for our *60-90 minutes together as a group.* Let us look at these 6 integrated parts for leading an effective group encounter.

Welcome.

1. Personally Welcome people to your house.

Welcome people as they arrive to your house. It is preferable that <u>you</u> meet your guests at the door. It shows that you value them.

- Ask them how they are?
- Ask them about their day?
- Ask them how they feel?
- Ask them follow up questions about their family's welfare? Always start with the person and then branch out to the immediate family and other circumstances.

2. Connect people during this time.

Use this welcoming time to help the group to be better <u>connected</u> with each other as well, especially in the beginning phase of them meeting together.

- **Friendliness** - The purpose is to make them feel welcome and that you feel blessed that they are there. Remember, we want to shepherd them through the Word, by the Holy Spirit Gifts and through natural means. We are blessed to have people come to us. Treat them with honor and respect their time and effort.
- **Hospitality** - One of the best ways to show hospitality is to offer them something to <u>drink</u>. The purpose is not to have

a tea drinking party, but just a way of showing hospitality and to let people settle in and relax. It is just to make people feel relaxed and welcome. Even a glass of water will work.

3. Officially, Welcome Everyone.

Draw all the various conversations to a close, once all your expected guests have arrived, by *raising your voice slightly* and *welcoming them all* for coming. Always declare your gathering open by saying something expectant and positive. "*I am so excited for this time together. I believe the Holy Spirit is really going to minister to each one of us today,*" or "*I have been so blessed with the Word today. I look forward to sharing God's Word with us today,*" Or "*We are so blessed to be able to gather together, and to share this time together as friends.*"

The purpose of this process of welcoming is to *help people relax, forget about the challenges, struggles*, and *concerns of their day*, and *settle in* on the purpose of them being there.

Welcoming people sincerely *opens their hearts to you and to God.*

4. Opening Prayer

It is always a great idea to open every gathering in prayer to set the tone and affirm the purpose for coming together. You might want to open your gatherings with prayer or ask one or more of your group to open in prayer. The purpose of this time of prayer is to welcome the Lord in your midst, and to commit your hearts to worship Him, to Hear from Him, to avail yourselves to be instruments through whom He may minister to build and encourage others.

Worship.

Declare your purpose for worshipping together.

Immediately after welcoming and praying, draw the attention of your people to *the purpose* of your gathering, which is to *Worship God, Hear from Him, Learn from Him, and committing yourselves unto His service.*

Leading worship

Very few people actually have confidence in leading worship, so, if you have someone to lead the group in a time of singing songs of worship, count yourself highly fortunate. For the rest of us, we have to prepare to lead the singing of *2-3 songs* that is focused on bringing our praise and adoration to Jesus. You can use *worship music from your Christian Music collection* if it could be done seamlessly.

Make Worship simple.

My advice is to *make it as natural as possible*, because worship should not only be done when we gather together, *we should be worshippers of God everyday* of our lives. Singing *Accapella* (without music - voices only) is good. It helps people to hear their own voices as they worship God.

Heart-felt Worship

Worship should come from our hearts to touch the heart of God. Our time in Worship is devoted so that we can focus on Him, His Spirit and His Word. We want to *open our hearts and minds to Him.*

Be considerate in your worship

Be respectful when you meet in places where there are other people living in close vicinity to where you meet. In other words, don't sing so loud that you unnecessarily draw unwanted attention to your singing as to put people off at your inconsiderate worship. Worship should be done *at the same level as what you would present it to God during your own quiet times of Worship.*

Ensure people connect with God in Worship.

Ensure that the worship *leads people to connect with God.* As the Leader of the group, you should always be prayed up before every group meeting so that you could lead worship by your example, even though the person who is supposed to lead the worship might not be.

Remember that *the time of worship is to set the atmosphere for a time of ministry* to the people and between each other.

Sing from your heart and focus your attention on Him.

> John 4:23-24 "Yet a time is coming and has now come when the true worshipers will worship the Father in spirit and truth, for they are the kind of worshipers the Father seeks. God is spirit, and his worshipers must worship in spirit and in truth."

Focus on the Nature and Character of God in Worship.

One of the ways to lead worship is to choose a theme on the <u>nature</u> and <u>character</u> of God, and then worship God in song accordingly. Another way is to choose Scripture Songs, especially those we learned from the <u>Psalms</u>. They are often easy to learn and to remember. The purpose is to help the group give expression of their love and devotion to God, in song.

Ministry.

The time of ministry is one of the most impacting times of every meeting since *the needs of the people are met* by the <u>ministry</u> *of the Holy Spirit.*

Be an Instrument of God

Prepare to be an instrument through whom the Holy Spirit can meet the spiritual needs of your people. The Apostle Paul taught us that he desired to meet together, to impart some Spiritual gift to strengthen and encourage the believers. We should do the same during this time of ministry.

> Romans 1:11-12 "11 I long to see you so **that I may impart to you some spiritual gift to make you strong–** 12 that is, that you and I may be mutually encouraged by each other's faith."

Allow the Gifts of the Holy Spirit to operate.

May the Gifts of the Holy Spirit be used to build each other up. Be an example and encourage the group to minister to each other in an orderly way.

If you centre your time together around Jesus, the Word and His Holy Spirit, then He will build them up in their faith. Remember, we want more of Him in our lives!

This time of ministry will provide comfort, care, direction, encouragement and instruction.

Limit lone Rangers

Don't let any one-person minister alone or primarily. If there is to be that one person, it will be you, however, your goal is to encourage your group, who should all be filled with the Holy Spirit, and have discovered their spiritual gifts at some point in conclusion of them doing the Spiritual Gifts discovery weekend encounter.

Body ministry is key during this time.

Facilitate this time. Don't force it, however, led by your example. Ministry time is not spiritual counseling. It is hearing what the Holy

Spirit is saying to His people.

Encourage

Encourage one another. Build each other up.

Drawing Ministry Time to a Close.

Draw the ministry time to a *close by summarising*, as might be appropriate to share, what the Lord did and said during this time. It is always an easier way to draw this ministry time to a *close with a prayer of thanksgiving* that you lead.

Word.

Hearing and receiving the Word

Ministry time should **lead into hearing and receiving the Word** of the Lord.

Receiving instruction in the Word

During the Word time we initially, primarily teach our disciples the Discipleship Foundation Series materials from Step One and Step Two.
    * **Note to the teacher!** *During this weekend encounter phase, we unpack and internalise the weekend encounter material, especially how we might put it into practice. It will be advantageous if you prepare a suitable "Word" from some previous Step's material during this time.*

You are the initial sharer of the Word

During the teaching of Step 1 and 2 you will most certainly be the Primary Discipler. This might take you the better part of 6 months to complete. During the initial 6-9 months of your group meeting, you will be the primary teacher.

Directive to Facilitative

In the ***initial stage You will be highly <u>directive</u> during this teaching time***, however, as your disciples put things into practice and lead their own groups, you will find that a transition will take place as you provide a Word of encouragement to them, and then application to them fulfilling the call of God on their lives. ***The goal is for you to become more of a facilitator.***

Remember, we want to see our disciples become fully mature followers of Jesus. We desire to see that they hear from God clearly, and that they put into practice the very things they were taught. The only way that this is possible in this regard is to intentionally transition from leading in a highly directive way to becoming more of a leader who walk alongside your disciples as they put things into practice. This *"**walking alongside**"* is called facilitation.

Putting it into practice

It is essential that we always remember that our discussions around the Word should always culminate into the: ***How can I put this into practice in my life?*** If there be any sharing let it be the confession of commitment to putting it into practice.

This is ***not a time for arguments or opinions*** to be aired. The Word time should neither be a time of disciplining.

Let it be centered on the Bible

Our discussions should always be based on what the Word of God teaches. It is a time to learn the Word of God. ***The Bible form the backbone of all the Discipleship material*** we developed. Keep it void from self-interpretation and rather, like a child, receive the Word of God as God gave it to us.

Witness

Testify

Draw the Word time to a *close by asking people to* <u>testify</u> of what the Lord did for them during that meeting. Testimonies build people's faith as they hear, and proclaim, what the Lord has done for them.

One Minute testimonies

Share one-minute testimonies. Make sure that you get as many testimonies in as possible. It is sometimes easier to get people to share for one minute than to get them to share at all. It both offers a comfortable space and timing within to share as well as limit those who might cease an opportunity to take the floor.

Moderating sharing

It does happen at times that someone might extend the *one-minute time restriction*. Just be wise whether to allow it or to draw their testimony to a close. One of the best ways is to step in and say something like: *"Wow, it's amazing what the Lord did for you, let's hear from …. I see they are equally excited to share today."*

Testifying brings liberty

When people learn the value of sharing what the Lord did or do for them, *they become more liberated to share outside* the group with others about the Lord's goodness.

Testifying activates awareness of what God is doing

This exercise *brings a greater awareness, appreciation and recognition of the work of God* in our lives. People become much more aware of the work of God in their own lives as they hear the testimonies from others sharing.

Encourage everyone to share

Some will be more open to share than others. Our role is to draw people into sharing by highlighting to them what they sensed God did for them. *Get them to see it for themselves.* Initially we have to point it out to them, but later you will see them responding to this by themselves spontaneously.

Mission

We *conclude* our *60-90 minutes together* with *casting vision of our mission*. It is easy to ramble off the mission part, however, getting the group to take a moment to share in groups of two or three on the main areas where they can prayerfully trust the Lord to work in and through them, usually activates the Vision into them being on mission with God.

Prayer transitions our intentions into active participation

The *true impact* of *declaring our mission comes* when we *put action to our words of confession by praying* for, and with each other. The first, and *primary activity* to see any *Mission accomplished*, is when we unite our hearts to approach the Throne of God in *praying for it*.

- Our mission is to *seek and save the lost*, so, let the group form sub-groups of 3-4 and pray for each other's lost people to be saved.
- Our mission is to *make disciples of all nations*, so, in these groups pray for each other that God will bless each one with *the worthiest people to disciple*, to advance the Kingdom of God.
- Our mission is to *preach the gospel*, so, pray for boldness to

be able to *use every opportunity to share your faith* with outsiders.
- Our mission is to *be examples for others to follow*, so, we pray for each other that we will be worthy examples, *open letters*, that will present Christ in a worthy manner.

Close every discipleship gathering by reiterating the Mission God called us to.

Afterword

In conclusion, we need to be good stewards of our time together. Let us take a few moments and look at the recommended timelines within which to accomplish all of these six key elements to conclude a dynamically impacting meeting.

Timelines for gatherings

Welcome

The welcome should not extend over 10-15 minutes. The longer it takes, the harder it will be to refocus the attention of the people. *Let people arrive around 5 minutes prior to the set time,* and *welcome people on time so that we show respect for those who came on time.* If you slack on starting time, you might find that the worthiest of people will stop coming since the likelihood that you will then also run over time will be there.

The *rule of thumb* is this: *the worthier the people are that you minister to, the more likely they will be to follow a disciplined timeline.* Honor them since they are more likely to be able to teach other.

Worship

The worship time can be 10-15 minutes and should flow into

Ministry time seamlessly.

Ministry

Ministry should be done in a 10-15-minute timeframe, so that you could have a good 30 minutes to share the Word, or Teaching, for the day.

Word

Give yourself 30 minutes to teach the Word with enough time afterwards to discuss and internalise the Word or Teaching.

Witness

Give 5 minutes for people to share their testimonies of what the Lord did for them during their time together.

Mission

Secure at least 5-10 minutes at the end of your gathering time *to allow your people to pray with each other*, as well as to embrace their calling and mission together. If you overrun on other parts you will find people take the opportunity to excuse themselves during this vital conclusion.

This is probably the part that will catapult your disciples most into their mission and purpose for God. It *brings a sense of responsibility and mutual accountability* when they share and pray together.

If you can keep all of this under 90 minutes, then you will see great fruit from your good stewardship.

In Conclusion

In conclusion of this session, let us address two more essential elements which helps us immensely in leading our groups well:

Hospitality

Many *groups love socialising* after meetings, however, do not let this be the norm. *Rather meet on other occasions for fellowship and meals.* We all live in a time-constraint environment where every minute counts, therefor let us make the expectation clear that people don't feel rude or unsocial for not lingering beyond the 90 minutes.

There are always those who want to remain behind to further unpack or assimilate the happenings of the time together. We as Shepherds need to be prepared for it, and somehow welcome those moments as people come closer to Jesus, and their hearts more open to His Will and purpose.

Discipline

Sometimes we are required to bring correction to people who acted in an unacceptable way or manner, either themselves or to others during a meeting. If the opportunity arises then *ask them to meet with you during a mutually convenient time* to discuss the incident or occasion.

Discipline in private, Praise in public

Most *sheep are open to such correction and guidance.* Goats are never open to instruction and discipline. Remember, these are God's people who devoted their lives to Christ, and you are leading them on His behalf. *Remind them* that *you are there to care* for them, and that *their behavior or actions either advance or thwart the purpose of God*, both in their lives, as well as in the lives of the rest of the group. *Discipline in private* as far as is possible and appropriate. *Praise in public!*

Finally, enjoy the meetings, since it is here that you will see strangers become the family of God. It is here that you will observe the Grace of God in action. It is here with them that you will grow and mature in your faith and reliance on the Holy Spirit. *Enjoy!*

Assimilation Sheet for
The Practical Keys

1. Complete the sentence. *Set out the meeting place in a <u>circle</u> as opposed to a classroom setting.*

2. What does the acronym WWM represent? *<u>It represents two sets of WWM's: Welcome, Worship, Ministry, and Word, Witness and Mission.</u>*

3. Which are the four main ingredients to Welcoming well? *<u>1. Personally welcome people to your home; 2. Connect people during this time; 3. Officially welcome everyone; and 4. Open in Prayer.</u>*

4. Complete the sentence. *The purpose of this process of welcoming is to help people <u>relax</u>, forget about the challenges, struggles, and <u>concerns</u> of their day, and settle in on the purpose of them being there. Welcoming people <u>sincerely</u> opens their hearts to you and to <u>God</u>.*

5. Complete the sentence. *The purpose of your gathering is to <u>Worship</u> God, Hear from Him, <u>Learn</u> from Him, and committing yourselves unto His <u>service</u>.*

6. How do we know that it is the Will of God to take time to Worship? Provide a Scripture for your answer. *<u>We know it is the Will and desire of God since God is looking for Worshippers who would worship Him in Spirit and in Truth. John 4 verses 23-24.</u>*

7. What happens during the Ministry time, and by whose ministry? *<u>The needs of the people are met by the ministry of the Holy Spirit.</u>*

8. Body ministry is important during ministry time. Which Scripture exhorts us towards Body ministry? *<u>Romans 1 verses 11-12.</u>*

9. There are two key parts to closing the ministry time. How do we draw the Ministry time to a close? *<u>Draw the ministry time to a **close by summarising** what the Lord did and said during this time, and close with a prayer of thanksgiving.</u>*

10. There is an intentional transition that needs to take place in How we teach and equip our disciples during the Word time. How are we teaching initially and where do we intend to transition to? *<u>In the initial stage we will be highly directive in how we teach, and then we will transition to becoming more facilitative.</u>*

11. Which are two essential parts and focuses during the Word part? *How we put the teachings and Word into practice in our lives, as well as keeping it centered on the Bible.*

12. During the Witness time of our meetings, How long should we encourage the testimonies to be? *No longer than one minute.*

13. Name possible outcomes from this witnessing time? *When people learn the value of sharing what the Lord did or do for them, they become more liberated to share outside, as well as, this exercise brings a greater awareness, appreciation and recognition of the work of God in our lives.*

14. Complete the sentence. *The true impact of declaring our mission comes when we put action to our words of confession by praying for, and with each other.*

15. Name the four primary focuses of our Mission.

- *Our mission is to **seek and save the lost.***
- *Our mission is to **make disciples of all nations.***
- *Our mission is to **preach the gospel.***
- *Our mission is to **be examples for others to follow.***

16. Provide the suggested time allocation for each of the essential focuses of a group meeting.
   1. Welcoming - *10-15 minutes*
   2. Worship - *10-15 minutes*
   3. Ministry - *10-15 minutes*
   4. Word - *30 minutes*
   5. Witness - *5 minutes*
   6. Mission - *5-10 minutes*

17. Complete the sentence. *It brings a sense of responsibility and mutual accountability when they share and pray together.*

18. Complete the sentence. *Discipline in private and Praise in public!*

27

SESSION SIX: PRACTICAL APPLICATION

Leading a group is quite a challenging exercise which requires some understanding as well. In this final session we will look at two additional practical areas: *The Equipping process* as well as *the <u>stages</u> of forming a cohesive well-functioning group*. Both are equally essential for our understanding as well as keeping us sane during the tumultuous times that we all go through when we bring people from different backgrounds and values together, especially when it is to disciple them as Christ followers.

Equipping Process

The *equipping process* deals with the *intentional equipping* towards *transitioning <u>responsibility</u> and accountability* from ourselves to those we lead and care for. This is a particularly delicate process to lead, mostly adult people, from spiritually infancy to be fully mature followers of Christ.

As with children, during their *initial few years*, the relationship is led by us being *highly directive and instructive*. As our children *grow up*, we hold them *increasingly accountable* to hold their own. We initially brush their teeth, but after a while we teach them to brush it with our supervision, and still later, for many years in some cases, we have to ask them daily whether they brushed their teeth. There is a point though that this is no longer required under normal circumstances. This initial highly directive stage of instruction does not define us as controlling and manipulating, it is simply an essential role we need to play since we care for our children's well-being.

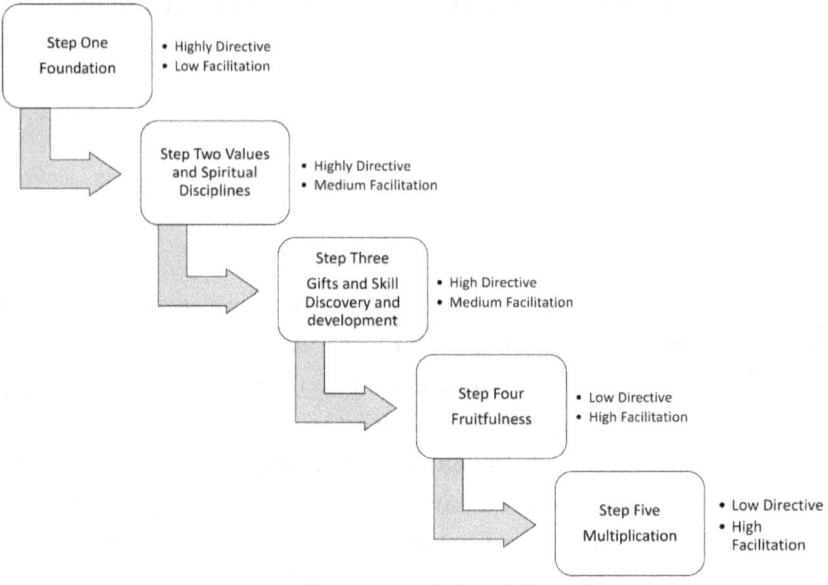

Equipping Process within the Five Discipleship Steps

The discipleship process develops from an initial **highly directive** and no facilitation approach, to ultimately relating with **low directive** instruction and **high facilitation**.

Directive Learning

Directive – meaning that you *direct the course of thought*. You instruct with a high sense of sharing irrefutable truth, meaning it is not up for discussion.

When we use directive learning, we equip our disciples by

teaching them the principles of God's Word, both by sharing the principles from God's Word, but more importantly by giving them a living example, through application in your own life. *In directive learning we <u>tell</u>, we <u>instruct</u>, and we direct the course of learning and understanding.*

Facilitative Learning

Facilitation – meaning that you *provide more emphasised <u>guidance</u>*, by *asking open-ended and <u>application</u> questions*, on how to apply the contents, more than on the information that is shared for assimilation.

For true transformation to take place in this equipping process we need to place a higher priority on creating and providing an example from whom others can learn, than being a conveyor of new information. This learning aspect through this equipping process is *more caught than taught*. It should be *seen and observed firsthand* for this to be effectively communicated, understood and received by others.

> *2 Timothy 1:5 I have been reminded of your **sincere faith, which** **first lived in** your grandmother Lois **and in your mother** Eunice and, I am persuaded, **now lives in you also**.*

The things that the Apostle Paul encouraged his spiritual son, Timothy, to teach was alive and observed by other in his family, and in him also. He was encouraged to teach the word but also with the emphasis to be an example to the Believers. Repeatedly we read about *'teaching'* and *'my way of life'* in the same phrase or sentence. These were coupled and this should be our approach as well.

> *2 Timothy 3:10 You, however, **know all about my teaching, my way of life**, my purpose, faith, patience, love, endurance,*

> *1 Timothy 4:11-13 11 **Command and teach these things**. 12 Don't let anyone look down on you because you are young, but **set an***

> *example for the believers in speech, in life, in love, in faith and in purity. 13 Until I come, devote yourself to the public reading of Scripture, to preaching and to teaching.*
>
> *1 Timothy 4:15-16 15 Be diligent in these matters;* ***give yourself wholly to them, so that everyone may see your progress.*** *16* ***Watch your life and doctrine closely.*** *Persevere in them, because if you do, you will save both yourself and your hearers.*

Nothing impacts others as much as a <u>living</u> **example.** We command and teach these things since they live in us.

Directive Process

When we start the Discipleship journey with new Believers, especially during **Step One and Two** where we **give them instruction** in **building a solid foundation** for their faith, as well as teach them the **Values of the Kingdom of God** and **Spiritual Disciplines** to maintain their growth and development in the Lord, **our approach** is to **provide highly directive instruction.** This highly directive approach will be appreciated and followed when we model the very things we teach. **The more visible our directive teaching can be observed** in our lives, **the more our teaching will impact** those whom we lead in the Lord.

When we proceed to **Step Three in the Discipleship process**, we equip them along **a shared pathway of instruction and <u>facilitation</u>.** We teach them and facilitate them to discover and develop ways to **put into practice what they learn,** especially as it relates to others. The key in this Step of Discipleship is that we not only equip them with skills but also with an understanding towards future implementation. It is therefore important to **add greater facilitation** during these **weekend equipping encounters** in order that the disciples will not just think on how it benefits them but also how they will help their disciples to grow.

Step Four and Five are low directive since we are working with **disciples who have become friends,** co-labourers and partners in advancing the Kingdom of God. We have *a low directive approach of equipping* since the emphasis is *leaning more towards encouragement* towards a being a better example and at the same time equipping your disciples with *skill sharpening tools* and *keeping them focused* on keeping intentionally focused on the task at hand. *The directive part is decreasing* as your *disciples assume their personal relationship with the Holy Spirit*, who is the ultimate teacher of us all.

We remain their Shepherds, and as such, we will always continue to lead them in their walk with God. *We will always provide care, guidance, protection and provision* for their growth and well-being, and this is where there will always remain *a low-directive component*. On the whole, effective leading at this stage of our disciple's growth, *facilitation is key*.

Facilitation Process

The facilitation only become of essence once you have given instruction in the ways, *principles* and *values of the Kingdom of God*. Once your disciples have been taught in an area, then only does the facilitation process start.

Open-ended Questions

The Facilitation process is grounded in *asking open-ended, observation and application questions. Open-ended questions* are those that typically start with *'How,' 'What,' 'When,' and 'Where,'* that requires *more than just a yes or no answer*.

Observation Questions

Observation questions are more invasive in that they require thoughtful answers. The '*Serendipity Bible*' is a good resource for observation and application questions, on almost every portion of Scripture in the Bible.

Observation questions ask the:

"What do I (first person) learn from this Scripture, or teaching?"
"What message in this Scripture is addressing areas of my life?"

Application Questions

<u>Application</u> *questions* and answers, primarily, will **provide solutions** or on the '*How to' put things into practice*. For example:

"How can I do this?"
"What do I need to do to put this into practice?"
"Where do I start?"
"What are the steps I need to take to make this true in my life and circumstances?"

Listening Skills

For these questions to have the ***transformational impact*** we pray for, we also need to apply our <u>*listening skills to hear*</u> what is communicated ***orally and non-verbally***. The Bible teaches us the importance of listening before we speak.

> *James 1:19 Listening and Doing* "*19 My dear brothers, take note of this:* <u>**Everyone should be quick to listen**</u>*, slow to speak and slow to become angry,*"

> *Proverbs 18:13 "13 He who answers before* **listening**— *that is his folly and his shame."*

For us to be effective in facilitating transformation in our disciples, we need to ***give our full attention when our people speak.***

Here we have a few good pointers on *How to be a good listener*:

- *Do not interrupt them* when they speak.
- *Discern the underlying spirit* from which they speak.
- *Pay attention* to their *non-verbal communication.*
- *Repeat the key points* of what they are saying, so that they know that *you are listening to them,* as well as it serves to communicate that *you heard their main concerns, struggles,* or *emphasis,* and *give an opportunity* to *clarify what you are hearing.*
- *Ask questions for clarification.* It usually *encourages them to speak more, especially* when *they have a sense that you seem to get something* that they attempted to communicate.
- *Do not jump to conclusions* too hastily.
- *Do not sit in judgement* over those people who took the courage to open up and speak up. *This is an opportunity to help their transformation,* especially when you *follow their openness up* with *words of mercy and grace,* and *offer practical advice* on next steps.

Good listening will often lead your disciples to deeper <u>openness</u> and self-revelation, which in turn could lead to a deeper and more meaningful relationship, and *a deeper relationship with the Lord.*

Remember the <u>JOHARI</u> Window!

Communication Skills

It is common knowledge that people remember only around *<u>7</u>% of what they hear* (**Verbal.**) The emphasis we place on our words (**non-verbal**), accelerates our words with another **55%**, however, the way in which we posture ourselves (**para-verbal**) adds another *<u>38</u>%* to our effective communication.

If you wish to break this down to further understand how we may use our *Verbal, Para-Verbal and Non-Verbal communication skills* to have the maximum impact when we share, we need to expand these three dimensions to many more to include *written* communication, *emotiona*l communication, and *listening* communication.

We all communicate every day, in every situation, whether we intentionally do so or not, we do. The awareness I wish to leave with you today is that **there are ways to communicate which are more effective and beneficial** for us to have a greater impact when we intend to lead people in their walk with God.

Things to consider when you communicate is:

- *Your choice* and *use of language* over that of any other person in the room.
- *The intentional use* and *meaning of the words* you choose to use when you speak.
- *The way we structure our sentences* has a determined impact.
- *The Pitch, tone and rhythm in our voice speaks volumes,* and has determined different meanings and impact.
- *The volume you use* (how *loud or soft*) can equally soften or impact a conversation.
- *The Speed with which we speak* has a determined impact on what and how we communicate.

What *is important, is that we balance these with a consistent predetermination* to, *equip by teaching things* that are both *real and observable in our lives*, as well as *ensure* that *our disciples actually learn* and *practice* these in their own lives.

We can be fool hardy to simply bring a teaching without observing whether they *"got it"* or whether they actually put it into observance. *Our calling is to ensure* that *they put into practice* what we teach. I once heard that: *"You have not taught until they have learned."*

Concluding communication skills

It is *always easier to teach, and Disciple, new Believers* than people who have been 'churched.' New Believers are like sponges in their new-found faith and open to learn all they can *'to be like Jesus.'*

My prayer is that *the Lord will use you to reach the 2/3 of the world population* who have never given their lives to the Lord. I pray that they will be like sheep and not goats. I pray that they will want to learn and that the seed of the Word will fall on good soil. I pray that you will fulfill the Call to *"teach them to obey everything I have taught you."*

Stages of forming a group

In leading and developing a group of disciples to form a cohesive body of Believers who live together in harmony and work towards a common goal and purpose, we need to also understand the various stages a group go through until they become that unified and on-purpose group.

Stages of Group Forming

Forming Stage

The first is the <u>forming</u> stage where *we bring people together who were previously unrelated.* During this stage people find themselves *being courteous and polite,* given that it is a Christian gathering, and they do not know much about each other. Typical *level 1 and 2 communication* will be experienced as *people speak in clichés* and as *they assess each other* regarding the *factual communication that transpires.*

Challenge Stage

The second stage is where people in the group *start to <u>challenge</u> each other* with *whatever they share, stand for, or even regarding their participation,* or non-participation, in the group. *The challenge stage is a courteous stage* where *people muscle each other* to *find some kind of pecking order* in the group.

This is not really the biggest challenge in forming and leading a unified and purposeful group. *The key* is to *bring every diversion back to the purpose of the group* and to *appeal to their decision* and *commitment to follow Christ* and to grow up in Him as their Lord and Master. During this stage you will *experience level 3 kind of relationship building* happen as *people start to share and assess ideas and <u>beliefs</u>.*

During *this stage of group development,* we need to keep in mind that *a.) these are sheep,* who need shepherding into their God-given life and purpose, and *b.) they are assimilating new ideas and concepts* that are for most parts *foreign to that taught in the world,* and *c.) they are doing this whilst growing and developing new relationships* within a new and often foreign relational environment. *They are challenged* and face these challenges *simultaneously* at a few different levels at the same time.

The challenge stage consists of being *relationally* challenged, *spiritually* challenged, and *culturally challenged.* They often feel *challenged personally* as it relates to their growth and assimilation of the Values and Disciplines of the Kingdom of God. They are *challenged relation-*

ally as they sense the synergy and mutual accountability being developed in the group.

As Shepherds, this calls for our deep prayer and intercession for and on behalf of them. *Many people* can be *overwhelmed* by this *accentuated process to change and transformation.*

Some fight and *some take flight* as they become aware of *the challenge that is calling them* to "*conflict through*" to *a new life in Christ.*

Conflict Stage

The Conflict stage is where personalities come to a <u>clash</u> with each other. The *tolerance level* of many people seems to be *tested beyond their spiritual maturity.* They often find themselves in *conflict with you* as the one bringing these new things into their lives.

Don't take it personal!

People often challenge you about *the things you teach* them, and *the ways of the Word* that you present to them. These, often *new concepts and values*, bring them to a place where they realise that *they need to make life-changing decisions.* They often, because of the Grace of God and the powerful work of the Holy Spirit, *repent, change and transform*, but sometimes *not before a major conflict* within *themselves* or *with others* with whom they do life with. *Expect the conflict*, but remember, it is because they are *transforming from darkness to light*, from death to life.

Restoring Stage

The Restoring stage is where things restore to the new <u>norm</u>. You will find that *they transition* from an *old lifestyle to a new*. You will see how *their language*, their *manners*, and their *behavior change.* You will see a new *eagerness and sincerity in their walk* with God. I always remember 2 Corinthians 7 when I see this *transformation*.

> *2 Corinthians 7:11 **See what this godly sorrow has produced in you:** what **earnestness**, what **eagerness** to clear yourselves, what indignation, what alarm, what **longing**, what **concern**, what **readiness** to see justice done. At every point you have proved yourselves to be innocent in this matter.*

During the Restoring stage you will see the disciples *actively engage the Word, the Holy Spirit, and Christian living.* You will observe their *earnestness and eagerness.* You will observe how they *accept each other in love.* You will see how *relationships are restored.* You will observe a **humility and humanity** within those who transitioned out of the conflict stage.

The *first signs of true transformation* will be their *eagerness to do something* to *make a difference.* It is these comments and conversations that will bring the group to the next stage of their forming, and that is *to become the Body of Christ* and to *fulfill their God-given purpose.*

Mission Stage

The Mission Stage is where you see these *disciples start sharing their faith, leading others to Christ, form their own discipleship groups,* and *committing themselves to be examples* against whom people measure their growth and development. *We have all been called for a purpose.* Fulfilling that purpose come on the back end of *a journey of forming,* being *challenged, waring through change, transforming into a committed follower of Jesus Christ,* and finally *desiring to serve Him,* and *fulfilling His Purpose* for our lives. God is calling each one of us to be on Mission with Him.

Conclusion

I pray that you will have seen these stages play out in your own life-group, and I pray that you will now be one of those gentle and wise Shepherds who will help and guide many through their transformation into pursuing Christ with all their hearts, minds and souls.

Session Six: Practical application | 333

Assimilation Sheet for
The Practical Application

1. Complete the sentence. *The equipping process deals with the intentional equipping towards transitioning <u>responsibility</u> and accountability from ourselves to those we lead and care for.*

2. Complete the sentence. *During their initial few years, the relationship is led by us being highly <u>directive</u> and instructive.*

3. Complete the sentence. *The discipleship process develops from an initial <u>highly</u> directive and <u>no</u> facilitation approach, to ultimately relating with <u>low</u> directive instruction and <u>high</u> facilitation.*

4. Complete the sentence. *In directive learning we <u>tell</u>, we <u>instruct</u>, and we direct the course of learning and understanding.*

5. Complete the sentence. *In Facilitation we provide more emphasised <u>guidance</u>, by asking open-ended and <u>application</u> questions.*

6. Which Equipping process is applicable when teaching through the Steps of the Discipleship Foundation Series?

- *<u>Step One - Salvation - High Directive and no facilitation.</u>*
- *<u>Step Two - Values and Spiritual Disciplines - High Directive and low facilitation.</u>*
- *<u>Step Three - Developing Gifts and Skills - Balanced between Directive and Facilitation learning.</u>*
- *<u>Step Four - Fruitfulness - Low Directive and High Facilitation.</u>*
- *<u>Step Five - Multiplication - Low Directive and medium facilitation.</u>*

7. Define Open-ended questions. *<u>Open-ended questions are those that typically start with 'How,' 'What,' 'When,' and 'Where,' that requires more than just a yes or no answer.</u>*

8. Define Observation Questions. Name one Good resource that you can use to help you ask good observation questions from the Bible? *<u>Observation questions are more invasive in that they require thoughtful answers. The Serendipity Bible is a good resource.</u>*

9. Define Application Questions. Give a few examples of good

application questions. *Application questions and answers, primarily, will provide solutions or on the 'How to' put things into practice. "How can I do this?" "What do I need to do to put this into practice?" "Where do I start?" "What are the steps I need to take to make this true in my life and circumstances?"*

10. What will release transformational power in our disciples when we ask these questions? <u>*Transformational impact will happen when we apply our listening skills to hear what is communicated orally and non-verbally.*</u>

11. Outline a few ways in which we could be better listeners.

<u>*• Do not interrupt them when they speak.*</u>
<u>*• Discern the underlying spirit from which they speak.*</u>
<u>*• Pay attention to their non-verbal communication.*</u>
<u>*• Repeat the key points of what they are saying, so that they know that you are listening to them, as well as it serves to communicate that you heard their main concerns, struggles, or emphasis, and give an opportunity to clarify what you are hearing.*</u>
<u>*• Ask questions for clarification. It usually encourages them to speak more, especially when they have a sense that you seem to get something that they attempted to communicate.*</u>
<u>*• Do not jump to conclusions too hastily.*</u>
<u>*• Do not sit in judgement over those people who took the courage to open up and speak up. This is an opportunity to help their transformation, especially when you follow their openness up with words of mercy and grace and offer practical advice on next steps.*</u>

12. What percentage impact does each of the following ways of communication have when we communicate?

- <u>7</u>% Verbal
- <u>55</u>% Non-Verbal
- <u>38</u>% Para-verbal

13. Name the Five Stages of Group Forming, with a brief description of the stage, as well as the type of communication that exist in each stage.

- *The first stage is the Forming Stage and refers to when strangers are brought together to start a journey together. Level 1 and Level 2 communication exist, which is defined by communicating through the use of clichés and then the assessing of the factual communication.*
- *The second stage is the Challenge Stage and is defined by when this newly formed group challenge each other to share their stories in a courteous manner. People muscle each other to determine some kind of pecking order, based on the experiences they share, their knowledge, their ideas and beliefs, and the confidence with which they uphold themselves. Typically we will find Level 3 type communication emerging and prevailing here where the predominant means of communication evolves around the valuing of shared ideas and beliefs. People are predominantly challenged by the variances, and How to adapt or adopt to these varied personalities, cultural differences, and emotional and relational adaptabilities. It simply challenges people to observe How others change and adapt to their new life in Christ. People learn and grow at varying speeds. These all challenge the best of us.*
- *The Third Stage is known as the Conflict Stage and refers to that period where personalities clash with each other. Their tolerance is tested beyond their maturity level. More often they warfare through as they are challenged and come to terms with the need to make life-changing decisions that will affect almost every part of their lives. This is a full-on war on everything they believed, stood for and lived for before they accepted Christ. Most people give expression to this conflict by making it personal, either with their leader or with others in the group. Level 4 communication takes place since people typically openly share their emotions, likes and dislikes. This vulnerability and openness creates the right atmosphere to move beyond the superficial masks people often wear, and creates a platform where transformational change can take place.*
- *The Fourth Stage is known as the Restoring Stage. The*

Restoring stage is where things restore to the new norm. You will see how their language, their manners, and their behavior change. You will see a new eagerness and sincerity in their walk with God. The first signs of true transformation will be their eagerness to do something to make a difference. During this stage we find Level 5 type of communication as there exist a lot of forgiveness, grace and acceptance of each other. Open and transparent communication develops and emerges.

- *The Fifth Stage is known as the Mission Stage. The Mission Stage is where you see these disciples start sharing their faith, leading others to Christ, form their own discipleship groups, and committing themselves to be examples against whom people measure their growth and development. In an atmosphere of acceptance and rest people find their united purpose and place in the Mission God called them to.*

SESSION SEVEN: CONSECRATION SESSION

Acts 20:28 Keep watch over yourselves and all the flock of which the Holy Spirit has made you overseers. Be shepherds of the church of God, which he bought with his own blood.

The Apostle Paul sums up His appeal to the gentile Elders in Ephesus with a few charges.

Firstly, he exhorts them to "keep watch" over themselves. Look after yourselves, spiritually, mentally, emotionally, and physically. Keep yourselves in step with what the Holy Spirit desires to do in and through you. Keep watch that you keep your conversations wholesome and seasoned, your example safeguarded, and your walk above reproach.

His second appeal is that they "keep watch" over all the flock of which the Holy Spirit has made them overseers. This is exactly what the Holy Spirit is doing and will be doing with each one of us, He will entrust sheep to our care and prayerful watch. We need to be careful to *"keep watch"* over those entrusted to our care. This might start with one or two disciples, but later it might extend to *"keeping watch"* over a whole congregation.

Finally, He reminds them that these "sheep" has been "bought with

His own Blood, " and as His Shepherds, we need to take care of His sheep.

We also have the exhortation of the Apostle Peter to his Jewish Brothers through his first pastoral letter to them.

> *1 Peter 5:2-4 Be shepherds of God's flock that is under your care, serving as overseers—not because you must, but because you are willing, as God wants you to be; not greedy for money, but eager to serve; 3 not lording it over those entrusted to you, but being examples to the flock. 4. And when the Chief Shepherd appears, you will receive the crown of glory that will never fade away.*

The Apostle Peter sums up the heart and call of the New Testament Shepherd within these few verses. His exhortation starts with a charge: **"Be Shepherds of God's flock."**

- The first instruction is to **"be a Shepherd."**
- The second exhortation is to **"take care"** of the sheep.
- The third is to "***serve.***" In the Kingdom of God, it's all about serving, not because we have to, but because we are **"willing."** Our **"willingness to serve"** is seen by the extent to which we are willing to serve those whom He place under our care and oversight. Many people shy away from this kind of responsibility and serving, but here we see that it is **"as God wants you to be."** God desires that we willingly and eagerly serve as overseers.
- The fourth observation from this portion of Scripture is the emphasis that we are actually **"entrusted"** with the care of His sheep. We need to live up to the entrustment.
- The fifth emphasis is on **"being examples to the flock."**
- The sixth emphasis is one a few cautionary notes. This highly directive portion of Scripture covers a few **"not's,"** **"not because you must,"** **"not greedy for money,"** and **"not lording it over those entrusted to you."**

- The final emphasis is on the reward for giving yourself to this cause and purpose. This portion ends with a wonderful promise of *"a Crown of Glory"* for those who served the Lord in this way. There might not be must glory in serving as a Shepherd in this life, but there will most certainly be a reward for those who willingly serve the Lord and His Sheep in eternity.

At one point the Apostle Paul gave a charge to his spiritual son Timothy, and with that we wish to give you a charge to take care of those whom the Lord will entrust to your care. The first portion of Chapter 4 of the First Letter to Timothy and Chapter 4 in the Second Letter to Timothy speaks amply on the stewardship and our part.

> *1 Timothy 4:11-16 Command and teach these things. Don't let anyone look down on you because you are young, but set an example for the believers in speech, in life, in love, in faith and in purity. Until I come, devote yourself to the public reading of Scripture, to preaching and to teaching. Do not neglect your gift, which was given you through a prophetic message when the body of elders laid their hands on you. Be diligent in these matters; give yourself wholly to them, so that everyone may see your progress. Watch your life and doctrine closely. Persevere in them, because if you do, you will save both yourself and your hearers.*

> *1 Timothy 6:11-13 Paul's Charge to Timothy "11 But you, man of God, flee from all this, and pursue righteousness, godliness, faith, love, endurance and gentleness. 12 Fight the good fight of the faith. Take hold of the eternal life to which you were called when you made your good confession in the presence of many witnesses. 13 In the sight of God, who gives life to everything, and of Christ Jesus, who while testifying before Pontius Pilate made the good confession, I charge you "*

> *2 Timothy 4:1-2 "1 In the presence of God and of Christ Jesus, who will judge the living and the dead, and in view of his appearing and his kingdom, I give you this charge: 2 Preach the Word; be prepared in season and out of season; correct, rebuke and encourage–with great patience and careful instruction."*

> *2 Timothy 4:5 But you, keep your head in all situations, endure hardship, do the work of an evangelist, discharge all the duties of your ministry.*

With these words we want to charge you to go and "**Be Shepherds over God's Flock,**" as willing servants of God, "**keep watch over the Sheep**" entrusted to your care. "**Be examples**" to the sheep in every aspect of your life, "**set an example for the believers in speech, in life, in love, in faith and in purity.**" May God grant you the strength to endure, the patience to persevere and the courage to preach the Word even though it might feel as if you are the only person on the planet pursuing God, His Will and His Word.

Remember, you are never alone! The Holy Spirit is with us always.

Go, and Shepherd God's People.

OTHER BOOKS BY DR HENDRIK J VORSTER

Discipleship Foundations - Step One - Salvation Disciple Manual

Step One - Salvation

This Course explores the "How to" be Born Again and to establish a solid Foundation for your faith in Jesus Christ. It is based on Hebrews chapter 6 verses 1 and 2, and explores:
    Repentance of dead works,
    Faith in God,
    Baptisms,
    Laying on of hands,
    Resurrection of the dead, and
    Eternal Judgement

Teacher Manuals and Video Teaching material are available through our website: www.churchplantinginstitute.com

Discipleship Foundations Step Two - Values and Spiritual Disciplines Disciple Manual

Step Two - Values and Spiritual Disciplines Disciple Manual

This Course explores the "How to" develop spiritual disciplines as well as 52 Values Jesus taught. It is based on the teachings of Jesus to His Disciples, and explores:

Spiritual Disciplines

The disciplines we explore are: Reading, meditating on the Word of God, Prayer, Stewardship, Fasting, Servanthood, Simplicity, Worship, and Witnessing.

Values of the Kingdom of God

Humility, Mournfulness, meekness, Spiritual Passion, Mercifulness, Purity, Peacemaker, Patient endurance, Example, Custodian, Reconciliatory, Resoluteness, Loving, Discreetness, Forgiving, Kingdom of God Investor, God-minded, Kingdom of God prioritiser, Introspective, Persistent, Considerate, Conservative, Fruit-bearing, Practitioner, Accountability, Faithful, Childlikeness, Unity, Servanthood, Loyalty, Gratefulness, Stewardship, Obedience, Carefulness, Compassion, Caring, Confidence, Steadfastness, Contentment, Teachable, Deference, Diligence, Trustworthiness, Gentleness, Discernment, Truthfulness, Generous, Kindness, Watchfulness, Perseverance, Honouring and Submissive.

Teacher Manuals and Video Teaching material are available through our website: www.churchplantinginstitute.com

Other Books by Dr Hendrik J Vorster | 343

Discipleship Foundations Step Three - Developing Gifts and Skills

Step Three - Developing Gifts and Skills

This course is run through five weekend encounters. These weekend encounters have been designed to help Disciples discover their spiritual gifts, as well as learn skills to use their gifts, and to serve the Lord for the extension of His Kingdom. The Weekend Encounters are:

Gifts Discovery Weekend Encounter

We learn about Ministerial Office gifts, Service gifts, and Supernatural Spiritual Gifts. We discover our own, and then learn How we may use them to build up the local Church.

Survey of the Bible Weekend Encounter

During this weekend we do a survey of the Bible, from Genesis to Revelation. We also learn about the History of the Bible as well as How we can make most of our time in the Word.

Sharing your Faith Weekend Encounter

During this weekend we learn about the Gospel message, and How to share our faith effectively.

Overcoming Weekend Encounter

During this weekend we deal with those thistles and thorns that smother the growth and harvest of the good seed sown into our lives. We address How to overcome fear, unforgiveness, lust and the cares of the world with faith and obedience.

Shepherd Leader Weekend Encounter

During this weekend encounter we learn about being a Good Shepherd, and How to best disciple in a small group.

Teacher Manuals and Video Teaching material are available from our website: www.churchplantinginstitute.com

344 | STEP THREE - DEVELOPING GIFTS AND SKILLS

Discipleship Foundations Step Four - Fruitfulness

Step Four - Fruitfulness

We were saved to serve. This course has been designed to mobilise Believers from Learners to Practitioners. These sessions have been prepared for individual use with those who are producing fruit.

We explore:
1. Introduction.
2. Walking with purpose.
3. Build purposeful relationships. Finding Worthy Men
4. Priesthood. Praying effectively for those entrusted to you.
5. Caring compassionately.
6. Walking worthily.
7. Walking in the Spirit.
8. Practicing hospitality.

Teacher Manuals and Video Teaching material are available from our website: www.churchplantinginstitute.com

Discipleship Foundation Step Five - Multiplication

Step Five - Multiplication

This course was designed to assist fruit-producing disciples to live a life that will encourage a lifetime of fruitfulness. It will also give disciples skills and guidelines to navigate their disciples through seasons of challenge and growth. We explore:

1. Vision and dreams.
2. Set Godly Goals.
3. Character development
4. Gifts development
Impartation and Activation
5. Fruitfulness comes through constant challenge.
6. Relationships
Family, Children and Friends
7. The Power of encouragement
8. Finances
Personal and Ministry finances
9. Dealing with setbacks

- How to deal with failure?
- How to deal with betrayal?
- How to deal with rejection?
- How to deal with trials?
- How to deal with despondency?

10. Eternal rewards

Teacher Manuals and Video Teaching material are available from our website: www.churchplantinginstitute.com

Values of the Kingdom of God
By Dr. Hendrik J Vorster

VALUES OF THE KINGDOM OF GOD

Dr. Hendrik J. Vorster

Everyone desires to be known as a pleasant to be around with kind of person. This book helps you develop values towards such a godly character. This book explores 52 Values of the Kingdom of God.

Books are available from our website: www.churchplantinginstitute.com

Spiritual Disciplines of the Kingdom of God
By Dr. Hendrik J Vorster

SPIRITUAL DISCIPLINES OF THE KINGDOM OF GOD

Every Believer desires to be a Fruit-producing branch in the Vineyard of our Lord. Developing spiritual disciplines is to develop spiritual roots from which our faith can draw sap to grow strong and fruit-bearing branches. This Book explores Nine Spiritual Disciplines of the Kingdom of God.

Books are available from our website: www.churchplantinginstitute.com

Other Books by Dr Hendrik J Vorster

Church Planting - by Dr Hendrik J Vorster

Church Planting - How to plant a dynamic, disciple-making church
By Dr Hendrik J Vorster

This is a handbook for those who wish to plant a disciple-making church. This book explores every aspect of church planting, and is widely used in over 70 Nations on 6 Continents. Here is a list of the areas that are explored:

1. The challenge to plant New Churches
2. Phases of Church Planting
3. Phase One of Church Planting - The Calling, Vision and Preparation Phase
4. The Call to Church Planting
5. Twelve Characteristics of Church Planting Leaders
6. Church Planting Terminology
7. Phase Two of Church Planting - Discipleship
8. The Process of Discipleship
9. Phase Three of Church Planting - Congregating the Discipleship Groups
10. Understanding Church Planting Finances
11. Understanding Church staff
12. Phase Four of Church Planting - Ministry development and Church Launching Phase
13. Understanding and Implementing Systems
14. Phase Five of Church Planting - Multiplication
15. Understanding the challenges in Church Planting
16. How to succeed in Church Planting
17. How to plant a House Church

Student Manuals and Video Teaching material are available from our website: www.churchplantinginstitute.com

ENDNOTES

3. The Service Gifts

1. https://biblehub.com/greek/4394.htm
2. https://www.biblestudytools.com/lexicons/greek/nas/didasko.html

9. The Authority of the Bible

1. Miller & Huber, Stephen & Robert (2003). *The Bible: the making and impact on the Bible a history*. England: Lion Hudson. p. 21. ISBN 0-7459-5176-7.
2. https://en.wikipedia.org/wiki/Nevi%27im
3. Neusner, Jacob, The Talmud Law, Theology, Narrative: A Sourcebook. University Press of America, 2005
4. Coogan, Michael D. A Brief Introduction to the Old Testament: the Hebrew Bible in its Context. Oxford University Press. 2009; p. 5
5. Coogan, Michael D. A Brief Introduction to the Old Testament: the Hebrew Bible in its Context. Oxford University Press. 2009; p. 5
6. https://theconversation.com
7. [6] What the Bible is All About Visual Edition by Henrietta C. Mears – Gospel Light Publications, 2007. pp. 438–39
8. Bart D. Ehrman (1997). *The New Testament: A Historical Introduction to the Early Christian Writings*. Oxford University Press. p. 8. ISBN 978-0-19-508481-8.
9. *Saint Justin Martyr*, Encyclopedia Britannica, Inc.
10. *Saint Justin Martyr*, Encyclopedia Britannica, Inc.

13. Sharing Our Faith In A Practical Way

1. https://www.beliefnet.com/faiths/christianity/galleries/7-reasons-christians-dont-share-their-faith.

14. The Practical Gospel Message

1. https://en.wikipedia.org/wiki/Apostles%27_Creed

www.ingramcontent.com/pod-product-compliance
Lightning Source LLC
Chambersburg PA
CBHW070959160426
43193CB00012B/1837